INDIA AND NUCLEAR ASIA

INDIA AND NUCLEAR ASIA

Forces, Doctrine, and Dangers

YOGESH JOSHI AND FRANK O'DONNELL

Georgetown University Press / Washington, DC

Library of Congress Cataloging-in-Publication Data

Names: Joshi, Yogesh (International relations specialist), author. |
O'Donnell, Frank (Writer on nuclear weapons), author.
Title: India and nuclear Asia : forces, doctrine, and dangers /
Yogesh Joshi and Frank O'Donnell.
Description: Washington, DC : Georgetown University Press, 2019. |
Series: South Asia in world affairs series | Includes bibliographical
references and index.
Identifiers: LCCN 2018017986 (print) | LCCN 2018032307 (ebook) |
ISBN 9781626166172 (pbk. : alk. paper) | ISBN 9781626166165
(hardcover : alk. paper) | ISBN 9781626166189 (ebook)
Subjects: LCSH: Nuclear weapons—India. | Nuclear arms control—India. |
Nuclear nonproliferation—India. | Deterrence (Strategy) | Nuclear
weapons—Pakistan. | Nuclear weapons—China. | India—Military policy.
Classification: LCC U264.5.I4 (ebook) | LCC U264.5.I4 J67 2019 (print) |
DDC 355.02/170954—dc23
LC record available at https://lccn.loc.gov/2018017986

∞ This book is printed on acid-free paper meeting the requirements of
the American National Standard for Permanence in Paper for
Printed Library Materials.

20 19   9 8 7 6 5 4 3 2 First printing

Printed in the United States of America.
Cover design by Martha Madrid.

To Ma and Papa.
—Yogesh Joshi

To my parents, Dominic and Kathy O'Donnell, and my wife, Kimberly.
—Frank O'Donnell

CONTENTS

TABLES

ACKNOWLEDGMENTS

This book is the culmination of a multiyear collaborative research project, also yielding a shorter monograph and several peer-reviewed articles and policy briefs. This project would not have been possible without the dedicated support and advice of our respective doctoral supervisors, Professors Harsh Pant and Rajesh Rajagopalan. Together, we applied for a UK Economic and Social Research Council grant that enabled us to conduct respective visits to India and the UK and build our research partnership. The outputs of our project have been beyond what either of us anticipated at its origination; for this, we thank Harsh and Rajesh for their mentorship, training, and encouragement. We also thank the UK Economic and Social Research Council for funding our initial research.

To further explore the evolution of India's nuclear policy and debates, the simultaneous transitions occurring in China and Pakistan, and the effects of these potential interactions on regional and US security, we then successfully applied for a US Army War College Strategic Studies Institute grant. This allowed us to conduct valuable research and interviews in New Delhi and Washington. While in Washington, George Perkovich and Toby Dalton kindly invited us to be visiting fellows at the Carnegie Endowment for International Peace. The Carnegie Endowment provided an ideal environment to learn more about how these topics were perceived in Washington, and we also benefited from the opportunity to share our early findings at an event chaired by George.

As our research has progressed, we have also benefited from interviews, conversations, and encouragement from many highly respected experts. We would like to thank C. Uday Bhaskar, Lisa Curtis, Nitin Gokhale, Bharath Gopalaswamy, Happymon Jacob, Saurav Jha, Manoj Joshi, Gurmeet Kanwal, Bharat Karnad, Paul Kerr, K. Alan Krondstadt, Raja Menon, Arun Prakash, Rajeswari Rajagopalan, R. Rajaraman, Iskander Rehman, Nilanthi Samaranayake, Lowell

Schwartz, and Ashley Tellis. We would also like to thank the Indian officials who preferred that their comments remain anonymous but whose input was invaluable. We have also benefited immensely from our sometimes collective and often individual interactions with Mansoor Ahmed, Rajesh Basrur, Atul Bhardawaj, Nicolas Blarel, Kartik Bommakanti, Matthew Bunn, Christopher Clary, David Holloway, Sharad Joshi, Shashank Joshi, S. Paul Kapur, Aditi Malhotra, Martin Malin, Steven E. Miller, Anit Mukherjee, Rohan Mukherjee, Vipin Narang, Swapna Kona Nayudu, Christian Ostermann, Avinash Paliwal, Kapil Patil, Barry Posen, Srinath Raghavan, Scott Sagan, Gary Samore, Samir Saran, Jayita Sarkar, Ajai Shukla, and Balazs Szalontai. Our conclusions and any mistakes, of course, remain our own.

Finally, we would like to thank our South Asia in World Affairs book series editor at Georgetown University Press, T.V. Paul, and senior acquisitions editor Donald Jacobs for their dedication, constructive feedback, and support for this project.

FRANK O'DONNELL

As well as the people listed previously, I offer my gratitude to my family for their constant encouragement and belief in me. I have always been inspired by the love and support given to me by my parents, Dominic and Kathy, and by their teaching of the value of education from an early age. My brother, Dom, is a great source of companionship and humor. My wife, Kim, has been a wonderful source of support, happiness, and love and a gift to have in my life. Finally, I am grateful for the opportunity to build what will be a long and fruitful research partnership with Yogesh.

YOGESH JOSHI

My parents have been a constant source of support and motivation for which I will always remain grateful. My sisters—Sangu, Kabbu, and Anu—and their better halves—Pradeep, Amrit, and Gaurav—have always lent their support to my academic work. To them, I offer my sincere gratitude. Thanks to Vibhu and Preety for being such wonderful friends. They have often been the first ones to hear of all my joys, sorrows, and complaints. Frank, of course, is a terrific academic to work with.

ABBREVIATIONS

AAD	advanced air defense
AEC	Atomic Energy Commission
AECA	US Arms Export Control Act
ATV	Advanced Technology Vessel
BARC	Bhabha Atomic Research Centre
BJP	Bharatiya Janata Party
BMD	ballistic missile defense
CBM	confidence building measure
CCS	Cabinet Committee on Security
CD	Conference on Disarmament
CPEC	China-Pakistan Economic Corridor
CTBT	Comprehensive Test Ban Treaty
DAE	Department of Atomic Energy
DND	Draft Nuclear Doctrine
DRDO	Defence Research and Development Organisation
FBR	fast breeder reactor
FMCT	Fissile Material Cut-Off Treaty
GoI	Government of India
GoP	Government of Pakistan
HEU	highly enriched uranium
IAEA	International Atomic Energy Agency
IAF	Indian Air Force
IBG	integrated battle group

ICBM	intercontinental ballistic missile
IGDMP	Integrated Guided Missile Development Program
INSTC	International North-South Transport Corridor
ISPR	Inter Services Public Relations, Government of Pakistan
JIC	Joint Intelligence Committee
MEA	Ministry of External Affairs
MIRV	multiple independently targeted reentry vehicle
MLRS	multiple launch rocket system
MoD	Ministry of Defence
MTCR	Missile Technology Control Regime
MwTh	megawatts thermal
NAI	National Archives of India
NAM	Non-Aligned Movement
NCA	Nuclear Command Authority
NDA	National Democratic Alliance
NFU	no first use
NMML	Nehru Memorial Museum and Library
NPT	Nuclear Nonproliferation Treaty
NSA	national security advisor
NSAB	National Security Advisory Board
NSC	National Security Council
NSCS	National Security Council Secretariat
NSG	Nuclear Suppliers Group
OVL	Oil and Natural Gas Corporation Videsh
PAD	Prithvi air defense
PIB	Press Information Bureau
PNE	peaceful nuclear explosion
PRP	Plutonium Recycle Project
PTI	Press Trust of India
RevCon	review conference
RgPu	reactor-grade plutonium
RSS	Rashtriya Swayamsevak Sangh

SAM	surface-to-air missile
SFC	Strategic Forces Command
SLBM	sea-launched ballistic missile
SPD	Strategic Plans Division (Pakistan)
SPS	Strategic Planning Staff (NCA)
SSBN	nuclear-armed submarine
UN	United Nations
UPA	United Progressive Alliance
WgPu	weapons-grade plutonium
WMD	weapon of mass destruction

INTRODUCTION

As India continues to rise in the international system, its foreign and security policy approaches will attain greater influence in shaping the regional and global security environment. These approaches will also frame how India is perceived as an international actor by its citizens, global partners, and adversaries. A central element of India's external policy approaches that has long been viewed domestically as an essential expression of Indian identity in global politics is its nuclear policy. The nuclear policy encompasses India's attitudes both toward its own nuclear weapon possession and toward restricting global nuclear proliferation. India's nuclear journey was a long one; it debated and discussed the option of going nuclear for almost four decades and therefore earned the distinction of being a "reluctant nuclear power."[1] Two decades after it declared itself a nuclear weapon state, India today faces multiple technical, strategic, and political challenges—as well as opportunities—related to its nuclear policy. Four factors complicate India's nuclear policy matrix.

First, Asia is witnessing a nuclear transition, which many have also called the "second nuclear age."[2] This nuclear age is distinct from the Cold War—the first nuclear age—in many ways. The 1998 nuclear tests broke the Cold War monopoly on the accepted nuclear powers as enshrined in the Nuclear Nonproliferation Treaty (NPT). Unlike the Cold War, during which the two superpowers spearheaded the global nuclear race, the current nuclear transition is manifested in many states going nuclear. This n-player game has consequences not only for global nuclear proliferation but also for strategic stability. Further, this nuclear transition is not taking place in a vacuum; a complex web of institutions, organizations, and treaties—collectively called the global nuclear nonproliferation regime—channels state behavior in the second nuclear age. And these new nuclear states do not behave in accordance with Cold War rulebooks. States like Pakistan and North Korea, for example, have used nuclear deterrence to undertake ever riskier foreign and military policies. If deterrence

1

induced caution among superpowers, the same cannot be said for some new nuclear powers. India's nuclear behavior, therefore, will be continuously influenced by how this transition unfolds.

Second, India is a unique nuclear power insofar as it is surrounded by two hostile nuclear neighbors: China and Pakistan. Security concerns about these countries were India's principal reason to go nuclear, and their nuclear profiles have transformed substantially in the past two decades. India has very distinct nuclear deterrence requirements against China and Pakistan, which translates into additional pressure on India's nuclear forces and deterrent strategies. How India is coping with the transformation in nuclear capabilities of its principal adversaries, therefore, is a matter of immense curiosity.

Third, India's nuclear profile has altered dramatically in the last two decades. With the Agni-V missile, it has achieved an intercontinental ballistic missile (ICBM) capability. It is close to operationalizing sea-based deterrence, with its nuclear-powered submarines presently undergoing sea trials. Its ballistic missile defense program is at an advanced stage of technological development. Yet how these technological achievements will be assimilated in India's nuclear force posture and doctrine has remained an area of speculation.

Fourth, since 1998 India has actively pursued accommodation in the global nuclear regime. With the 2008 Indo-US Civilian Nuclear Agreement, it has managed to integrate itself with the global nuclear nonproliferation regime, though only partially. It remains outside the Nuclear Suppliers Group (NSG) technology control regime and is actively lobbying to be granted membership. This integration in the global nuclear regime has created both opportunities and challenges for India's nuclear policy. On one hand, it has normalized India's nuclear status as a de facto nuclear power; on the other, India has also incurred additional responsibilities in areas of export controls and arms control. India's integration into the global nuclear nonproliferation regime, therefore, is an important variable in its nuclear policies.

India's responses to these nuclear policy challenges constitute the focus of this book. This study delivers a clear assessment of the contextual landscape within which Indian nuclear policy presently operates, investigating and clarifying core factors that shape this landscape. These factors include new Indian nuclear force posturing opportunities brought by technical force advancements at a time when nuclear policy governance structures are still being actively constructed. Another factor is the evolution of nuclear doctrinal debates and posturing intentions within India, Pakistan, and China. As we will see, there are growing disjunctures in these doctrinal debates with a resultant threat of crisis escalation due to deepening misperceptions. An additional factor is the emergence of new generations of Indian, Chinese, and Pakistani land-based nuclear and conventional force projection amid aggressive supporting trends in strategic thought. We also see an extension of these three countries' nuclear competition to join the growing and tense conventional competition in the naval domain. A further complicating factor of this landscape is the striking absence of trilateral strategic dialogue to reduce misperceptions and related tensions. Finally, contemporary global nonproliferation challenges pose difficult choices for Indian foreign policy in the twenty-first century.

This book investigates these challenges for Indian policymakers in detail. However, it also contributes to academic understandings of nuclear deterrence, the conventional-nuclear threshold, and misperception in nuclear strategy. In particular, it builds on our theoretical understanding of dynamics that can lead to unplanned escalation. The theoretical focus and overall arguments of the book are outlined in the following sections.

INADVERTENT ESCALATION

In his landmark work on escalation, *Inadvertent Escalation: Conventional War and Nuclear Risks*, Barry Posen argued that there are two primary routes to escalation in conflict: planned and unplanned. Planned escalation is a conscious decision by fully informed policymakers to expand the force commitments, geographic expanse, or political stakes of a given conflict. Unplanned escalation, however, was the focus of Posen's work and involved scenarios when escalation occurs in forms unanticipated by one or more parties to a conflict.

Posen looked particularly at what he termed "inadvertent escalation": conventional attacks on the nuclear forces or infrastructure of an adversary force. These conventional attacks could threaten the adversary's confidence in its ability to marshal nuclear defenses if needed and thus would prompt the adversary to introduce nuclear weapons, even if only to satisfy its military thinking, into the subsequent conflict.[3] Posen established three principal causes of inadvertent escalation: the natural offensive preferences of militaries, the security dilemma problem of assuming adversary actions are intentionally escalatory, and "fog of war" challenges of operating with incomplete information. Posen proceeded to identify inadvertent escalation risks in US-Soviet posturing and strategic thought.[4]

However, applications of this concept to the South Asian context, and especially to the India-China-Pakistan triangular nuclear competition, remain limited. Iskander Rehman has investigated the dangers of contemporary Indian and Pakistani intentions to field nuclear-armed naval forces.[5] Rehman's works are limited to this bilateral naval environment, however, and only briefly discuss China in the context of its role in supporting Pakistan's nuclear force development. In other contributions Feroz Hassan Khan and P. R. Chari separately apply Posen's inadvertent escalation pathways to study risks emerging from Indo-Pakistani competition in the land and air domains.[6]

While scholarly research on the India-Pakistan bilateral context thus evidences the inadvertent escalation concept, the literature on Sino-Indian strategic competition has especially awaited substantial research on this theme. Kalyan Kemburi briefly outlines some dual-use perceptual challenges of cruise missile platforms in India and China but does not extend this into a systematic analysis of unplanned escalation risks in their nuclear rivalry.[7] Recent works by Arun Sahgal and Ashley Tellis on contemporary Sino-Indian force balances also do not consider factors relevant to unplanned escalation dynamics.[8]

Indeed, broader contemporary surveys of Chinese and Indian strategic thought and planning similarly do not focus specifically on inadvertent escalation risks. Nevertheless, they reveal developments that illustrate the necessity of a study on this topic. For example, Liping Xia briefly notes the Chinese debate regarding the potential review of its no-first-use (NFU) policy in the event of a conventional attack on its nuclear forces.[9] In his exploration of current Indian nuclear perceptual and planning issues, Vipin Narang indicates that inadvertent escalation could obtain from the aggressive adversary missile targeting intentions of Indian commanders. However, this point forms a limited observation, and the full scope of potential regional inadvertent escalation risks are not the primary focus of Narang's study.[10]

The academic literature therefore lacks a significant analysis of potential inadvertent escalation dangers emanating from the contemporary trilateral South Asian strategic competition. However, as this study finds, three principal factors generate conditions conducive to inadvertent escalation in nuclear South Asia.

The first is the looming extension of the India-China-Pakistan nuclear competition to the naval domain. India and China are fielding a new generation of nuclear-armed submarines (SSBNs) and will necessarily learn about their operation partly through trial and error. Pakistan is seeking its own nuclear naval forces, most likely through commissioning dual-use Chinese submarines. All three states deploy strident maritime practices or doctrines. India has long viewed itself as a primary naval leader in the Indian Ocean, with its most recent Maritime Security Strategy extending its aegis to identify the South and East China Seas as an "area of maritime interest." Pakistan has a tradition of using high-risk naval maneuvers to force adversaries to back down, and its general maritime force modernization uses antiaccess/area-denial capabilities. China's Indian Ocean ambitions include regular submarine forays close to Indian littorals. The true nuclear naval intentions, seaborne deterrent patrol routes, constitution of nuclear naval forces, and maritime territorial boundaries to be defended by all three states remain unclear. There is little regional dialogue focused on establishing a mutual understanding of these aspects or managing a contingency in which a conventional boat comes into hostile contact with a nuclear-armed vessel of another state.

The second factor is the rising prominence of potential dual-use platforms in regional nuclear competition. At sea nuclear weapons can be carried aboard surface ships and future submarine platforms of all three states. On land it remains unclear whether Indian conventional missiles, such as the Prahaar, Brahmos, and Nirbhay, will be assigned nuclear missions. China prioritizes conventional ballistic missiles, including dual-use platforms such as the DF-21, in its offensive strike planning.

The third factor is the reported intentions of all three states to conduct early consequential strikes on adversary territory, seize the operational initiative, and force termination on their terms at the outset of a conflict. Chinese military thinking prioritizes substantial conventional ballistic missile strikes on adversary population centers, command and control facilities, and force concentrations at the outset of a conflict. Indian conventional force commanders will reportedly seek to destroy any missile units and launching areas within adversary territory quickly in a conflict and are developing plans and capabilities to launch missile barrages similar to those recommended in Chinese thinking. While not a deep conventional strike, Pakistan's plans to field nuclear-armed sixty-kilometer-range ballistic missile forces should be added to this discussion given their potential to substantially alter and escalate a regional conflict, even if they are only deployed for signaling purposes. The understanding by all three states of the escalatory significance of these initiatives, as they are likely to be perceived by the adversary, is unclear.

ACCIDENTAL ESCALATION

A second form of unplanned escalation is accidental escalation. Herbert Lin defines this concept generally as "when some operational action has direct effects that are unintended by those who ordered them."[11] This concept is different from inadvertent escalation because it accords greater comparative weight to the perceptions of the political leadership and the surrounding security community, rather than those of operational military forces, as a driver of unplanned escalation.

The first South Asian regional factor conducive to accidental escalation is the near absence of strategic dialogue among India, China, and Pakistan. Dialogues, when they occur, are bilateral (India-Pakistan, India-China, or

China-Pakistan), are intermittent, and often do not involve nuclear policy discussions. Without a clear understanding of the nuclear doctrinal and force-posturing intentions of the other countries and without understanding of conventional territorial and conflict threshold red lines, opportunities for misperception and for planning nuclear forces according to worst-case assumptions of an adversary's dark nuclear intentions are rife. To give examples of current regional nuclear misunderstanding, Pakistan doubts the reality of India's declared NFU policy, India doubts the applicability of China's NFU policy to conventional conflicts involving India, and China refuses to even recognize India as a state that possesses nuclear weapons. The absence of strategic dialogue also amplifies the opportunities for inadvertent escalation flowing from the merging of nuclear with naval competition, the rising prominence of dual-use capabilities, and shared regional interests in issuing a devastating offensive strike to settle a conflict early, without understanding of how an adversary would perceive and respond to this strike.

The second driver of accidental escalation risk is new developments in nuclear-posturing and doctrinal debates within all three states. Indian nuclear doctrine, which has been unchanged since 2003, includes an NFU policy and massive retaliation to adversary first use. Early views of an Indian force posture characterized by minimum deterrence—ensuring the ability to respond to adversary nuclear use with the smallest possible nuclear forces in numerical size and destructive capacity—are increasingly being challenged by calls for an emphasis on credibility as the organizing concept. Among other recommendations, supporters of the credibility approach want to see an end to the NFU commitment and a larger, more technically diverse nuclear force. While the 2003 doctrine remains unrevised despite these pressures, new technical capabilities in the context of this debate and in the absence of a new public Indian nuclear doctrine suggest a certain level of Indian strategic interest in counterforce—war-fighting—capabilities. India's defense scientific agency has an explicit interest in fielding multiple-warhead nuclear missiles and in making missiles such as the ballistic Prahaar or cruise Brahmos and Nirbhay platforms nuclear-capable. The growing ambiguity, at least in the academic and policy debates, regarding India's ultimate nuclear intentions—which would be best settled by an official public defense review—generates opportunities for adversaries to misperceive what these intentions are.

Pakistan reportedly builds into its force sizing plans Indian fissile material stocks from both civil and military nuclear energy programs, despite Indian claims that the two programs are fully separate. Pakistan is also moving from credible minimum deterrence to full spectrum deterrence. While Islamabad's first-use policy remains intact, its full spectrum deterrence organizing concept includes a specialized nuclear force capability for every potential rung of conflict with India. This would dramatically lower the bilateral nuclear threshold to essentially exclude any conventional conflict from having nuclear implications, freezing most uses of India's conventional superiority (as the existence of this superiority is perceived by Islamabad) for fear of nuclear escalation. This new concept is best symbolized by the sixty-kilometer-range Nasr nuclear ballistic missile, intended to escalate local Indian conventional attacks to the nuclear level and thus deter them. Pakistan's nuclear threshold red lines remain ambiguous, sketched in various scenarios of substantial maritime, land, economic, or conventional force losses. It remains generally unclear, even to well-informed Pakistani analysts, how much general conventional damage Pakistan will tolerate before considering first use.

India refuses to accept full spectrum deterrence and what the Nasr represents in its force planning. This refusal is a clear example of India's deliberate decision to adopt, if not a misperception of Pakistani nuclear intentions, certainly a perception different from the intentions declared by Islamabad. Further, Indian conventional force commanders continue to focus on training exercises to enable the military to fight through nuclear use, signaling to Pakistan that New Delhi will be undeterred by the Nasr's use in pursuit of wartime objectives. Pakistan, by contrast, continues to claim that full spectrum deterrence will deter Indian conventional attacks on Pakistan. As Michael Krepon has previously argued, only one state can be correct.[12]

China's nuclear doctrine emphasizes NFU and a more stringent form of minimum deterrence than India's credible minimum deterrence. However, a similar ambiguity is growing regarding its nuclear and conventional intentions. As part of wide-ranging military reforms announced in December 2015, Beijing is reorganizing all land-based conventional and nuclear missile forces under a single rocket force and merging its previous two India-facing military commands into one western command with a more aggressive operational concept. As well as the aforementioned nuclear-armed submarine fleet, China is introducing a new generation of more precise, multiple-warhead, and more mobile ground nuclear forces. Chinese nuclear missile testing since January 2016 has particularly featured conditions like those of missile bases with India targeting missions, and recent discourse suggests that Chinese strategists could see adversary conventional attacks on nuclear-capable units or bases—as is reportedly promised by Indian conventional force commanders—as amounting to nuclear first use: the classic Posen scenario of inadvertent escalation.

The present South Asian nuclear context, therefore, offers fertile ground for deepening our theoretical understanding of escalatory pressures and of the potential for ambiguous nuclear doctrines and force-planning intentions to generate regional instability. This book highlights how the interacting nuclear doctrines and evolving postures of India, China, and Pakistan, in a near absence of effective strategic dialogue, are creating new conditions conducive to inadvertent and accidental escalation.

RECOMMENDATIONS

As well as elucidating these dynamics and developing the literature on unplanned escalation, this book also makes two policy recommendations. First, we propose that New Delhi, Beijing, and Islamabad initiate nuclear and naval strategic dialogues to discern mutual nuclear and territorial intentions and thus reduce the risk of conflict emerging from misperception. These dialogues would be a worthy risk-reduction and confidence-building initiative to counteract the multiple interlocking challenges that this book identifies. Challenges include growing ambiguity in regional nuclear intentions arising from new debates on nuclear doctrine; the fielding of a new generation of nuclear forces; the multiple technical posturing and doctrinal options presented by dual-use ballistic missiles, naval platforms, and air platforms; and the opportunities for adversary misperception of ultimate nuclear intentions and risk of unplanned nuclear escalation within this context. Convening regular dialogues would especially support nuclear risk-reduction efforts by preventing the misperception of a conventional for a nuclear mission, or vice versa; this potential misperception is one of the core emerging concerns in both the land and the sea domains. Because the nuclear forces of India, China, and Pakistan may come into direct contact more frequently through nuclear-armed naval fleets, institutionalizing trilateral nuclear dialogues can potentially prevent a nuclear crisis or reduce tensions if one occurs.

Second, to fully integrate this complex and evolving regional strategic context into Indian defense planning, we recommend that an official public Indian defense review be conducted. This review would include an assessment of India's rapidly shifting regional environment to inform conventional and nuclear force planning. In exploring these conditions, the review should lead to the adoption of a posturing response that clearly separates conventional from nuclear threats and assigns response packages to conventional and nuclear forces, respectively. This latter exercise should reiterate that Indian nuclear forces only obtain credibility as a tool of last resort and should be thought of solely in the minimum terms of deterring specifically nuclear threats. Stronger conventional defenses and renewed effort to building these defenses should form the Indian response to nonnuclear threats. As well as disaggregating and prioritizing the specific regional threats posed to Indian security and generating a more efficient use and development of defense resources in response, the review process would reduce the capability-led and doctrine-led ambiguity regarding nuclear thresholds that is emerging. A review will also help India address political and technical questions regarding its nuclear force capabilities that influence its stances toward the Comprehensive Test Ban Treaty (CTBT) and Fissile Material Cut-Off Treaty (FMCT), as we will see in chapter 6, on Indian nonproliferation policy approaches.

CHAPTER SUMMARIES

This book will explore the Indian nuclear force's technical advancements, the nuclear doctrinal evolution and force developments of Pakistan and China, the history and present contours of Indian nuclear thought, and India's approach to global nonproliferation policy. Chapter 1 investigates the Indian nuclear force's technical development and finds that in 2017 India's nuclear force scaled new heights of technical achievement at an unprecedented rate. Progress in delivery vehicles is seemingly constrained only by present limits in technical knowledge. India today stands on the brink of possessing ICBMs, a potential new generation of short-range nuclear-capable missiles, and a seaborne nuclear-armed submarine fleet. While some measures of restraint, such as the testing moratorium practiced since 1998, are in place, the wide scope and ambition of nuclear force development are increasingly difficult to reconcile with India's stated nuclear posture of credible minimum deterrence.

Chapters 2 and 3 investigate in detail the Indian nuclear doctrinal and force pressures posed by Pakistan and China. Both states are modernizing their nuclear forces and honing the nuclear and conventional threats they pose to India, albeit in different ways. These chapters particularly highlight that in the land and emerging naval domains, the line between conventional and nuclear thresholds is increasingly blurred as states harbor different ideas about where these thresholds are and should be. Further, as dual-use platforms become more prominent, it becomes more difficult to discern the conventional or nuclear mission of an adversary force concentration. Without the establishment of a trilateral nuclear and defense dialogue, the factors conducive to accidental and inadvertent escalation outlined previously are likely to further develop.

Chapters 4 and 5 explore India's nuclear doctrinal debate from 1964 until present. During this period there has been a gradual transition from early near-universal policymaker and expert support for minimum deterrence to growing interest in establishing the technical credibility of the nuclear force rather than its continued "minimum" status. This debate is reflected in differences between the 1999 and 2003 Indian nuclear doctrines and in the tenor of current doctrinal debates. Indian nuclear planners are approaching a juncture where they must decide how to balance the continued substantial support for minimum deterrence with rising pressures to elevate the role of nuclear weapons in Indian defense in a worsening regional strategic context.

Finally, chapter 6 outlines India's approach to global nonproliferation policy. It finds that India has long been dedicated to policies to limit external proliferation but has traditionally conditioned the scope of its efforts on an overarching view of India's broader national interests, such as perceived needs to retain a nuclear weapon capability and not virtually terminate all relations with a state of proliferation concern. This approach has also involved a willingness to develop and enforce nonproliferation policies unilaterally, rather than through many of the principal international nonproliferation regime structures. Although India has a unique nonproliferation policy history and record of engagement with these international structures, this balancing of nonproliferation policy objectives with broader strategic interests explains much of the Indian trajectory and continues to characterize India's approach today. Political and technical questions regarding nuclear force size and reliability continue to affect current Indian debates on the CTBT and FMCT, highlighting again the need for an official defense review.

We will now turn to survey the Indian nuclear force's technical development as it stood in 2017 and explore the questions current nuclear projects raise for Indian security planners and the use of India's nuclear force in South Asia.

NOTES

1. Stephen P. Cohen and Sunil Dasgupta, *Arming without Aiming: India's Military Modernization* (Washington, DC: Brookings Institution Press, 2014), 97.
2. Paul Bracken, *The Second Nuclear Age: Strategy, Danger, and the New Power Politics* (New York: Times Books, 2012), 3; Ashley J. Tellis, "No Escape: Managing the Enduring Reality of Nuclear Weapons," in *Strategic Asia 2013–14: Asia in Second Nuclear Age*, ed. Ashley J. Tellis, Abraham M. Denmark, and Travis Turner (Washington, DC: National Bureau of Asian Research, 2014), 4.
3. Barry R. Posen, *Inadvertent Escalation: Conventional War and Nuclear Risks* (Ithaca, NY: Cornell University Press, 1991), 1–4. For early discussions highlighting the general relevance of unplanned escalation dynamics to a primarily bilateral India-Pakistan nuclear context, see particularly Mahesh Shankar and T.V. Paul, "Nuclear Doctrines and Stable Strategic Relationships: The Case of South Asia," *International Affairs* 92, no. 2 (January 2016): 1–2; Vipin Narang, "Five Myths about India's Nuclear Posture," *Washington Quarterly* 36, no. 3 (Summer 2013): 151; Bhumitra Chakma, "Escalation Control, Deterrence Diplomacy and America's Role in South Asia's Nuclear Crises," *Contemporary Security Policy* 33, no. 3 (2012): 555–56; Rajesh Rajagopalan, "The Threat of Unintended Use of Nuclear Weapons in South Asia," *India Review* 4, no. 2 (2005): 215; P. R. Chari, *Nuclear Crisis, Escalation Control, and Deterrence in South Asia* (Washington, DC: Stimson

Center, August 2003), https://www.stimson.org/sites/default/files/file-attachments /escalation_chari_1_1.pdf; and Michael Krepon, *The Stability-Instability Paradox, Misperception, and Escalation Control in South Asia* (Washington, DC: Stimson Center, May 2003): 8–20, https://www.stimson.org/sites/default/files/file-attachments/stability -instability-paradox-south-asia.pdf. An edited version of this paper, with the same title, is also available as a chapter in *Prospects for Peace in South Asia*, ed. Rafiq Dossani and Henry S. Rowen (Stanford, CA: Stanford University Press, 2004): 261–79.

4. Posen, *Inadvertent Escalation.*

5. Iskander Rehman, *Murky Waters: Naval Nuclear Dynamics in the Indian Ocean* (Washington, DC: Carnegie Endowment for International Peace, 2015); Iskander Rehman, "Drowning Stability: The Perils of Naval Nuclearization and Brinkmanship in the Indian Ocean," *Naval War College Review* 65, no. 4 (Autumn 2012): 77–80.

6. Feroz Hassan Khan, "Reducing the Risk of Nuclear War in South Asia," in *Pakistan's Nuclear Future: Reining in the Risk*, ed. Henry D. Sokolski (Carlisle, PA: US Army War College Strategic Studies Institute, 2009), 63–102; Chari *Nuclear Crisis*, 22–23.

7. Kalyan Kemburi, "Recalibrating Deterrence Theory and Practice: The View from India," in *The China-India Nuclear Crossroads*, ed. Lora Saalman (Washington, DC: Carnegie Endowment for International Peace, 2012), 87–89.

8. Ashley J. Tellis, *Troubles, They Come in Battalions: The Manifold Travails of the Indian Air Force* (Washington, DC: Carnegie Endowment for International Peace, 2016); Arun Sahgal, "China's Military Modernization: Responses from India," in *Strategic Asia 2012– 13: China's Military Challenge*, ed. Ashley J. Tellis and Travis Tanner (Seattle: National Bureau of Asian Research, 2012), 277–305.

9. Xia Liping, "China's Nuclear Doctrine: Debates and Evolution," Carnegie Endowment for International Peace, June 30, 2016, http://carnegieendowment.org/2016/06/30 /china-s-nuclear-doctrine-debates-and-evolution-pub-63967. See also Forrest E. Morgan, Karl P. Mueller, Evan S. Medeiros, Kevin L. Pollpeter, and Roger Cliff, *Dangerous Thresholds: Managing Escalation in the 21st Century* (Santa Monica, CA: RAND, 2008), 61–65, 80.

10. Narang, "Five Myths," 151.

11. Herbert Lin, "Escalation Dynamics and Conflict Termination in Cyberspace," *Strategic Studies Quarterly* 6, no. 3 (Fall 2012): 53.

12. Krepon, *Stability-Instability Paradox*, 16.

1

TWO DECADES OF INDIAN NUCLEAR FORCE DEVELOPMENT

The Emerging Posture and Looming Decision Points

After India conducted a series of nuclear weapon tests in 1998, many prognosticated a grim future for India's nuclear forces and its status as a nuclear weapon state. India was called a "third-tier nuclear state" and "a low-level nuclear power."[1] Some doubted India's ability to expand its nuclear arsenal and its intention to be counted as a major nuclear power. In fact, India's slow drive for weaponization was conflated with its limited capabilities. Given India's nascent nuclear arsenal, compared to the technological sophistication and doctrinal clarity other nuclear powers had achieved, it was also suggested that India would not command the same respect that other major nuclear powers had. Some observers forecasted that Pakistan would remain the singular focus of India's nuclear forces, and hence, India's nuclear deterrent at best would be confined to South Asia.[2] The reasons for these assumptions were mainly material: shortage of fissile material, technological incapacity to produce reliable delivery systems, ineffective bureaucratic structures (especially in its scientific enclave), and rudimentary command and control systems. Progress on these components was assumed to be severely restricted by India's dire economic health and the necessity to cater to more important demands of Indian democracy: the need for economic development and reduction of the chronic poverty that formed the dark underbelly of a nuclear India. Further, the hostile international reaction to India's overt nuclearization threatened to restrict or even punish efforts to further develop Indian nuclear capabilities.

Moralistic considerations were also availed to argue that development of a robust deterrent would remain hesitatingly slow. While addressing an attentive audience at the India International Center just after the nuclear tests, India's foremost strategic thinker—K. Subrahmanyam—claimed, "Nuclear weapons is not the issue. . . . It is a question of India's dignity and sovereignty. India has the right to be equal with any other major power of the world because it represents one sixth of humanity and that is the issue, because a nuclear weapon is not a weapon of war."[3] Such ex post facto reasoning, especially coming from the center of realpolitik thinking in India, made India's aspirations for nuclear status appear as mere symbolism—all rhetoric, no substance—further validating the assumptions that India had neither the intentions nor the will to expand its nuclear forces. Subrahmanyam also made a number of other claims: for projecting effective deterrence, only a few nuclear weapons would suffice; having managed to enter the "mainstream paradigm" of nuclear weapon states, India could now "change the paradigm itself" (read "pursue effective disarmament"); on the "basis of a perception of mutual deterrence," India and Pakistan would now have peace; and India could now sign the CTBT and vouch for a nuclear weapon convention.[4]

Beyond these material and moralistic rationales for a rudimentary nuclear force, there was the notion that India was a different kind of nuclear power compared to the expansionist Cold Warriors and that India's force development would be haltingly slow.[5] India's strategic restraint in past conflicts and its abhorrence of the use of nuclear weapons were often cited as proof that force development would not gain a lot of momentum. India's limited use of force during the Kargil War gave further boost to the idea that even small nuclear forces could deter states from escalating the conflict, whether it was Pakistan or India that did the escalating. And therefore, India's nuclear forces would not see a major accretion.

Twenty years hence India's trajectory as a nuclear weapon state is drastically different from the initial pictures painted by many in the aftermath of the 1998 nuclear tests. Many initial assumptions have been undermined by growing instability in Indo-Pakistan relations, the shift in focus of India's nuclear forces from Pakistan to China, and the shallow treatment disarmament receives in India's current nuclear politics. What is glaringly conspicuous in India's twenty years as a nuclear weapon state is progress in technical force development and expansion of the nuclear arsenal.

Today India boasts an expanding nuclear portfolio designed to extend beyond South Asia. Indeed, the ambitions of India's nuclear weapon designers invite questions about whether political limits guide the program. The emerging nuclear force structure appears to be moving away from the stated postures of credible minimum deterrence and assured retaliation, that is, ensuring a minimum deterrent able to retaliate against nuclear first use by China or Pakistan. Instead, recent development projects—such as multiple independently targeted reentry vehicle (MIRV) warheads, the 700-kilometer-range Shourya nuclear missile, and the potentially nuclear-capable short-range Prahaar,

Brahmos, and Nirbhay missiles—indicate Indian interest in a war-fighting capacity. The government is facing growing pressure from within India to include war-fighting options in its nuclear approach, and a retired army officer and nuclear expert has argued that the Shourya and Prahaar "confer a war-fighting capability."[6] Even if these missiles are assigned solely conventional missions, they would still enable an enhanced Indian capability to launch conventional counterforce strikes. Shivshankar Menon, a former Indian national security advisor (NSA), published a memoir (discussed in detail later) outlining these emerging elements of Indian nuclear discourse and suggesting Indian interest in counterforce targeting, even including preemptive counterforce strikes.[7]

India is advancing all aspects of its technical nuclear capabilities. It is planning and unveiling ballistic missiles of ever-greater range, and its long-awaited nuclear-armed submarine fleet is finally taking operational form with the launch of INS *Arihant*. More subtle improvements are also being made in supporting infrastructure. The Defence Research and Development Organisation (DRDO), responsible for missile development, is working on warhead miniaturization, which could lead to a tactical nuclear weapon capability. The Department of Atomic Energy (DAE) is upscaling its uranium enrichment capabilities, which could accelerate India's fissile material production. A sense of momentous and fast-moving technical progress is in the air.

India's land-based ballistic missile portfolio attracts most of the public limelight. In 1998 New Delhi hosted just three platforms—the Prithvi, Agni-I, and Agni-II—limited in range to targets in Pakistan. Today New Delhi is building the Agni-V, able to reach all targets in China, and working on the Agni-VI, intended to extend even farther. The missiles enjoy a certain patriotic symbolism, with each successive unveiling of a new platform attracting celebratory statements from the Prime Minister's Office and favorable coverage in Indian media. However, there are questions concerning the governance of this missile program. India's political masters appear not to have set an upper limit for the state's missile aspirations. The operational credibility of these new missiles is doubtful given the limited DRDO testing program before entry into service. Despite the reported formation of several combined civil-military nuclear planning cells in the last decade, these issues persist and raise concerns regarding the missile program's correspondence with Indian strategic intentions.

The air-based leg of India's emerging nuclear triad has not dramatically changed since 1998 and is still the most reliable of the three legs. The platform relies on nuclear gravity bombs dropped by Jaguar IS/IB and Mirage 2000H aircraft. Additional aircraft currently under Indian procurement, such as the Sukhoi Su-30MKI and Rafale, are also nuclear-capable and could serve a future role in India's nuclear force. As the full induction of new land-based and sea-based platforms will likely take decades, the Indian Air Force (IAF) will continue to serve as the backbone of India's nuclear force in the medium term.

India's sea-based platforms, the least operationalized of the three legs, are still mainly theoretical. *Arihant*, the flagship of India's indigenous nuclear-armed submarine fleet, is currently out for sea trials. Indian sailors are gaining operational knowledge of a nuclear submarine by trialing *Akula*, a nuclear attack submarine on loan from Russia. The Sagarika and K-4 seaborne missiles to be hosted on the *Arihant*-class SSBN fleet are still under development, and the highly limited range of the Sagarika suggests further work is needed before a satisfactory SSBN force is ready.

While efforts to operationalize the nuclear triad continue, India is also developing a ballistic missile defense (BMD) system. DRDO announced in 2011 that a limited BMD capability, combining radar technology acquired through international cooperation with interceptor units developed by the Indian missile program, would be fielded around New Delhi and Mumbai by early 2014. DRDO did not deliver this capability in 2014 and has not publicized an updated official time estimate.[8] Like the later Agni platforms, the BMD system may not have the operational credibility DRDO claims it has. Concerns about BMD and the Agni portfolio have arisen around whether these projects are being conceived, directed, and monitored by the Prime Minister's Office, Strategic Forces Command (SFC), and the Ministry of Defence in accordance with preexisting strategic doctrine or whether they are being conceived and developed by a more autonomous Indian defense scientific establishment with looser central political and technical oversight.

These new systems will affect India's great power profile and relationships with key allies and adversaries, further elevating the importance of the governance questions they raise. In analysis of the progress and credibility of India's developing nuclear capabilities, a recurrent question is, In what direction is India's nuclear force heading? A strategic defense review, including a new assessment of the role of nuclear weapons and current nuclear force projects in India's wider defense posture, is needed.

INDIAN NUCLEAR FORCES IN 2018: OVERVIEW

This chapter seeks to provide an empirical analysis of India's technical force development trajectory. This analysis will provide the technical background against which the broader Indian doctrinal debate (discussed in chapters 4 and 5) is conducted. This chapter seeks to answer the questions: What does the Indian nuclear force look like in 2018? What is envisioned for its future? What are the technological and governance issues shaping the nuclear force?

Nuclear Warheads and Fissile Material Capabilities

India is presently estimated to hold 90 to 120 nuclear warheads, a weapons-grade plutonium (WgPu) stockpile of 540 kilograms (1,190 pounds, enough for around 110 bombs), and a highly enriched uranium (HEU) stockpile of 800 kilograms (1,763 pounds, enough for around 50 bombs).[9] This estimate can be taken as a minimum against a more ambitious assessment by R. Rajaraman. According to Rajaraman, India has more than 600 kilograms (1,323 pounds) of WgPu and more than 1,300 kilograms (2,866 pounds) of reactor-grade plutonium (RgPu).[10] Given that one of the nuclear devices in the 1998 tests used RgPu and one warhead would use 5–7 kilograms (11–15 pounds) of fissile material, India could potentially have a nuclear arsenal comparable to that of China: something close to a capability of 300 to 350 nuclear warheads.

The two main WgPu-producing reactors in India have been CIRUS and DHRUVA. CIRUS, commissioned in 1963 and decommissioned in December 2010, could generate 40 megawatts thermal (MwTh). DHRUVA started producing WgPu in 1988 and runs at 100 MwTh.[11] According to a 2008 estimate by Rajaraman, if both CIRUS and DHRUVA were operated at an average capacity of 70 percent, these two reactors would produce 9 kilograms and 22 kilograms (20 and 48 pounds) of WgPu a year, respectively.[12] According to Rajaraman, by 2008 CIRUS had produced close to 342 kilograms (754 pounds) (except for the period 1997–2003, when it was closed for refurbishing), and DHRUVA 437 kilograms (937 pounds) of WgPu, bringing India's total WgPu stocks to 779 kilograms (1,717 pounds). Given that close to 131 kilograms (289 pounds) of fissile material were consumed during India's nuclear tests and preparations, India's nuclear warhead inventory consisted of approximately 648 kilograms (1,429 pounds) of fissile materials as of 2008.[13]

India also has a huge inventory of RgPu. Its pressurized heavy water reactors, or CANDU-type reactors, are ideal for producing spent fuel that is rich in plutonium Pu239 but that is accompanied by several plutonium isotopes, such as Pu240, Pu241, and Pu242.[14] The presence of these isotopes renders the RgPu inefficient for weapon design as the isotopes' radioactive decay life is considerably shorter, making them unsuitable for weapons. However, it is possible to fabricate low-yield nuclear fission devices using RgPu;[15] in fact, it has been widely reported that one of the tests conducted during 1998 used RgPu.[16] India has an RgPu inventory of around 13 tons.[17] However, India's annual RgPu production from CANDU reactors eventually went down from 2 tons (4,810 pounds) in 2009 to 1.14 tons (2,513 pounds) by 2014, as more and more reactors were safeguarded under the Indo-US nuclear deal.[18] Of the twenty-two CANDU-type reactors currently in operation, India plans to safeguard only fourteen under the Indo-US deal. It will keep eight of them without any international oversight, and possibly for military purposes.[19] These eight reactors will continue producing unsafeguarded RgPu. In addition, the RgPu accumulated before the deal came into effect will not be safeguarded. India, if the need arises, can use this inventory of RgPu for weapons as it did with the one device in the 1998 tests.

India is also developing a fast breeder reactor (FBR) program. If this program is successful, a single breeder reactor, like the one being constructed at Kalpakkam, will generate more than 140 kilograms (309 pounds) of plutonium with a fissile content of more than 95 percent annually.[20] India has not officially rejected using the FBR program for its strategic needs. In fact, during the tense negotiations of the Indo-US nuclear deal, DAE fought strongly to keep the FBR program outside the purview of the International Atomic Energy Agency (IAEA). Anil Kakodkar, then chairman of DAE, claimed that the FBRs were important not only for India's energy security but also for its "strategic" needs (possibly weapons).[21]

In addition, India has two gas centrifuge facilities producing HEU in Mumbai and Rattehalli.[22] India started its uranium enrichment program in 1967–68 under Vikram Sarabhai, and for at least two decades, the program failed to yield any desired results.[23] Three factors delayed the progress in mastering uranium enrichment.[24] First, India's nuclear energy program had traditionally revolved around natural uranium, plutonium, and the thorium cycle, also called a three-stage nuclear program.[25] Therefore, the Bhabha Atomic Research Centre (BARC) had neither technical necessity nor any capability to produce enriched uranium to begin with. Second, for a long time, nuclear scientists experimented with inefficient enrichment technologies such as the gaseous diffusion method and nozzle enrichment. Last, by the time India seriously considered uranium enrichment through the centrifuge method in the late 1970s, a strict nonproliferation regime had been established by advanced nuclear technology states. It was only in the mid-1980s that scientists at BARC were able to produce enriched uranium using indigenous centrifuge technology at a pilot scale. Since then India's uranium enrichment program has grown in both quality and quantity.[26] Commissioned in the year 1990, the Rare Materials Plant at Rattehalli caters to the fuel needs of India's nuclear submarine project, producing 20–40 percent enriched uranium. However, reports suggest that some of this HEU was also used in the 1998 nuclear weapon tests.[27]

According to David Albright and Susan Basu, India has both enlarged its centrifuge capability and improved the sophistication of its centrifuge technology. In 2006 India ran 2,000–3,000 centrifuges with a capacity of 9,600 separative work units a year (SWU/y), enough to produce 48 kilograms (106 pounds) of 90 percent HEU annually.[28] M. V. Ramana provided a more conservative estimate. According to him, the enrichment capacity of the Rattehalli plant is approximately 4,500 SWU/y, capable of producing only 22 kilograms (48 pounds) of 90 percent HEU and 40–70 kilograms (88–154 pounds) of 45 percent enriched uranium.[29] At the other extreme, in 2015 former IAEA inspector Robert Kelley surveyed new construction at Rattehalli and found a total capacity of 42,000 SWU/y and around 183 kilograms (403 pounds) of weapons-grade uranium. Kelley's assessment is calculated by assuming efficient operation of a new generation of centrifuges. A third enrichment facility at Challakere is being built presently, although its intended output levels are unclear.[30]

This discussion of fissile material capability suggests more than a modest inventory of fissile material stocks. However, two factors must be accounted for. First, historically speaking, even when India has had huge stocks of fissile material, it has always been conservative about using it for weapons. As Rajesh Rajagopalan has argued, "The small size of the Indian nuclear force is the consequence of deliberate choice rather than because of any fissile material shortage."[31] If India's intentions for number of weapons are modest, the technical requirements of India's three-stage energy program, which includes breeder reactors, necessitate a high inventory of fissile material.[32] As far as its uranium enrichment program is concerned, it is primarily geared toward production of fuel for its nuclear submarines.

Nuclear Delivery Vehicles

Table 1.1 provides details of India's current nuclear delivery vehicles, inducted and developing. As we can see, these delivery vehicles are diversifying, rendering the overall trajectory of Indian nuclear force development uncertain. Is India headed toward a limited reliable triad supporting a posture of assured retaliation or toward a diversified posture more suggestive of war-fighting capabilities?

LAND-BASED DELIVERY VEHICLES

Indian missile development has overcome substantive barriers caused by financial limitations and external technology sanctions to feature diverse and ambitious projects today. At the time of the 1998 nuclear tests, India had a principally Pakistan-centric force that relied on air-delivered gravity bombs and ballistic missiles with a maximum range of 700 kilometers (435 miles). Contemporary Indian missile advancements, such as the 5,000-kilometer (3,107-mile) range Agni-V and the prospective 6,000-kilometer (3,728-mile) range Agni-VI, now signify a growing focus on China.[33] A former SFC chief recently commented: "It's not Pakistan we are looking at most of the time, like most

TABLE I.I
Indian Nuclear Forces in 2018

Type	Range	Payload	Current status
Land-based missiles			
Prithvi-I	150 km (93 mi)	1,000 kg (2,204 lb)	Deployed with the army's 333rd and 355th Missile Groups. Fewer than 50 launchers believed to be deployed.
Agni-I	700 km (435 mi)	1,000 kg (2,204 lb)	Deployed with the army's 334th Missile Group from 2004. Around 10–20 launchers believed to be deployed.
Agni-II	2,000 km (1,243 mi)	1,000 kg (2,204 lb)	Deployed with the army's 335th Missile Group. Around 10 launchers believed to be deployed.
Agni-II+	2,000+ km (1,243+ mi)	1,000 kg (2,204 lb)	Under development.
Agni-III	3,000 km (1,864 mi)	1,500 kg (3,307 lb)	Presently being inducted.
Agni-IV	3,500 km (2,175 mi)	1,000 kg (2,204 lb)	Presently being inducted.
Agni-V	5,000 km (3,107 mi)	1,500 kg (3,307 lb)	Under development.
Agni-VI	6,000 km (3,728 mi)	1,500 kg (3,307 lb)	Under development.
Sea-based missiles			
Dhanush	350 km (217 mi)	500 kg (1,102 lb)	Induction under way but not operational
K-15 (Sagarika)	700 km (435 mi)	500–600 kg (1,102–1,323 lb)	Development complete; integration with *Arihant*-class nuclear submarine under way
K-4	3,500 km (2,175 mi)	1,000 kg (2,204 lb)	Under development.
K-5	5,000 km (3,107 mi)	N/A	Under development.
Aircraft			
Mirage 2000H	1,800 km (1,118 mi)	6,300 kg (13,889 lb)	Squadron 1 or 7 of 40th Wing, deployed at Gwalior Air Station, is reported to have been assigned a nuclear mission. The Mirage fleet is undergoing capability improvements, adding twenty years to its life span, from July 2011.
Jaguar IS/IB	1,600 km (994 mi)	4,775 kg (10,527 lb)	Reports suggest two squadrons at Ambala Air Force Station are assigned nuclear missions. The Jaguar fleet is undergoing capability improvements, which will extend its life span past 2030.
MiG-27	1,760 km (1,094 mi)	3,500 kg (7,716 lb)	Some MiG-27s may be assigned nuclear roles; however, safety issues have led to a decision to phase out the MiG-27.
Sukhoi Su-30 MKI	3,000 km (1,864 mi)	8,000 kg (17,637 lb)	The Strategic Forces Command has assigned a nuclear role to 40 Sukhois. India intends a fleet size of 272 planes.
Rafale	3,700 km (2,299 mi)	9,525 kg (21,000 lb)	The Rafale is nuclear-capable, although there is no present evidence they will have nuclear roles. India intends a fleet size of at least 36 planes.

TABLE I.I *(continued)*

Sources: Data are from Puneet Bhalla, "India Chooses Rafale," *Scholar Warrior*, Spring 2012, 117–22, http
://www.claws.in/images/journals_doc/SW%20J.139-144.pdf; Laxman Kumar Behera, "Modernisation
of the Indian Air Force," *Defence Review Asia*, January 17, 2013, http://www.defencereviewasia.com/arti
cles/200/Modernisation-of-the-Indian-Air-Force; Gautam Datt, "More Teeth for Jaguar: Nearly 120 of the
Indian Air Force Jets Are Being Modernised," *Mail Online India*, September 10, 2012, http://www.daily
mail.co.uk/indiahome/indianews/article-2200832/More-teeth-jaguar-Nearly-120-Indian-Air-Force-jets
-modernised.html; Gautam Datt, "Indian Air Force Lost Half of MiG Fighter Jets in Deadly Crashes,"
India Today, May 3, 2012, http://indiatoday.intoday.in/story/iaf-lost-half-of-mig-fighter-jets-in-deadly
-crashes/1/187061.html; Ministry of Defence (MoD), *Annual Report 2014–15* (New Delhi: Government
of India [GoI], 2015), 75–77; MoD, *Annual Report 2013–14* (New Delhi: GoI, 2014), 86–87; International
Institute for Strategic Studies (IISS), *The Military Balance 2015* (London: IISS, 2015), 219, 248; Shannon N.
Kille, Phillip Schell, and Hans M. Kristensen, "Indian Nuclear Forces," in *SIPRI Yearbook 2012: Armaments,
Disarmament and International Security* (Oxford: Oxford University Press, 2012), 332–36; Rajat Pandit,
"High Cost of Mirage-2000 Upgrade Raises Eyebrows," *Times of India*, March 5, 2013, https://timesof
india.indiatimes.com/india/High-cost-of-Mirage-2000-upgrade-raises-eyebrows/articleshow/18804336
.cms; Chidanand Rajghatta, "Nuclear Weapons: India Keeps Pace with Pakistan, but Focuses on China,"
Times of India, June 3, 2013, https://timesofindia.indiatimes.com/india/Nuclear-weapons-India-keeps
-pace-with-Pakistan-but-focuses-on-China/articleshow/20404208.cms; Ajai Shukla, "Advanced Agni-6
Missile with Multiple Warheads Likely by 2017," *Business Standard*, May 8, 2013, http://www.business
-standard.com/article/economy-policy/advanced-agni-6-missile-with-multiple-warheads-likely-by-2017
-113050800034_1.html; Dassault Aviation, "Rafale Specifications and Performance Data," accessed
December 14, 2017, http://www.dassault-aviation.com/en/defense/rafale/specifications-and-perfor
mance-data/; Sukhoi Company, "Su-30MK Aircraft Performance," accessed December 14, 2017, http://
www.sukhoi.org/eng/planes/military/su30mk/lth/; Hans M. Kristensen and Robert S. Norris,
"Indian Nuclear Forces, 2015," *Bulletin of the Atomic Scientists* 71, no. 5 (September 2015): 77–83; and Hans
M. Kristensen and Robert S. Norris, "Indian Nuclear Forces, 2012," *Bulletin of the Atomic Scientists* 68, no. 4
(July–August 2012): 96–101.

in the West presume. . . . Beijing has long managed a thermonuclear program, and so this is one of many options India should push forwards with, as well as reconsidering our nuclear defense posture, which is outdated and ineffective. We have to follow the technological curve. And where China took it, several decades before us, with the hydrogen bomb, India has to follow."[34] However, Indian missile development does not merely entail ever-greater size and range extensions. Nor do India's broadening nuclear aspirations mean Pakistan is overlooked as a strategic target. A growing interest in short-range missile development threatens new frictions with Pakistan.

India's present missile platforms emanate from the Integrated Guided Missile Development Program (IGDMP), established in 1983 to organize military projectile development. Initial IGDMP projects included the Prithvi (short-range surface-to-surface), Agni (intermediate-range ballistic), Trishul (short-range surface-to-air), Akash (medium-range surface-to-air), and Nag (antitank) missile platforms. Of these platforms, the Prithvi and Agni were intended to be nuclear-capable.[35] The Prithvi and Agni served as the two operative missile platforms leading up to India's 1998 nuclear tests. Their limited ranges and positioning near Pakistan indicated the centrality of Pakistan to Indian nuclear and strategic planning in this period.[36] However, successive Indian governments in the 1990s were reluctant to subject these platforms to regular tests, and this caused observers to doubt their operable capability. Governments, on the other hand, feared that conducting launch tests would generate geopolitical tension and accusations of nuclear aggression. The consequent opacity surrounding the number of Prithvi and Agni missiles available, their technical reliability, and their specific attributes reflected India's general approach to nuclear policy in the 1990s. India would neither confirm nor deny its possession of nuclear weapons, and thus, it refrained from visible efforts to deploy a nuclear arsenal, including launch tests.

A new coalition government, led by the Bharatiya Janata Party (BJP), entered office in March 1998 and initiated a nuclear policy based on developing an overt nuclear arsenal. This policy involved a series of tests of nuclear devices in May 1998 with a range of yields (see table 1.2). The tests intended to provide greater technical certainty about Indian nuclear capabilities and to symbolize the dawning of a new era of India as a nuclear power. The series, operated by a joint DRDO-DAE team of scientists, included a single thermonuclear test. The yield from this test was initially reported as meeting design specifications of forty-five kilotons. However, K. Santhanam, a senior DRDO member of the test team, publicly disavowed this stated yield in 2009. He claimed the yield was instead a "fizzle," or significantly lower than that intended by the test team.[37] There is no present effort to independently test the credibility of DAE claims regarding the performance and reliability of their warheads; thus, technical doubts permeate India's nuclear force development. Following the 1998 tests, the Prithvi and Agni programs were accelerated. The Agni-I was formally commissioned in 1999. The government also approved a test of the Agni-II in April 1999 and announced it would be commissioned in August 1999.[38]

DRDO has continued missile research, developing longer-range platforms ranging from the Agni-III to the prospective Agni-VI. As DRDO has every bureaucratic interest in expanding its missile portfolio to acquire greater budget allocations and political prestige, the only limit to Indian missile aspirations at present appears to be technical knowledge.[39] A recent DRDO chief, remarking on potential limits to Indian missile development, said that "DRDO does not wait for the threat to become a reality before it starts the development," and thus, it intends to "develop capabilities to meet futuristic threats."[40]

The rapid improvements in technical knowledge afforded by the more supportive stance of post-1998 governments for nuclear force development, plus this seeming tendency for missile decisions to move into DRDO operational discretion, could account for the acceleration of the missile program over the past few years. More recent missile platforms, beginning with the Agni-III, have

TABLE I.2

Shakti (Power) Nuclear Testing Round, May 1998

Date	Identifier	Description
May 11, 1998	Shakti I	Two-stage thermonuclear device with fusion boosted primary; 45 kt yield
May 11, 1998	Shakti II	Lightweight pure fission device; 12 kt yield
May 11, 1998	Shakti III	Experimental pure fission device; 0.3 kt yield
May 13, 1998	Shakti IV	Experimental device; 0.5 kt yield
May 13, 1998	Shakti V	Experimental device; 0.2 kt yield

Source: Data from Nuclear Weapon Archive, "India's Nuclear Weapons Program: Operation Shakti: 1998," last modified March 30, 2001, http://nuclearweaponarchive.org/India/IndiaShakti.html.

been subjected to only a few tests. While these latest platforms are important for understanding the direction of Indian nuclear force development, their full operational credibility and deployment is still a ways off.[41]

These new missiles, given their ranges and DRDO remarks about them, are more clearly focused on Chinese targets.[42] This became especially obvious when DRDO unveiled the Agni-V (5,000-kilometer [3,107-mile] range) missile, the first missile able to reach east coast Chinese metropolitan targets like Beijing or Shanghai. As a further sign of robust intent against potential Chinese aggression, DRDO is reportedly developing MIRV warheads. Several existing Agni missile models are unable to host MIRVs without substantial redesign and miniaturization of warheads, but DRDO has nevertheless expressed its intention to pursue this project.[43] Although the National Security Council Secretariat (NSCS) includes a planning cell that makes recommendations about nuclear force structure, this cell does not appear to have set an upper ceiling for Indian missile range and destructive capability.[44]

These large, long-range ballistic missiles garner the greatest media attention, but substantive developments in short-range ballistic and cruise missiles could also affect Indian security and relations with neighbors. The 150-kilometer-range Prahaar ballistic missile, for example, is intended to replace the Prithvi nuclear-capable missile. Flight trials for the Prahaar are currently being planned, and the potential nuclear mission of this missile is still unclear.[45] With a warhead capacity of 200 kilograms (441 pounds), the Prahaar is currently defined by DRDO as a purely conventional missile. This is because the agency has not yet mastered warhead miniaturization to smaller than 500 kilograms (1,102 pounds), not because there are political limitations against fielding tactical nuclear missiles.[46] Former DRDO head V. K. Saraswat has confirmed that the Prahaar can host "different types of warheads," and a retired Indian army officer has described the missile as providing a nuclear war-fighting option.[47]

An Indian defense analyst has outlined potential Indian Army thinking behind the development and induction of the Prahaar. The missile can assume the burden of local target strikes from the IAF and permit the IAF to focus its attention on deeper strikes within the adversary territory:

> During a future round of all-out hostilities (which are likely to be of limited duration, not lasting more than two weeks), the Army wants to reduce as much as possible its traditional reliance on the Indian Air Force (IAF) for close air support and tactical battlespace interdiction during the first 72 hours and wants to acquire its own integral ground-launched firepower assets that are available on demand under all weather conditions. This in turn will free the IAF to realise its larger objective of shaping the multi-theatre battlespace by decapitating the enemy's tactical airpower through relentless offensive air superiority and counter-base air campaigns.[48]

Another short-range Indian missile platform to be inducted as part of the Indian posture against China is the Brahmos. The Brahmos is a hypersonic cruise missile jointly designed with Russia with a range of 600 kilometers (373 miles). Like the Prahaar, the Brahmos may not be able to host nuclear warheads, although a Russian official has said that the missile is "capable of carrying a nuclear warhead."[49] The Indian Army plans to induct at least five Brahmos regiments, each consisting of thirty-six Brahmos missiles and at least one stationed in Arunachal Pradesh as part of India's force posturing against China.[50] A new variant of the Brahmos, the Block-III, is designed with a "steep-dive" capability that can reach targets on the rear side of a mountain. As well as targeting adversary force concentrations and facilities, this variant is supposedly ideal for blocking mountain pathways.[51] The Block-III is intended for induction into the Mountain Strike Corps.[52]

Indeed, Chinese media have recently expressed concern regarding the assignment of a Brahmos regiment to the Indian Army's Forty-First Artillery Division in Arunachal Pradesh, close to the Line of Actual Control with China.[53] Furthermore, a forthcoming Brahmos-II (K) missile is designed to eliminate "hardened targets such as underground bunkers and weapons storage facilities."[54] This variant suggests Indian interest in using the missile for deep conventional strikes, especially if it is launched from Sukhoi fighters.

The 1,000-kilometer (622-mile) range Nirbhay land-, air-, and sea-launched cruise missile, however, is the most likely of the short-range platforms to be assigned a nuclear mission. Both the Nirbhay and Brahmos presently use Russian technology, which means India is restricted in its ability to use them as nuclear missiles under the Missile Technology Control Regime (MTCR). However, efforts are under way in both missile programs to indigenize the technology.

While marking a significant advance in the technical sophistication of Indian missiles, full indigenization would also permit the Nirbhay and Brahmos to be added to India's nuclear arsenal. India is presently testing a new domestically developed turbofan engine to replace the Nirbhay's existing engine, which is the missile's last component of foreign origin. The Brahmos's more advanced ramjet engine has been identified by Indian defense scientists as an obstacle in the path to indigenization.[55]

These technical points, however, do not diminish the potential for these three platforms to be assigned nuclear missions in the future or for Pakistan and Chinese commanders to view them as nuclear-armed and to misinterpret their deployment in a crisis. Even if they are attributed as solely conventional missions, the Prahaar and Brahmos platforms are well suited to potential counterforce strike packages, and their deployment or related preparations could be interpreted in this light by adversaries. The Brahmos-II (K) appears especially intended for operations against high-value military targets. The impending assignment of these missiles to Sukhoi fighters and the nuclear missions attached to these fighters by the SFC creates further ambiguity around potential Sukhoi missions that could prove dangerous in a crisis. Therefore, Indian forces' intention to make greater use of these missiles could substantially blur the threshold between conventional and nuclear conflict for India's targeted adversary.

Indian missile developments are therefore reaching new heights of technical maturity. However, only the Prithvi, Agni-I, and Agni-II have been fully inducted, meaning the full integration of the later Agni platforms into India's nuclear force is at this point only a future aspiration. Nevertheless, the announcement of the Agni platforms and the Prahaar indicates the Indian government's intention to field a diversified missile force. Political limits to the eventual size, range, and destructive yield of this force are difficult to identify. Moreover, projects such as MIRV warheads raise questions about whether "credible minimum deterrence" is an apt descriptive term for the direction of India's nuclear force and whether India is interested in a nuclear war-fighting capacity.

AIR-BASED DELIVERY VEHICLES

The IAF serves as the oldest and most technically dependable leg of India's nuclear arsenal. Indeed, this is a common development chronology: the American B-52, British V-bomber, and French Mirage IV-A acted as the backstop for their respective nuclear forces while more-advanced land-based missile and sea-based nuclear platforms were being developed. A former SFC chief, remarking on the operational status of India's nuclear force, affirmed, "Today it is the air which would be the greater reliance factor as far as India is concerned, the answer to that would be yes."[56] This reliance on air-based delivery of nuclear warheads looks set to continue in the near term as India extends the life spans of two nuclear-capable aircraft, the Mirage 2000H and Jaguar IS/IB, and as land-based induction proceeds at a slow place.

The Mirage 2000H nuclear-capable bomber, with a range of 1,800 kilometers (1,119 miles), is of French origin. Mirages have been historically assigned nuclear missions by the French air force.[57] Two Mirage 2000H squadrons are currently deployed at Gwalior Air Force Station, 270 kilometers (168 miles) southeast of New Delhi. This location and the aircraft's range allow nuclear-armed Mirage 2000H bombers to strike Pakistan and parts of southwest China. In 2010 an agreement was concluded with France to upgrade India's entire Mirage fleet of fifty-one aircraft.[58] The refurbishments will extend the life span of the fleet by twenty to twenty-five years. The refitted Mirage 2000H bombers will also reportedly be able to carry intermediate-range missiles, which could be nuclear-armed. Air-launched missiles currently in development include the short-range (1,000 kilometer, or 622 mile) Nirbhay and the Brahmos. If a nuclear-armed version of these missiles is mated to Mirage 2000H bombers, India will be able to significantly extend its air-launched nuclear strike capacity into Chinese territory.[59]

Jaguar IS/IB nuclear-capable aircraft, with a range of 1,600 kilometers (994 miles), were originally jointly developed by France and Britain. Jaguars are organized in four operational squadrons. Two of these squadrons are deployed at Ambala Air Force Station, located 525 kilometers (326 miles) from Islamabad, and could be certified for nuclear missions.[60] India received its first Jaguar aircraft on loan from Britain in 1979. It currently has ninety-five Jaguar IS/IB planes and is upgrading its entire fleet of Jaguar aircraft. This will extend their life span past 2030. As part of the upgrades, the Rolls-Royce Adour-811 turbofan engines are being replaced with more powerful Honeywell F124IN engines.[61]

These two aircraft are the most likely to have nuclear roles, but other elements of the IAF are also nuclear-capable. The MiG-27, an 800-kilometer-range nuclear-capable bomber initially fielded by the Soviet Union in the 1970s, could potentially have nuclear roles. However, persistent safety issues—extensive enough that a retired wing commander has labeled the plane a "flying coffin"—have led to the decision to phase out the MiG-27 at the end of its natural life span, around 2030.[62]

The Sukhoi Su-30MKI, a multirole fighter jet, is being inducted close to the China border, and certain Sukhois are being assigned nuclear missions. India is aiming for a total Sukhoi fleet of 272 aircraft.[63] The Sukhoi features a maximum range of 3,000 kilometers (1,864 miles) without refueling and 8,000 kilometers (4,971 miles) with two refuelings.[64] India is developing a variant of the potentially nuclear-capable Nirbhay missile to be fitted to certain Su-30MKI aircraft.[65] The SFC has ordered that forty aircraft be assigned for nuclear missions, and forty Sukhois are being modified to carry Brahmos missiles.[66] Sukhois are being stationed at the Tezpur and Chabua airbases in Assam state, close to the eastern Line of Actual Control region, and at Bareilly in Uttar Pradesh, near the central region.[67]

India also committed to purchasing thirty-six French Rafale fighters in April 2015.[68] The Rafale is assigned to carry the ASMP-A nuclear cruise missile in the French air force.[69] As India continues to bolster its air force and general military presence along borders with Pakistan and China, the air leg will continue to play a crucial role in Indian nuclear deterrence.[70]

SEA-BASED DELIVERY VEHICLES

India's draft nuclear doctrine, released in 1999 by the National Security Advisory Board (NSAB), stated that a nuclear triad was required for effective projection of India's nuclear deterrent.[71] Land-based missiles and aircraft delivery systems constitute the first two legs of the nuclear triad, and an underwater nuclear launch capability mounted on nuclear submarines forms the third. A retired admiral has noted that the sea-based nuclear launch capability is important because it provides a "post-surprise attack-survivable force" and, hence, has a "deep stabilising effect" on nuclear deterrence in the region.[72]

India's defense planners and the Indian navy agree. In the 2004 Indian Maritime Doctrine, the Indian navy presented the possession of a submarine-based nuclear delivery capability as "an unstated axiom" of "an independent foreign policy."[73] The 2007 Indian Maritime Strategy similarly states that "it is vital for a nation to possess nuclear submarines capable of launching missiles with nuclear warheads" for effective deterrence to be achieved.[74] The most recent iteration of the maritime strategy, issued in 2015, also includes this emphasis on the importance of sea-based nuclear deterrence.[75]

In the Indian case, there are three main reasons for developing a force of SSBNs with the concomitant armament of long-range ballistic missiles tipped with nuclear warheads.[76] First, the removal of India's nuclear forces from the mainland would effectively neutralize the enemy's nuclear targeting. More nuclear weapons at sea would automatically mean less vulnerability. Second, a naval nuclear force based on nuclear submarines is very difficult to detect and destroy, which provides for "unhurried retribution" after careful evaluation to ensure that the "effect on the enemy would be catastrophic." These characteristics of a sea-based nuclear force complement India's nuclear doctrine, which calls for massive and assured retaliation. The invulnerability of an SSBN fleet to an enemy first strike and its being a reliable second-strike platform also figured prominently in the 2009 Maritime Doctrine of the Indian navy.[77] Third, a robust naval nuclear force would render the need of a large nuclear arsenal redundant. Since nuclear submarines are hard to detect, India need not fear attrition in its nuclear deterrent capability owing to a first strike by the enemy. A minimal nuclear arsenal would suffice to project deterrence. In fact, some experts have argued that once India achieves the capability to fire a nuclear-tipped ballistic missile from the depths of the ocean, the "country's deterrence could shift entirely underwater and realign its strategy to those of Britain and France."[78]

In the last decade, India has made some notable gains in developing the sea-based component of its nuclear deterrence force. India's drive toward a nuclear submarine force dates back to the early 1980s, when it began developing fast-moving, deep-diving nuclear-powered attack submarines that could be used for hunting surface naval ships.[79] But India did not formally declare its intention to develop SSBNs until the end of 2008. According to one analyst, India avoided making a formal declaration—except in its nuclear doctrine, which put the need for SSBNs in extremely vague language—before it consummated the Indo-US nuclear deal in 2008.[80] This way India could avoid complicating its accommodation in the global nuclear regime via the deal with the United States.

The Advanced Technology Vessel (ATV) is India's flagship project in its sea-based nuclear deterrence force. Several S-class submarines will be developed by 2030–35 as part of this project.[81] The first vessel in this class—the S-2, popularly known as *Arihant* (destroyer of enemies)—was launched by Prime Minister Manmohan Singh on July 26, 2009. *Arihant* is 10 meters (33 feet) in width, 106 meters (348 feet) in length, and has a displacement of 5,000–6,000 tons.[82] The cost of INS *Arihant* has been estimated at $2.9 billion.[83]

Arihant is powered by an 80–85 MW pressurized water reactor running on HEU.[84] The reactor fuel for the vessel comes from DAE's uranium enrichment facilities at the Rare Materials Plant at Rattehalli.[85] The International Panel on Fissile Materials estimates that India's inventory of HEU stands at around 1 ton of 90 percent enriched U235.[86] As mentioned earlier, the Rattehalli plant has a current capacity of 4,500 SWU/y and can produce 22 kilograms (49 pounds) of 90 percent enriched uranium annually.[87] Although this amount is sufficient for *Arihant* alone, it will be inadequate for the fleet of four to six SSBNs that the Indian navy envisages in the near future.[88] However, India has made both qualitative and quantitative changes to its HEU-producing capacity.

Russia has been particularly helpful in India's quest for an undersea nuclear deterrent capability. Russian expertise and technical assistance facilitated *Arihant*'s reactor design.[89] India has also leased nuclear submarines from Russia in

TABLE I.3

Design Specifics of INS *Arihant*

Displacement	5,000–6,000 t
Length	106 m (347.8 ft)
Hull width	10 m (32.8 ft)
Reactor type and power	pressurised water reactor, 80–85 MW
Reactor fuel	Highly enriched uranium
Fuel replenishment period	10 years
Turbines	47,000 hp, 70 MW
Diving depth	300 m (984.2 ft)
Endurance	100 days
Weapons	12 k-15 Sagarika SRBMs, 4 k-4 IRBMs[a]

[a]SRBM = short-range ballistic missile; IRBM = intermediate-range ballistic missile.

Source: Data from Frank O'Donnell and Yogesh Joshi, "Lost at Sea: The Arihant in India's Quest for a Grand Strategy," *Comparative Strategy* 33, no. 5 (2014): 470–71.

order to learn how to operate this complex technological system and then train Indian navy personnel in nuclear submarine operation.[90] In 1988 the Soviet Union provided India with a Project 670 Skat attack nuclear submarine (NATO Charlie I class) that remained with the Indian navy till the end of 1990.[91] Currently, India operates a Project 971 Schuka-B SSBN (NATO Akula II class), renamed INS *Chakra*, leased from Russia for ten years. INS *Chakra* joined the Indian navy in April 2012.[92] India and Russia are now negotiating a lease of a second nuclear submarine.[93] India is the only country to have operated a foreign SSN (a submarine that is nuclear-powered but not nuclear-armed).[94]

The reactor for India's nuclear submarine program was developed by a joint team of personnel from the Indian navy and DAE at the Indira Gandhi Center for Atomic Research at the Prototype Testing Center (PTC) in Kalpakkam. Their work was conducted under the guise of the Plutonium Recycle Project (PRP). The marine propulsion reactor was conceived in the late 1980s, but the project gathered momentum only in the 1990s. The land-based version of the PRP submarine reactor became operational in November 2003, and subsequently, efforts were made to integrate it with the hull of the first S-class nuclear submarine, *Arihant* (see table 1.3).[95] Launched in 2009, *Arihant* initiated sea trials in 2014. Work on the second and third SSBNs—the S-3 and S-4—is already under way.[96]

Arihant has four sea-launched ballistic missile (SLBM) tubes. These tubes can host up to twelve short-range ballistic missiles capable of hitting targets at a range of 500–1,000 kilometers (311–622 miles) or four intermediate-range ballistic missiles with a range of 3,500–4,000 kilometers (2,175–2,486 miles).[97] DRDO is responsible for developing the delivery vehicles used with *Arihant*.

The short-range ballistic missile, code-named K-15 and recently rechristened BO-5, is also called the Sagarika (Oceanic).[98] The Sagarika is 10.4 meters (34.1 feet) in length and can carry a five-ton warhead 750 kilometers (466 miles).[99] It is a two-stage ballistic missile with an underwater boost mechanism propelled by liquid fuel and an atmospheric phase propelled by solid fuel.[100] After the November 2012 missile tests, DRDO claimed that the Sagarika was almost ready for integration with INS *Arihant*.[101] About fifteen Sagarika tests from submerged pontoons were conducted between 1998 and November 2015.[102] The K-4/K-X intermediate-range ballistic missile, with a range of 3,500 kilometers (2,175 miles) is also under development; its design borrows heavily from the technological lessons learned during the Agni project and is based on the Agni III.[103] A further-reaching SLBM, the 5,000-kilometer (3,107-mile) range K-5, is also reportedly being studied by DRDO.[104]

In April 2016, for the first time, DRDO conducted an SLBM launch from on board *Arihant*, signaling integration of missile components with India's first SSBN.[105] The K-4 is small enough to be hosted on *Arihant* without substantial modifications, but the K-5 likely cannot be modified to fit the SSBN. The K-5 will therefore have to wait for the larger, redesigned S-5 SSBN, the fourth boat in the *Arihant* class.[106]

Once DRDO has developed and successfully integrated its MIRV technology with the existing missile systems, India's ability to deliver nuclear payloads in the second-strike mode will be significantly increased. With MIRV technology, India's ability to deliver nuclear payloads from sea or land will substantially exceed the twelve nuclear warheads presently envisaged on each nuclear submarine.

Still, delays often beset India's major technological projects, including the ATV. Since 2008 projections have continually been made about when INS *Arihant* would become fully operational, but the SSBN is still in trials. Given these delays, it is likely that a fully operational force of four to six submarines will take at least a decade to be fielded.[107]

Four technical hurdles will need to be overcome before an active and capable sea-based nuclear force—and nuclear triad—can be achieved. The first, which has been overcome with the April 2016 SLBM test, is the successful integration of ballistic missiles with the nuclear submarine.[108] Second is the operational success of the miniaturized nuclear reactor under the duress of extensive sea operations.[109] Third is the fact that the first few submarines, including INS *Arihant*, are unlikely to be a major component of India's nuclear deterrence force. Various authorities concerned with the project have characterized INS *Arihant* as a technology demonstrator rather than a robust deterrent projector.[110] Some also doubt the performance of the S-class vessels given that INS *Arihant* and the others belong to the first and second generation of SSBNs. As one analyst argues, "It is only when the S-5 vessel with a new design and a powerful nuclear reactor is launched, which could be two decades away, can India hope to have a semblance of sea-based deterrence against China."[111]

Fourth is the "grossly insufficient" range of India's SLBMs for effective deterrence.[112] The limited range of Sagarika, many argue, is a cause of concern because the submarines would have to move closer to enemy shores to fire these missiles for effective targeting of the opponent.[113] This would in turn make the SSBNs extremely vulnerable to detection and ultimately destruction through antisubmarine warfare. Many are also concerned with the nuclear delivery capacity of the K-15 and missiles for *Arihant*.[114] These concerns are mainly regarding the size of the nuclear warhead that will be delivered by these ballistic and cruise missiles. Has India sufficiently miniaturized warhead designs to successfully integrate them with small missile platforms?

Once these technical problems have been addressed, other questions remain about the eventual role of *Arihant* in India's defense posture. Indian strategic discourse has suggested several potential missions for the SSBN, ranging from offering greater technical assurance to India's nuclear deterrence to demonstrating symbolic resolve against Chinese incursions in the Indian Ocean.[115] The government needs to provide more guidance on the specific mission of the *Arihant*-class fleet in Indian defense and to recognize its inherent limits as a last-resort nuclear backstop. This reflects the recurring problem in Indian nuclear force development: the ambitions of technical nuclear force development do not appear to correspond with the credible minimum deterrence posture.

Command and Control

India has set up a robust command and control structure to manage decision making regarding its nuclear force. However, this structure, designed to channel the decisions of the top political officials, will operate only as well as the attentions of these officials permit.[116] This flaw in the structure is shown by the growing disjuncture between nuclear force development and doctrinal statements.

Following the 1998 nuclear tests, the Indian government established new institutions to manage nuclear policymaking. These institutions replaced a previous informal command chain concentrating authority in the Prime Minister's Office. In the wake of the tests, the government decided that a more transparent command structure was necessary to reassure the world that India understood, in the words of a former NSAB chair, "the very nature of nuclear deterrence as practiced by a civilian democracy dictates that decisions relating to the nature and scope of the arsenal, its deployment and use, be anchored in the larger architecture of democratic governance."[117] The two new institutions, publicly announced in the 2003 iteration of India's nuclear doctrine, were the Nuclear Command Authority (NCA) and SFC.[118] The NCA is the civilian body that considers and issues nuclear deployment orders.[119] The SFC, led by military service chiefs, receives and executes orders from the NCA and manages the operationalization of the nuclear force.[120]

NCA membership consists of two tiers: a political council chaired by the prime minister and an executive council chaired by the NSA. The political council includes the Cabinet Committee on Security (including the prime minister, defense minister, home minister, finance minister, and external affairs minister) and the NSA. The executive council advises the political council and organizes the execution of its orders. The executive council is chaired by the NSA and typically includes the cabinet secretary, the principal scientific advisor, the foreign secretary, and the chiefs of DAE, DRDO, the Research and Analysis Wing, the Intelligence Bureau, the Joint Intelligence Committee, and the SFC.[121] A Strategic Planning Staff (SPS) exists within the NCA and provides "strategic inputs on the quality and reliability of India's nuclear weapons and delivery systems, foreign intelligence, global arms control and disarmament initiatives, and long term planning for the arsenal."[122]

The SFC is headed by a rotating military chair and the three service chiefs and organizes the military execution of orders emanating from the NCA. In the event of a decision to use nuclear weapons then, the command structure is organized so that the decision is made solely by the NCA political council; its execution is organized by the NCA executive council; and its ultimate execution is conducted by the SFC.[123]

The NCA meets intermittently to review aspects of nuclear force development; one report specifies that meetings are held "every three to six months."[124] The functioning of the NCA and SFC remains a work in progress. Notable efforts have been made to build security into agency operations. NCA council meetings occur at hardened facilities, and an alternate NCA command chain has been established in the event hostilities disrupt the first chain laid out previously. NCA processes are also reportedly aided by two NSCS groups (located in the Prime Minister's Office): the Strategy Program Staff and the Strategic Armament Safety Authority. The former group includes both military and civilian officials and examines potential future Indian nuclear force postures. The latter group assesses the quality of nuclear armaments storage.[125]

The existence of civil-military coordination mechanisms within the NCA structure and the two dedicated planning groups have been cited as evidence that the Indian government has achieved more effective political and technical oversight over nuclear force development today as compared to previous eras. The structural participation of the military in these multiple elements of the nuclear command chain, in this reading, suggests its greater involvement in nuclear force development.[126]

However, there are still limits to this trend. At present the Office of the Chairman of the Joint Chiefs of Staff Committee coordinates the execution of joint SFC–armed forces procedures to mate warheads to delivery vehicles in the event of an order to do so from the NCA. This chairman position is currently held by the most senior of the three existing armed forces chiefs, leading to a higher turnover rate, with chairmen occasionally serving less than a year in post. The chairman also currently retains operational responsibility for his own service during this tenure.

The prime minister was reportedly briefed in late May 2014 on the need to appoint a four-star chairman of the Joint Chiefs of Staff Committee for a two-year term to assume operational management of the nuclear arsenal, with service responsibility to be assigned to a different service chief. SFC officials and external analysts think such a reform will enhance the focus and coordinative ability of the chairman in implementing NCA directives. Nevertheless, this recommendation was in a "planning" stage as of 2017.[127]

The existence of these new structures, however, has also left one of the core problems of Indian nuclear force development—the discrepancy between the respective levels of confidence of DRDO and the military in the technical reliability of nuclear missiles—unaddressed. DRDO conducts few tests of its missiles before announcing them ready for military induction; its director general remarked in July 2015, "To declare a missile proven, we need three consecutive successful tests."[128] By comparison the US Minuteman-I ICBM had been tested fifty-six times by 2002, and the Trident-II D5 SLBM, carried aboard American and British SSBNs, had been successfully tested 155 times by February 2015.[129] The military has historically not shared the confidence of DRDO in this technical reliability certification system.[130] Commenting on the Agni-I and Agni-II missiles in 2008, a retired army officer observed that they had "been tested five times, which is inadequate to generate confidence in a nuclear capable missile."[131] A retired naval officer and nuclear expert noted in 2012, "There is no adequate user acceptance system in place for inducting missiles into the strategic arsenal."[132]

Concerns regarding warhead performance join the concerns with general missile reliability. The prime minister reportedly established a committee to investigate claims regarding underperformance of the thermonuclear device tested in 1998 made by retired DRDO scientist K. Santhanam in 2009.[133] While the new civil-military structures and planning cells may aid some elements of nuclear force planning, their existence has evidently not led to resolution of the differences between the defense scientific agencies and the military regarding missile reliability standards, one of the most prominent issues in contemporary Indian nuclear force development. Moreover, the prime minister's decision to set up a new committee to investigate warhead performance raises additional questions regarding the ability of existing entities to ensure reliability. It therefore appears premature to suggest that these new oversight structures are successfully addressing the political and technical governance questions about Indian nuclear force development raised throughout this chapter.

Ballistic Missile Defense

India is currently involved in research, procurement, and development of indigenous and external BMD systems.[134] However, it is unclear if a government assessment of the full interactions of different BMD postures with India's conventional and nuclear force policies has shaped these programs. Several recent concerns have raised India's interest in these systems: China's and Pakistan's growing nuclear arsenals; chances of accidental launch from Pakistan; fears of a bolt-from-the-blue strike on India; Pakistan's unstable political situation; and the growing influence of non-state actors, especially in the Pakistani body politic.[135] However, DRDO's seeming operational discretion to build and test indigenous BMD systems also creates reliability concerns regarding the accuracy of its capability claims. India's BMD programs, like its nuclear force development, need to be directed by a strategic defense review and regularly evaluated to ensure they meet national defense goals.

India's interest in BMD systems goes back to the initiation of the IGMDP in 1983.[136] IGMDP not only led to the development of offensive missile platforms, like the Prithvi and Agni series, but also had a defensive component in the form of Akash surface-to-air missiles (SAMs) initially planned for air defense measures and equipped with the potential for conversion to a theater missile defense system.[137] In the 1990s DRDO started conceptualizing a missile defense plan for India. Subsequently, DRDO and the Indian military also entered negotiations for BMD platforms and associated technologies with Israel and Russia.[138]

Currently, the Indian system boasts both exo-atmospheric and endo-atmospheric BMD capability, providing India with two layers of defense.[139] Whereas Prithvi air defense (PAD) is supposed to tackle incoming missiles at a range of 50–80 kilometers (31–50 miles) (exo-atmospheric interception), the advanced air defense (AAD) mainly consists of Akash SAMs and can kill incoming missiles at the range of 15–30 kilometers (9–18 miles) (endo-atmospheric interception).

Clearly, the PAD system is devised for midcourse interception, and the AAD is a terminal phase interception system that can only counter incoming missiles after their entry into the atmosphere. In their present configuration, these systems are designed to counter missiles with ranges close to 2,000 kilometers (1,243 miles) and speeds from Mach 3 to Mach 8. However, DRDO has recently announced its intentions to intercept missiles with over 5,000-kilometer (3,107-mile) range.[140] These systems, named AD-1 and AD-2, could counter missiles with a velocity of up to Mach 12 to 15.[141]

To bolster its missile-tracking capabilities, India imported in 2002 and 2005 two Green Pine radars, which Israel uses in its Arrow missile defense system.[142] India had quietly initiated technical collaboration with Israel to develop a long-range tracking radar and with France to develop a guidance control radar before the 1998 nuclear weapon tests.[143] The Swordfish long-range tracking radar (LRTR), based on Green Pine radar technology, can reportedly track more than 200 objects with a minimum two-inch (five-centimeter) diameter at a range of 600–800 kilometers (373–497 miles). DRDO plans to further extend the range of this radar system to 1,500 kilometers (932 miles). India had previously acquired the Phalcon airborne warning and control system (AWACS) from Israel at a cost of $2 billion. This system provided India low-level detection of hostile missile platforms and considerably enhanced the response time for missile interception.[144]

Although these indigenous efforts have been primarily to develop midcourse and terminal phase interception capabilities, India has also looked abroad for more limited or pinpoint defenses. India uses the Barak antimissile defense system on its naval ships and has purchased S-300 antimissile systems from Russia.[145] The George W. Bush administration expressed interest in selling US PATRIOT (Phased Array Tracking Radar to Intercept on Target) Advanced Capability (PAC-2) anti-ballistic-missile systems to India at the end of the Next Steps in Strategic Partnership (NSSP) process in December 2004.[146] At this point, India is more interested in the more advanced PAC-3 system.[147]

India is also studying the Israeli Arrow missile defense system, but because this system was codeveloped with the United States, sale of this system to India would require US permission.[148] Still, the US has generally shown increasing openness to joint missile defense system development with India in recent years.[149]

These foreign systems are ineffective for interception of long-range ballistic missiles. Their usefulness instead lies in intercepting tactical ballistic missiles of short range and medium velocities and in augmenting India's endothermic missile interceptions, thereby increasing redundancy in missile interception.[150] They may be used only in pinpoint defenses. Despite these limitations, regular engagement with the US, Israel, and Russia regarding system development allows India to observe general missile defense technology evaluation in these countries.

Since 2006 India has been actively testing components of its indigenous ballistic missile defense program (see table 1.4). DRDO has conducted over ten missile interception tests, the latest in March 2017.[151] The agency has claimed that more recent tests have been executed in a deployment mode, with members of the Indian Army and IAF observing the tests.[152] During a 2012 test series, DRDO demonstrated its capability to simultaneously intercept multiple targets using both AAD and PAD systems.[153] Soon after these tests, V. K. Saraswat, then director general of DRDO, declared that by early 2014 India would be ready to field area BMD systems, specifically systems able to protect Delhi and Mumbai.[154] It is uncertain at the time of writing in spring 2018 when such systems will be actually operable. Indeed, similar claims about BMD have been made before; in fact, members of India's defense scientific enclave tend to make premature declarations of capability regarding missile interception programs.[155]

Further, DRDO has claimed that its BMD systems have a 90 percent accuracy level. Given that missile defense systems in other advanced-technology states have an accuracy level of about 70 percent, external analysts are skeptical of DRDO's claims.[156] Also, because tests of the systems have been conducted in controlled environments, critics question DRDO claims that these systems are ready for deployment.[157] The missiles targeted in these interceptions are slow-moving Prithvi missiles; indigenous BMD systems may not be as successful against missiles with solid-fuel booster mechanisms that travel at far greater speeds.

The Indian government is so confident in its technical claims regarding indigenous capabilities and the time frame for their induction perhaps in part because it is planning to buy Russian missile interception systems. The Ministry of Defense approved purchase of up to five Russian S-400 Triumph air and missile defense systems in December 2015 at an estimated cost of $4.5–7 billion.[158] The IAF reportedly urged this purchase because its leadership doubted progress in developing indigenous BMD capabilities.[159] A subsequent agreement for India to buy five systems from Russia for $6 billion was reported in October 2016.[160] Three systems would be positioned in the West in support of Indian defenses against Pakistan, and two systems would be allocated to the East for defense against China.[161] An analyst noted, "The S-400 outperforms India's AAD on nearly all counts, including flight speed when fitted with the upgraded 48N6 interceptor."[162] In December 2015 a cooperation agreement was signed between Reliance Defense, an Indian defense contractor, and Almaz-Antey

TABLE I.4

Ballistic Missile Interception Tests by DRDO

System	Date	Results
PAD	November 2006	Successful interception at 50 km (31 mi)
AAD	December 6, 2007	Successful interception at 15 km (9.3 mi)
PAD	March 6, 2009	Successful interception at 75 km (46.6 mi)
AAD	March 15, 2010	Tests aborted (hostile missile lost trajectory)
AAD	July 26, 2010	Successful interception at 15 km (9.3 mi)
AAD	March 6, 2011	Successful interception at 16 km (9.9 mi)
AAD	February 10, 2012	Successful interception at 15 km (9.3 mi)
PAD/AAD	November 23, 2012	Multiple interceptions accomplished by destroying incoming projectiles at altitudes 15 and 120 kms (9.3 and 74.5 mi). Whereas AAD was a physical interception, the PAD test was an electronic simulation.
Prithvi Defense Vehicle (PDV)	April 27, 2014	Unsuccessful "near miss" of target
AAD	April 6, 2015	Unsuccessful miss of target
AAD	November 22, 2015	Unclear whether interception occurred
AAD	May 15, 2016	Successful interception at 20–40 km (12.4–24.8 mi)
PDV	February 12, 2017	Successful interception at 100 km (62 mi)
AAD	March 1, 2017	Successful interception at 65 km (40.4 mi)

Sources: Data from Franz-Stefan Gady, "India Successfully Tests Supersonic Interceptor Missile," *The Diplomat*, March 2, 2017, http://thediplomat.com/2017/03/india-successfully-tests-supersonic -interceptor-missile-2/; Franz-Stefan Gady, "India Successfully Tests Prithvi Defense Vehicle, A New Missile Killer System," *The Diplomat*, February 15, 2017, http://thediplomat.com/2017/02/india -successfully-tests-prithvi-defense-vehicle-a-new-missile-killer-system/; Rahul Bedi, "India Successfully Tests Ballistic Missile Shield," *Jane's Defence Weekly*, May 16, 2016, http://www.janes.com/; Rahul Bedi, "Indian BMD System Suffers Test Failure," *Jane's Defence Weekly*, April 8, 2015, http://www.janes .com/; Hemant Kumar Rout, "AAD Interceptor Missile Test Fired," *New Indian Express*, November 23, 2015, http://www.newindianexpress.com/states/odisha/2015/nov/23/AAD-Interceptor-Missile-Test -Fired-846821.html; and Saurav Jha, "Some Notes on DRDO's PDV Ballistic Missile Defence Interceptor," *IBNLive*, August 30, 2014, http://www.news18.com/blogs/india/saurav-jha/some-notes-on-drdos-pdv -ballistic-missile-defence-interceptor-10879-748578.html.

JSC, a Russian defense firm that holds the S-400 technology license. Reliance Defense specifically identified the S-400 system as a target for cooperation. It also identified the Tor 1-M SAM system, which can intercept some terminal-phase cruise missiles, as a second potential focus of cooperation.[163] The Indian government's readiness to commit substantial financial resources to off-the-shelf, foreign BMD systems, at the reported behest of IAF, suggests limits to its confidence in the reliability and deliverability of the indigenous systems promised by DRDO.

THE FUTURE OF INDIAN BALLISTIC MISSILE DEFENSE

As far as the scope of missile interception is concerned, there are indications that India will opt for limited coverage rather than development of a national missile interception capability.[164] Three reasons underpin this development trajectory. First, for Indian strategists, a limited missile interception would better complement India's nuclear doctrine.[165] Second, and perhaps more determinatively, development of a national missile interception capability is simply beyond India's economic means. With increasing capabilities in the booster strength of its ballistic interceptors and of its ground radars, it is hard to foresee a mission creep in India's ballistic missile interception program. This is in contrast to the emerging technical mission creep visible in India's nuclear force development. Last, some have argued that limited defenses may help in augmenting strategic stability in South Asia.[166]

Nevertheless, that economic reasoning is the best guide to understanding the contours of India's future BMD program reflects again the evolution of India's defense scientific enclave with no clear national defense objectives. This is an important point as India's BMD capabilities, while still nascent and arguably mostly unproven, can still affect regional deterrence relationships and thus Indian nuclear policy. A Pakistani analyst has written of the deterrence challenge of a hypothesized Indian Cold Start conventional attack shielded from retaliation by BMD.[167] The current Pakistani permanent representative to the United Nations (UN) has also remarked on the perceived Indian BMD threat in justifying Pakistan's nuclear arsenal growth.[168] China's neuralgia regarding BMD systems as a threat to its minimum deterrent posture has also been well documented.[169] For a BMD capability to most effectively serve Indian defense, it must be assessed as part of a wider strategic defense review and its development subsequently guided by the holistic structuring of strategic priorities and projects.

CONCLUSION

Today's Indian nuclear force is scaling new heights of technical achievement at an unprecedented rate. Progress in delivery vehicles is seemingly constrained only by present limits in technical knowledge. India stands on the brink of possessing ICBMs, a potential new generation of short-range nuclear-capable missiles, and a seaborne nuclear-armed submarine fleet. While some measures of restraint, such as the testing moratorium practiced since 1998, are in place, the wide scope and ambition of India's nuclear force development are increasingly difficult to reconcile with the country's stated nuclear posture of credible minimum deterrence.

Despite the impressive progress made in delivery vehicle development, the Indian nuclear force is affected by governance issues. DRDO and DAE evidently enjoy broad discretion in conceiving, planning, and fielding new nuclear capabilities. Their technical ambitions, now entering the realms of thermonuclear and multiple-warhead ICBMs and short-range nuclear weapons, threaten to undermine India's stated nuclear doctrine of restraint. Also, as it is in their bureaucratic interest to announce eye-catching new nuclear projects, the rapid successive unveiling of the later Agni models has not been matched with equal effort in ensuring their full operational credibility. Only the Prithvi, Agni-I, and Agni-II have graduated from the developmental stage to full military deployment. A third wrinkle is the technical doubt surrounding the viability of Indian thermonuclear warheads following the 1998 "fizzle," which is perpetuated by the opacity of India's strategic enclave and its resistance to any kind of external peer review of its claims.

Other governance issues surface in the study of India's nuclear command chain. Although the command chain establishes clear principles of elected civilian decision-making supremacy and transparency in the flow of orders, ad hoc practices characterize the irregular NCA meeting times and SFC staffing, which is determined by interservice haggling. India's unique civil-military relations, featuring an overweighting of the civil over the military, also influence the command chain, with military expertise relegated to the NCA's second tier and having little institutional voice in other elements of Indian nuclear decision making. Like concerns over the technical hardware of Indian nuclear force development, these "software" concerns involving effective governance demonstrate that full operationalization of India's stated capabilities remains a work in progress.

Nevertheless, the growing diversity of India's delivery vehicles generates questions about whether its nuclear posture is still one of credible minimum deterrence or whether a transition toward fielding war-fighting capabilities is taking place. Developments at the lower end of the spectrum—such as the potential nuclear capability of the Prahaar, Brahmos, and Nirbhay—threaten to blur the line between conventional and nuclear conflict. At the upper end of the spectrum, no range limit appears to have been set for the Agni series. A strategic defense review, including a reassessment of Indian nuclear policy, is required to clarify the Indian nuclear doctrine and posture given its changing delivery vehicle portfolio and to ensure India's nuclear force remains categorized as a last-resort tool.

India's expanding strategic footprint is, however, not entirely driven by an abstract technological quest; it is equally influenced by myriad security challenges the state faces in the nuclear domain, especially from its nuclear adversaries: Pakistan and China. The next chapter will look in detail at the security challenges posed by Pakistan and the way these amplify questions regarding how India will situate its nuclear force in its regional context.

NOTES

1. Amit Gupta, "India's Third-Tier Nuclear Dilemma: N Plus 20?" *Asian Survey* 41, no. 6 (November–December 2001): 1044–63; Amit Gupta, "Communication: Building a Nuclear Triad; India's Draft Nuclear Doctrine," *Pacifica Review: Peace, Security and Global Change* 12, no. 2 (June 2000): 189–95.
2. Gupta, "India's Third-Tier Nuclear Dilemma," 1044–63.
3. K. Subrahmanyam, "Nuclear Tests: What Next?" *India International Centre Quarterly* 25, no. 2/3 (Summer/Monsoon 1998): 52.
4. Ibid., 53, 54, 58, 59.
5. Raja Menon, "Parallel Stories: Soldiers, Scientists and Nuclear Logic," *India International Centre Quarterly* 25, no. 2/3 (Summer/Monsoon 1998): 78.
6. Ali Ahmed, "Taking Nuclear War-Fighting Seriously," *Indian Defence Review* 27, no. 1 (March 2012), http://www.indiandefencereview.com/spotlights/taking-nuclear-war -fighting-seriously/; Gaurav Kampani, *China-India Nuclear Rivalry in the "Second Nuclear Age,"* IFS Insights no. 3 (Oslo: Norwegian Institute for Defence Studies, November 2014), 6, https://brage.bibsys.no/xmlui/bitstream/handle/11250/226454/1 /Insight2014_3.pdf.
7. Shivshankar Menon, *Choices: Inside the Making of India's Foreign Policy* (Washington, DC: Brookings Institution Press, 2016), 110, 117; Vipin Narang, "Beyond the Nuclear Threshold: Causes and Consequences of First Use" (remarks delivered to Carnegie International Nuclear Policy Conference, Carnegie Endowment for International Peace, March 20, 2017), https://southasianvoices.org/wp-content/uploads/2013/08/Vipin -Narang-Remarks-Carnegie-Nukefest-2017.pdf; Shashank Joshi, "India's Nuclear Doctrine Should No Longer Be Taken for Granted," *The Interpreter* (blog), March 22, 2017, https://www.lowyinstitute.org/the-interpreter/indias-nuclear-doctrine-should -no-longer-be-taken-granted; Rajesh Rajagopalan, "India's Nuclear Strategy: A Shift to Counterforce?" *Expert Speak* (blog), March 30, 2017, http://www.orfonline.org /expert-speaks/india-nuclear-strategy-shift-counterforce/.
8. Rahul Bedi, "India's Nirbhay Cruise Missile Fails Third Test Flight," *IHS Jane's Missiles and Rockets*, October 19, 2015, http://www.janes.com/.
9. International Panel on Fissile Materials, "Countries: India," last modified February 2013, http://fissilematerials.org/countries/india.html. See also M. V. Ramana, "India," in *Assuring Destruction Forever*, 2015 ed., ed. Ray Acheson (Geneva: Reaching Critical Will, 2015), 38–43; Hans M. Kristensen and Robert S. Norris, "Indian Nuclear Forces, 2015," *Bulletin of the Atomic Scientists* 71, no. 5 (September 2015): 77–83.
10. R. Rajaraman, "Estimates of India's Fissile Material Stocks," *Science and Global Security* 16, no. 3 (December 2008): 76–79.

11. R. Rajaraman, "India's Nuclear Arms Control Quandary," *Bulletin of the Atomic Scientists* 66, no. 2 (March 2010): 31.

12. Rajaraman, "Estimates of India's Fissile Material," 76. In another assessment, the estimated capacities of fissile material have been projected slightly higher: 9.2 kilograms (20.3 pounds) for CIRUS and 23 kilograms (50.7 pounds) for DHRUVA. See Zia Mian, A. H. Nayyar, R. Rajaraman, and M. V. Ramana, "Fissile Materials in South Asia and the Implications of the U.S.-India Nuclear Deal," *Science and Global Security* 14, no. 2/3 (January 2007): 121.

13. Rajaraman, "Estimates of India's Fissile Material," 76. CIRUS was decommissioned in 2010 and would have produced an additional 18 kilograms (39.6 pounds) of WgPu by 2010. On the other hand, if DHRUVA had continued to operate at a similar capacity in 2008–13, it would have churned out an additional 154 kilograms (339.5 pounds) of WgPu by the middle of 2015, taking India's stocks of fissile material up to 955 kilograms (2,105.4 pounds). If one subtracts the three-year cooling period for spent fuel from these reactors before WgPu could be separated at a reprocessing facility, 66 kilograms (145.5 pounds) of this WgPu remains in the spent fuel. Approximately 131 kilograms (288.8 pounds) of this WgPu has been consumed in India's nuclear weapon tests. Hence, India's current WgPu inventory should stand at about 758 kilograms (1,671 pounds). If 4–5 kilograms (8.8–11 pounds) of WgPu is considered enough fissile material for one warhead, India has an inventory to produce 150–90 nuclear warheads. On the other hand, if one goes by Ashley Tellis's assertion that India's unsophisticated nuclear designs consume 6–7 kilograms (13.2–15.4 pounds) of WgPu, India could have an inventory of fissile material sufficient for 110–26 nuclear warheads. See Ashley J. Tellis, *India's Emerging Nuclear Posture: Between Recessed Deterrence and Ready Arsenal* (Santa Monica, CA: RAND, 2001), 486.

14. Rajaraman, "India's Fissile Material Stocks," 78.

15. Richard L. Garwin, "Reactor Grade Plutonium Can Be Used to Make Powerful and Reliable Nuclear Weapons: Separated Plutonium in the Fuel Cycle Must Be Protected as if It Were Nuclear Weapons," Council on Foreign Relations, August 26, 1998, http://www.fas.org/rlg/980826-pu.htm.

16. Nuclear Weapon Archive, "India's Nuclear Weapons Program: Operation Shakti: 1998," last modified March 30, 2001, http://nuclearweaponarchive.org/India/India Shakti.html.

17. Rajaraman, "India's Fissile Material Stocks," 79. In another assessment published in 2010, Rajaraman estimates fourteen tons of RgPu stocks. See Rajaraman, "India's Nuclear Arms Control Quandary," 30.

18. Rajaraman, "India's Fissile Material Stocks," 81.

19. R. Rajaraman, "Implications of the Indo-US Nuclear Deal for India's Energy and Military Programmes," in *Indo-US Nuclear Deal: Seeking Synergy in Bilateralism*, ed. P. R. Chari (New Delhi: Routledge, 2013), 127–46.

20. Alexander Glaser and M. V. Ramana, "Weapon-Grade Plutonium Production Potential in the Indian Prototype Fast Breeder Reactor," *Science and Global Security* 15, no. 2 (November 2007): 105.

21. G. Balachandran, "On Fast Breeder Programme, Begin a Civil Debate," *Indian Express*, February 10, 2006, http://archive.indianexpress.com/oldStory/87591/.

22. Mian et al., "Fissile Materials in South Asia," 124.

23. "Summary of Records of the Meeting Held in the Planning Commission for Discussion

of Fourth Plan Proposal of the DAE (Confidential)," December 16, 1969, Subject File 131, Asok Mitra Papers, Nehru Memorial and Museum Library, New Delhi.

24. Interview with a senior nuclear scientist, Mumbai, April 9, 2017.

25. The three-stage program involved a development trajectory that in the first phase used natural uranium (U-238) as the primary fuel for India's nuclear reactors. Irradiation of this natural uranium produced plutonium as spent fuel and upon reprocessing could generate a highly fissile isotope called Pl-239. The second stage intended to use Pl-239 as fuel in breeder reactors alongside natural uranium and thorium. Irradiation of thorium in breeder reactors resulted in U-233, which was as good a fissile material as was naturally occurring U-235. Therefore, for the third and the last stage, Bhabha envisioned nuclear reactors using U-233 as the primary fuel. A good summary of India's three-stage atomic energy program is available in G. Venkataraman, *Bhabha and His Magnificent Obsessions* (Hyderabad: Universities Press India, 1994), 156–57.

26. David Albright and Susan Basu, "India's Gas Centrifuge Enrichment Program: Growing Capacity for Military Purposes" (Washington, DC: Institute for Science and International Studies, January 18, 2007), http://isis-online.org/publications/southasia/indiagrowingcapacity.pdf.

27. M. V. Ramana, "An Estimate of India's Uranium Enrichment Capacity," *Science and Global Security* 12, no. 1/2 (2004): 116.

28. Albright and Basu, "India's Gas Centrifuge Enrichment Program."

29. Ramana, "India's Uranium Enrichment Capacity," 120–21.

30. Adrian Levy, "Experts Worry That India Is Creating New Fuel for an Arsenal of H-bombs," Center for Public Integrity, December 16, 2015, http://www.publicintegrity.org/2015/12/16/18874/experts-worry-india-creating-new-fuel-arsenal-h-bombs.

31. Rajesh Rajagopalan, *Nuclear Non-proliferation: An Indian Perspective*, FES Briefing Paper 10 (New Delhi: Friedrich Ebert Stiftung, October 2008), 3, http://library.fes.de/pdf-files/iez/global/05793.pdf.

32. Jaideep A. Prabhu, "Fast Forwarding to Thorium," *The Hindu*, November 3, 2015, http://www.thehindu.com/opinion/op-ed/fast-forwarding-to-thorium/article7834156.ece.

33. Chidanand Rajghatta, "Nuclear Weapons: India Keeps Pace with Pakistan, but Focuses on China," *Times of India*, June 4, 2013, https://timesofindia.indiatimes.com/india/Nuclear-weapons-India-keeps-pace-with-Pakistan-but-focuses-on-China/articleshow/20404208.cms.

34. Levy, "India Is Creating New Fuel."

35. DRDO, *IGMDP: Integrated Guided Missile Development Program* (New Delhi: DRDO, 2008); Gaurav Kampani, "Stakeholders in the Indian Strategic Missile Program," *Nonproliferation Review* 10, no. 3 (Fall–Winter 2003): 48.

36. Vipin Narang, "Pride and Prejudice and Prithvis: Strategic Weapons Behavior in South Asia," in *Inside Nuclear South Asia*, ed. Scott D. Sagan (Stanford, CA: Stanford University Press, 2009), 163.

37. Sachin Parashar, "Pokhran II Not Fully Successful: Scientist," *Times of India*, August 27, 2009, https://timesofindia.indiatimes.com/india/Pokhran-II-not-fully-successful-Scientist/articleshow/4938610.cms.

38. Frank O'Donnell and Harsh V. Pant, "Evolution of India's Agni-V Missile: Bureaucratic Politics and Nuclear Ambiguity," *Asian Survey* 54, no. 3 (May–June 2014): 607.

39. Ibid., 594–99.

40. Avinash Chander, "Quality Our Concern," interview by T. S. Subramanian, *Frontline* 29, no. 10 (May 19–June 1, 2012), http://www.frontline.in/static/html/fl2910/stories/20120601291003600.htm.

41. For a fuller exploration of the implications of limited testing for Indian nuclear force reliability, see Frank O'Donnell, "Aim for Higher Testing Standards," *Pioneer*, July 27, 2015, http://www.dailypioneer.com/columnists/oped/aim-for-higher-testing-standards.html.

42. T. S. Subramanian, "Agni-V and Neighbours," *Frontline* 29, no. 9 (May 5–18, 2012), http://www.frontline.in/static/html/fl2909/stories/20120518290912800.htm.

43. Gaurav Kampani, "Is the Indian Nuclear Tiger Changing Its Stripes?" *Nonproliferation Review* 21, no. 3/4 (2014): 386–87; Verghese Koithara, *Managing India's Nuclear Forces* (New Delhi: Routledge, 2012), 130; Y. Mallikarjun, "Agni-V to Be Modified to Attack Multiple Targets," *The Hindu*, May 28, 2013, http://www.thehindu.com/news/national/agniv-to-be-modified-to-attack-multiple-targets/article4758676.ece.

44. Shyam Saran, "Is India's Nuclear Deterrent Credible?" (remarks delivered at the India Habitat Centre, New Delhi, April 24, 2013), 11, http://krepon.armscontrolwonk.com/files/2013/05/Final-Is-Indias-Nuclear-Deterrent-Credible-rev1-2-1-3.pdf.

45. Ministry of Defence (MoD), *Annual Report 2013–14* (New Delhi: Government of India [GoI], 2014), 87.

46. Frank O'Donnell, "Managing India's Missile Aspirations," *IDSA Comment*, February 10, 2013, http://www.idsa.in/idsacomments/ManagingIndiasMissileAspirations_fodonnell_100213; Surya Gangadharan, "Prahaar India's Counter to Pak's Nasr Missile?" News18.com, July 27, 2011, http://www.news18.com/blogs/india/surya-gangadharan/prahaar-indias-counter-to-paks-nasr-missile-11878-745907.html.

47. Narang, "Five Myths," 145; Ahmed, "Taking Nuclear War-Fighting Seriously."

48. Prasun K. Sengupta, "'Prahaar' NLOS-BSM Explained," *Tris* (blog), September 17, 2011, http://trishul-trident.blogspot.com/2011/09/prahaar-nlos-bsm-explained.html.

49. Narang, "Five Myths," 146.

50. "More Brahmos to Come: India Gets Two New Supersonic Cruise Missiles," *Sputnik*, April 1, 2016, https://sputniknews.com/asia/201604011037324740-russia-india-brahmos-missile/.

51. Saurav Jha, "India's Missile Build Up Gathers Pace with Monday's Brahmos Test by the Indian Army," News18.com, April 9, 2014, http://www.news18.com/blogs/india/saurav-jha/indias-missile-build-up-gathers-pace-with-mondays-brahmos-test-by-the-indian-army-10879-748397.html.

52. Vishal Thapar, "India to Arm Counter-China Corps with Steep Dive BrahMos Cruise Missile," *Arming India*, July 18, 2015, http://armingindia.com/India-To-Arm-Counter-China-Corps-With-Steep-Dive-BrahMos-Cruise-Missile-18-07-15.htm.

53. Rezaul H. Lashkar, "China Warns India against Deploying Brahmos Missile in Arunachal Pradesh," *Hindustan Times*, August 23, 2016, http://www.hindustantimes.com/india-news/china-warns-india-against-deploying-brahmos-missile-in-arunachal-pradesh/story-ui0psBJZ3WOvn3aJzLCqiJ.html.

54. Rahul Singh, "India Successfully Test-Fires Brahmos Supersonic Cruise Missile," *Hindustan Times*, March 11, 2017, http://www.hindustantimes.com/india-news/india-successfully-test-fires-brahmos-supersonic-cruise-missile/story-B3ERwFWxKpQAasgOxmho7I.html.

55. Jugal R. Purohit, "A View from the Brahmos Missile Factory," *India Today*, February 19,

2017, http://indiatoday.intoday.in/story/bramos-missile-russia-military/1/886323
.html; Vivek Raghuvanshi, "India Extends Homemade Missile Program Despite Failed
Test," *Defense News*, January 11, 2017, https://www.defensenews.com/naval/2017/01
/11/india-extends-homemade-missile-program-despite-failed-test/; "Indian Army
Acquiring More Land Attack Brahmos Supersonic Missiles," *Indian Defence Update*,
September 14, 2016, http://defenceupdate.in/indian-army-acquiring-land-attack
-brahmos-supersonic-missiles/; Toby Dalton and George Perkovich, "India's Nuclear Options and Escalation Dominance," Carnegie Endowment for International
Peace, May 19, 2016, http://carnegieendowment.org/2016/05/19/india-s-nuclear
-options-and-escalation-dominance-pub-63609; Gurmeet Kanwal, "India's Nuclear
Force Structure 2025," Carnegie Endowment for International Peace, June 30, 2016,
http://carnegieendowment.org/2016/06/30/india-s-nuclear-force-structure-2025
-pub-63988; Lashkar, "China Warns India."

56. Hans M. Kristensen, "India's Nuclear Forces 2008," *Strategic Security* (blog), Decem-
ber 4, 2008, http://blogs.fas.org/security/2008/12/india/#comment-658; Vishal
Thapar, "N-capable Agni-III Ready, but Aircraft Remain First Choice," News18.com,
May 8, 2008, http://www.news18.com/videos/india/missile-288735.html.

57. Dassault Aviation, "Mirage 2000 Family," accessed December 14, 2017, https://www
.dassault-aviation.com/en/defense/customer-support/operational-aircraft/mirage
-2000/.

58. "India's Fighter Upgrades: Mirage 2000s Grounded for Parts, Waiting for Upgrades,"
Defense Industry Daily, September 27, 2016, http://www.defenseindustrydaily.com
/indias-fighter-upgrades-mirage-2000s-next-02891; Rajat Pandit, "High Cost of Mi-
rage-2000 Upgrade Raises Eyebrows," *Times of India*, March 5, 2013, https://timesof
india.indiatimes.com/india/High-cost-of-Mirage-2000-upgrade-raises-eyebrows/ar
ticleshow/18804336.cms.

59. US National Air and Space Intelligence Center (NASIC), *Ballistic and Cruise Missile
Threat 2009* (Wright-Patterson Air Force Base, OH: NASIC, 2009), 29.

60. Kristensen and Norris, "Indian Nuclear Forces, 2015," 78; Hans M. Kristensen and
Robert S. Norris, "Indian Nuclear Forces, 2012," *Bulletin of the Atomic Scientists* 68, no.
4 (July–August 2012): 100.

61. Greg Waldron, "Aero India: Honeywell Tenders for Jaguar Engine Upgrade," *Flight
Global*, February 7, 2013, http://www.flightglobal.com/news/articles/aero-india
-honeywell-tenders-for-jaguar-engine-upgrade-382049/; IISS, *Military Balance 2015*,
251; Gautam Datt, "More Teeth for Jaguar: Nearly 120 of the Indian Air Force Jets
Are Being Modernised," *Mail Online India*, September 10, 2012, http://www.dailymail
.co.uk/indiahome/indianews/article-2200832/More-teeth-jaguar-Nearly-120-Indian
-Air-Force-jets-modernised.html.

62. Gautam Datt, "Indian Air Force Lost Half of MiG Fighter Jets in Deadly Crashes,"
India Today, May 3, 2012, https://www.indiatoday.in/india/north/story/iaf-lost-half
-of-mig-fighter-jets-in-deadly-crashes-100926-2012-05-03.

63. Indo-Asian News Service, "IAF Inducts Second Sukhoi Squadron in Northeast," *Strat-
Post*, March 1, 2011, http://www.stratpost.com/iaf-inducts-second-sukhoi-squadron
-in-northeast.

64. Airforce Technology, "Su-30MKI Multirole Fighter Aircraft, India," accessed December
14, 2017, http://www.airforce-technology.com/projects/su-30mki-multirole-fighter
-aircraft-india/.

65. Douglas Barrie and Neelam Mathews, "Su-30MKI to Get Indian Nirbhay Cruise Missile," *Aviation Week*, May 10, 2010, http://aviationweek.com/awin/su-30mki-targeted -indian-nirbhay-cruise-missile.

66. Rakesh Krishnan Simha, "How the Su-30 MKI Is Changing the IAF's Combat Strategy," *Russia Beyond*, January 5, 2014, https://www.rbth.com/blogs/2014/01/05/how _the_su-30_mki_is_changing_the_iafs_combat_strategy_32099.

67. Rajat Pandit, "With Eye on China, India Deploys Akash Missiles in Northeast," *Times of India*, August 2, 2014, https://timesofindia.indiatimes.com/india/With-eye-on -China-India-deploys-Akash-missiles-in-northeast/articleshow/40645978.cms.

68. Ankit Panda, "India Will Buy 36 Ready-to-Fly Dassault Rafale Fighters from France," *The Diplomat*, April 13, 2015, http://thediplomat.com/2015/04/india-will-buy-36 -ready-to-fly-dassault-rafale-fighters-from-france/.

69. "France's Rafale Fighters: A Courant in Time?" *Defense Industry Daily*, April 29, 2013, http ://www.defenseindustrydaily.com/frances-rafale-fighters-au-courant-in-time-05991/.

70. IISS, *Military Balance 2016*, 250–51.

71. NSAB, "Draft Report of National Security Advisory Board on Indian Nuclear Doctrine," August 17, 1999, http://www.mea.gov.in/in-focus-article.htm?18916/Draft +Report+of+National+Security+Advisory+Board+on+Indian+Nuclear+Doctrine.

72. Raja Menon, *A Nuclear Strategy for India* (New Delhi: Routledge, 2000).

73. Indian Navy, *Indian Maritime Doctrine*, INBR 8 (New Delhi: GoI, 2004), 49.

74. Indian Navy, *Freedom to Use the Seas: India's Maritime Military Strategy* (New Delhi: GoI, 2007), 76.

75. Indian Navy, *Ensuring Secure Seas: Indian Maritime Security Strategy* (New Delhi: GoI, 2015), 4850.

76. Tellis, *India's Emerging Nuclear Posture*; Menon, *Nuclear Strategy for India*.

77. Indian Navy, *Indian Maritime Doctrine*, 27.

78. Menon, *Nuclear Strategy for India*.

79. Yogesh Joshi, *The Imagined Arsenal: India's Nuclear Decision-Making, 1973–76*, Nuclear Proliferation International History Project Working Paper No. 6 (Washington, DC: Woodrow Wilson International Center for Scholars, 2015), 31–37, https://www.wil soncenter.org/sites/default/files/WP6--The%20Imagined%20Arsenal_2.pdf; Mark Gorwitz, "The Indian SSN Project: An Open Literature Analysis," Federation of American Scientists, December 1996, accessed December 14, 2017, http://www .fas.org/nuke/guide/india/sub/ssn/part01.htm.

80. Andrew C. Winner, "The Future of India's Undersea Nuclear Deterrent," in *Strategy in the Second Nuclear Age: Power, Ambition, and the Ultimate Weapon*, ed. Toshi Yoshihara and James R. Holmes (Washington, DC: Georgetown University Press, 2013), 168.

81. Pravin Sawhney and Vijay Shankar, "Is the Navy's Newest Sub Worth the Price?" *The Hindu*, April 4, 2012, http://www.thehindu.com/opinion/op-ed/is-the-navys-new est-sub-worth-the-price/article2829121.ece.

82. PTI, "India's First Nuke Submarine INS Arihant Launched," NDTV, July 26, 2009, https:// www.ndtv.com/india-news/indias-first-nuke-submarine-ins-arihant-launched-398648.

83. PTI, "PM Launches INS Arihant in Visakhapatnam," *Times of India*, July 26, 2009, https://timesofindia.indiatimes.com/city/hyderabad/PM-launches-INS-Arihant-in -Visakhapatnam/articleshow/4820660.cms; Naval Technology, "Arihant Class Submarine," accessed December 14, 2017, http://www.naval-technology.com/projects /arihant-class/.

84. World Nuclear Association, "Nuclear Powered Ships," last modified November 2017, http://www.world-nuclear.org/information-library/non-power-nuclear-applica tions/transport/nuclear-powered-ships.aspx.

85. Ramana, "India's Uranium Enrichment Capacity," 115.

86. International Panel on Fissile Materials, "Countries: India," last modified January 15, 2016, http://fissilematerials.org/countries/india.html.

87. PTI, "Navy to Operate Five Nuclear Submarines by End of Decade," *Economic Times*, April 5, 2012, https://economictimes.indiatimes.com/news/politics-and-nation/navy -to-operate-five-nuclear-submarines-by-end-of-decade/articleshow/12547328.cms.

88. Ramana, "India's Uranium Enrichment Capacity," 120–21.

89. GlobalSecurity.org, "Arihant—Advanced Technology Vessel (ATV)—Boat," last modi fied February 12, 2017, accessed December 14, 2017, http://www.globalsecurity.org /military/world/india/atv.htm.

90. Yogesh Joshi, "Leased Sub Key to India's Naval Modernization," *World Politics Review*, June 1, 2012, http://www.worldpoliticsreview.com/articles/12014/leased-sub -key-to-indias-naval-modernization.

91. Nuclear Threat Initiative, "India's Submarine Capabilities," September 30, 2015, http://www.nti.org/analysis/articles/india-submarine-capabilities/.

92. "INS Chakra Inducted into Indian Navy," *The Hindu*, April 5, 2012, http://www.the hindu.com/news/national/ins-chakra-inducted-into-navy/article3280078.ece.

93. Vladimir Radyuhin, "India in Talks with Russia on Lease of a Second Nuclear Sub marine," *The Hindu*, March 13, 2013, http://www.thehindu.com/news/international /india-in-talks-with-russia-on-lease-of-second-nuclear-submarine/article4505333.ece.

94. However, it is important to note that such transfers come with riders attached. India is forbidden to use INS *Chakra* in cases of war and hostilities and even to place nuclear weapons aboard.

95. T. N. Rohit, "India Built N-Sub in Kalpakkam under Codename 'PRP,'" *Times of India*, August 3, 2009, https://timesofindia.indiatimes.com/india/India-built-N-sub -in-Kalpakkam-under-codename-PRP/articleshow/4850142.cms.

96. S. Anandan, "Second Nuclear Submarine Headed for Year-End Launch," *The Hindu*, January 14, 2013, http://www.thehindu.com/news/national/Second-nuclear -submarine-headed-for-year-end-launch/article13364895.ece.

97. Winner, "India's Undersea Nuclear Deterrent," 172.

98. Missile Threat, "Sagarika (K-15)," October 29, 2012, https://missilethreat.csis .org/missile/sagarika-shaurya/.

99. Frank O'Donnell and Yogesh Joshi, "Lost at Sea: The Arihant in India's Quest for a Grand Strategy," *Comparative Strategy* 33, no. 5 (2014): 470.

100. Naval Technology, "Indian Navy's K-15 SLBM Successfully Completes Develop ment Trials," January 29, 2013, http://www.naval-technology.com/news/news indian-navys-k-15-slbm-successfully-completes-development-trials.

101. Y. Mallikarjun, "India to Integrate K-15 Missiles into Nuclear Submarine Soon," *The Hindu*, November 20, 2012, http://www.thehindu.com/todays-paper/tp-na tional/india-to-integrate-k15-missiles-into-nuclear-submarine-soon/article4113618 .ece.

102. Hemant Kumar Rout, "First Ejection Test of Underwater Missile from Arihant Submarine Successful," *New Indian Express*, November 27, 2015, http://www.new indianexpress.com/states/odisha/2015/nov/27/First-Ejection-Test-of-Under

water-Missile-From-Arihant-Submarine-Successful-848950.html; Pallava Bagla, "A White Rocket Rose from the Water," *Outlook*, February 11, 2013, https://www .outlookindia.com/magazine/story/a-white-rocket-rose-from-the-water/283764.

103. Saurav Jha, "Trends in Missile Development in India: An Interview with DRDO's Missile Man Avinash Chander," News18.com, February 7, 2013, http://www.news18 .com/blogs/india/saurav-jha/ballistic-missile-programme-10879-747567.html; Rehman, *Murky Waters*, 13.

104. Winner, "India's Undersea Nuclear Deterrent," 168.

105. Ankit Panda, "India Successfully Tests Intermediate-Range Nuclear-Capable Submarine-Launched Ballistic Missile," *The Diplomat*, April 10, 2016, http://thediplomat .com/2016/04/india-successfully-tests-intermediate-range-nuclear-capable-submarine-launched-ballistic-missile/.

106. Rehman, *Murky Waters*, 13.

107. PTI, "Navy to Operate."

108. Jaideep A. Prabhu, "India's Nuclear Triad—Are We Blowing the Trumpet Too Soon?" *Tehelka Blog*, January 13, 2013, http://blog.tehelka.com/indias-nuclear-triad-are-we -blowing-the-trumpet-too-soon/.

109. M. V. Ramana, *The Power of Promise: Examining Nuclear Energy in India* (New Delhi: Penguin Books India, 2013).

110. Sandeep Unnithan, "India's Secret Undersea Weapon," *India Today*, January 17, 2008, http://indiatoday.intoday.in/story/The+secret+undersea+weapon/1/3659.html.

111. Sawhney and Shankar, "Worth the Price?"

112. Arun Prakash, "India's K-15 Launch: Defence Scientists Do Nation Proud," *India Strategic*, January 2013, http://www.indiastrategic.in/topstories1894_India_K-15 _launch_defence_scientists_do_nation_proud.htm.

113. Raja Menon, "Just One Shark in the Deep Blue Ocean," *Outlook*, August 10, 2009, https://www.outlookindia.com/magazine/story/just-one-shark-in-the-deep-blue -ocean/261048.

114. Arun Prakash, "India's K-15 Launch and Dangers Beyond," *Gulf News*, January 30, 2013, http://gulfnews.com/opinion/thinkers/india-s-k-15-launch-and-the-dangers -beyond -1.1139370.

115. O'Donnell and Joshi, "Lost at Sea," 475–77.

116. O'Donnell and Pant, "Evolution of India's Agni-V Missile," 606–7.

117. Saran, "Is India's Nuclear Deterrent Credible?" 10.

118. Press Information Bureau (PIB), "Cabinet Committee on Security Reviews Progress in Operationalizing India's Nuclear Doctrine," January 4, 2003, http://mea.gov.in /press-releases.htm?dtl/20131/The_Cabinet_Committee_on_Security_Review s_perationalization_of_Indias_Nuclear_Doctrine.

119. Rajat Pandit, "Manmohan Singh Takes Stock of Country's Nuclear Arsenal," *Times of India*, May 17, 2011, https://timesofindia.indiatimes.com/india/Manmohan-Singh -takes-stock-of-countrys-nuclear-arsenal/articleshow/8380273.cms.

120. Josy Joseph, "India Sets Up Strategic Forces Command," *Rediff*, January 4, 2003, http://www.rediff.com/news/2003/jan/04nuke1.htm.

121. Cabinet Secretariat, "Composition of Cabinet Committees," September 11, 2017, https://cabsec.nic.in/shownewpdf.php?type=cabinetcommittees&id=1285&spec ial; Koithara, *Managing India's Nuclear Forces*, 101–2.

122. Gaurav Kampani, "India's Evolving Civil-Military Institutions in an Operational

Nuclear Context," Carnegie Endowment for International Peace, June 30, 2016, http://carnegieendowment.org/2016/06/30/india-s-evolving-civil-military-institu tions-in-operational-nuclear-context-pub-63910.

123. Harsh V. Pant, "India's Nuclear Doctrine and Command Structure: Implications for Civil-Military Relations in India," *Armed Forces and Society* 33, no. 2 (January 2007): 249.

124. Pandit, "Manmohan Singh Takes Stock."

125. Saran, "Is India's Nuclear Deterrent Credible?" 11.

126. Kampani, "Nuclear Tiger," 393–94.

127. Rajat Pandit, "4-Star General for Tri-services Issues?" *Times of India*, July 22, 2015, https://timesofindia.indiatimes.com/india/4-star-General-for-tri-services-issues /articleshow/48167519.cms; Praveen Swami, "Modi Briefed on Nuclear Command Structure," *The Hindu*, June 4, 2014, http://www.thehindu.com/news/national/Modi -briefed-on-nuclear-command-structure/article11635715.ece.

128. Ajay Banerjee, "N-Sub INS Arihant to Test-Fire Missile," *Tribune*, July 9, 2015, http:// www.tribuneindia.com/news/nation/n-sub-ins-arihant-to-test-fire-missile/104454 .html.

129. Lockheed Martin, "Navy's Trident II D5 Missile Marks 155 Successful Test Flights," February 23, 2015, http://www.lockheedmartin.com/us/news/press-releases/2015 /february/ssc-space-trident.html; Anthony H. Cordesman, *Strategic Threats and National Missile Defenses: Defending the U.S. Homeland* (Westport, CT: Praeger, 2002), 300; O'Donnell, "Aim for Higher Testing Standards."

130. Bharat Karnad, *India's Nuclear Policy* (Westport, CT: Praeger, 2008), 98; Cohen and Dasgupta, *Arming without Aiming*, 33; Koithara, *Managing India's Nuclear Forces*, 128– 29, 219–22.

131. Bharat Verma, "How DRDO Failed India's Military," *Rediff*, January 15, 2008, http:// www.rediff.com/news/2008/jan/15guest.htm; O'Donnell, "Aim for Higher Testing Standards."

132. Koithara, *Managing India's Nuclear Forces*, 151.

133. Kampani, "Nuclear Tiger," 385.

134. Anand Sharma, *Ballistic Missile Defence: Frontier of the 21st Century* (New Delhi: Centre for Air Power Studies and Knowledge World, 2011).

135. Balraj Nagal, "India and Ballistic Missile Defence: Furthering a Defensive Deterrent," Carnegie Endowment for International Peace, June 30, 2016, http://carnegieendow ment.org/2016/06/30/india-and-ballistic-missile-defense-furthering-defensive-deter rent-pub -63966.

136. Gurmeet Kanwal, "A Strategic Imperative: Ballistic Missile Defence and India's War Preparedness," Centre for Land Warfare Studies, June 3, 2008, http://www.claws .in/64/a-strategic-imperative-ballistic-missile-defence-and-indias-war-preparedness -brig-gurmeet-kanwal.html.

137. Bharath Gopalaswamy, "Missile Defense in India," *Bulletin of the Atomic Scientists*, February 27, 2009, http://www.thebulletin.org/web-edition/features/missile-defense-india.

138. Kampani, "Stakeholders," 48–70.

139. The concept of layered defense is also known as defense in depth. Multiple layered missile defense increases the chances of successful interception of incoming missiles. Redundancy, therefore, is accepted as a virtue in BMD systems.

140. PTI, "India to Have Shield from Missiles of 5,000km Range," *Times of India*, June 16, 2013, https://timesofindia.indiatimes.com/india/India-to-have-shield-from-missiles

-of-5000km-range/articleshow/20619039.cms; Rajat Pandit, "DRDO Faces Four Critical Tests in Coming Months," *Times of India*, April 30, 2013, https://timesofindia .indiatimes.com/india/DRDO-faces-four-critical-tests-in-coming-months/article show/19435681.cms.

141. Frank O'Donnell and Yogesh Joshi, "India's Ballistic Missile Defence: Is the Game Worth the Candle?" *The Diplomat*, August 2, 2013, http://thediplomat.com/2013/08 /indias-missile-defense-is-the-game-worth-the-candle/?allpages=yes.

142. Eric Auner, "India's Missile Defense Program Advances," *Arms Control Today*, January 15, 2013, http://www.armscontrol.org/act/2013_01-02/Indian-Missile-Defense -Program-Advances.

143. Sharma, *Ballistic Missile Defence*, 232–37; Ashok Sharma, *India's Missile Defence Programme: Threat Perceptions and Technological Development*, Manekshaw Paper No. 15 (New Delhi: Center for Land Warfare Studies, 2009), http://www.claws.in/images /publication_pdf/1262760881MP_15___111209.pdf, 4.

144. Narayan Menon, "Ballistic Missile Defence System for India," *Indian Defence Review* 27, no. 3 (July–September 2012), http://www.indiandefencereview.com/spotlights /ballistic-missile-defence-system-for-india/.

145. Sharma, *India's Missile Defense Programme*, 4.

146. Gulshan Luthra, "Advanced Patriots on Offer," *Tribune*, March 16, 2005, http://www .tribuneindia.com/2005/20050316/edit.htm#6.

147. Seema Sirohi, "Patriot Games," *Outlook*, December 27, 2004, https://www.outlookin dia.com/magazine/story/patriot-games/226097.

148. Erie Igozi, "Will Israel Be Able to Sell the Arrow System to India?" *IsraelDefense*, January 22, 2012, http://www.israeldefense.co.il/en/content/will-israel-be-able-sell-ar row-system-india.

149. PTI, "US Says It Is Open to Work with India on Missile Shield," *Times of India*, January 18, 2012, https://timesofindia.indiatimes.com/india/US-says-it-is-open-to-work -with-India-on-missile-shield/articleshow/11536963.cms.

150. Sharma, *India's Missile Defense Programme*, 9.

151. Doug Richardson, "AAD Tested against a Two-Missile Threat," *Jane's Missiles and Rockets*, November 27, 2012, http://www.janes.com; T. S. Subramanian, "DRDO to Conduct Eighth Ballistic Interceptor Missile Test This Month," *The Hindu*, November 10, 2012, http://www.thehindu.com/news/national/drdo-to-conduct-eighth-ballistic -interceptor-missile-test-this-month/article4082298.ece.

152. T. S. Subramanian, "Mission Success," *Frontline* 29, no. 4 (February 25–March 9, 2012), http://www.frontline.in/navigation/?type=static&page=flonnet&rdurl=fl2904 /stories/20120309290402900.htm; Mihir Shah, "The Indian Missile Shield: Nothing to Be Baffled About," News18.com, August 8, 2012, http://www.news18.com/blogs /india/saurav-jha/guest-post-2-the-indian-missile-shield-nothing-to-be-baffled -about-by-mihir-shah-10879-747086.html.

153. Saurav Jha, "India's Ballistic Missile Shield: DRDO: 2, Enemy Missiles: 0," News18 .com, November 23, 2012, http://www.news18.com/blogs/india/saurav-jha/indias -ballistic-missile-shield-drdo-2-enemy-missiles-0-10879-747387.html.

154. Debak Das, "India: How Credible Is Its Ballistic Missile Defence?" Institute of Peace and Conflict Studies, November 29, 2012, http://www.ipcs.org/article/nuclear/in dia-how-credible-is-its-ballistic-missile-defence-3768.html.

155. After the success of the first two tests, DRDO claimed that the first phase of missile

interception technology would be ready by 2011. Siddharth Srivastava, "India Hones Its Missile Shield," *Asia Times*, April 16, 2011, http://www.atimes.com/atimes/South _Asia/MD16Df01.html.

156. Amit Gupta, "Special Commentary: India's Missile Defence," Institute of Peace and Conflict Studies, April 12, 2013, http://www.ipcs.org/article/india/special-commen tary-indias-missile-defence-3880.html.

157. Manoj Joshi, "Government Baffled over DRDO Chief's Claims on Missile Shield," *India Today*, July 18, 2012, http://indiatoday.intoday.in/story/government-baffled-over -drdo-chief-claim-on-missile-shield/1/208850.html.

158. Alexandra Katz, "Putin-Modi Talks a Success, but No 'Triumph,'" *Russia Beyond*, December 26, 2015, http://in.rbth.com/economics/cooperation/2015/12/25/putin-modi -talks-a-success-but-no-triumph_555015; Ilya Arkhipov, Natalie Obiko Pearson, and Nc Bipindra, "Modi Meets Putin in Moscow as India Seeks Russian Arms Deals," *Bloomberg Business*, December 24, 2015, http://www.bloomberg.com/news/articles/2015-12-24 /modi-meets-putin-in-moscow-as-india-seeks-russian-weapons-deals.

159. Bedi, "India's Nirbhay Cruise Missile Fails."

160. Kallol Bhattacherjee and Suhasini Haidar, "India to Buy S-400 Missiles from Russia," *The Hindu*, October 16, 2016, http://www.thehindu.com/news/national/India-to -buy-S-400-missiles-from-Russia/article16072929.ece.

161. Rahul Bedi, "S-400s among USD10 Billion in Procurements Approved by Indian MoD," *Jane's Defence Weekly*, December 17, 2015, http://www.janes.com.

162. Ankit Panda, "India Tests Supersonic Advanced Air Defense Missile," *The Diplomat*, November 23, 2015, http://thediplomat.com/2015/11/india-tests-supersonic-ad vanced-air -defense-missile/.

163. Jon Grevatt, "India's Reliance and Russia's Almaz-Antey to Collaborate on Missile Systems," *Jane's Defence Industry*, December 28, 2015, http://www.janes.com/.

164. Rajesh Basrur, *Minimum Deterrence and India's National Security* (Stanford, CA: Stanford University Press, 2006).

165. Happymon Jacob, "Deterrence Debates and Defence," *The Hindu*, April 21, 2014, http://www.thehindu.com/opinion/lead/deterrence-debates-and-defence/arti cle5931349.ece; Yogesh Joshi and Alankrita Sinha, "India and Ballistic Missile Interception: From Theory to Practice," *Nuclear Notes* 2, no. 1 (June 2012): 27–28, https:// www.ciaonet.org/attachments/21076/uploads.

166. Jacob, "Deterrence Debates."

167. Zafar Nawaz Jaspal, "Ballistic Missile Defense: Implications for India-Pakistan Strategic Environment," *National Defence University Journal 2011*, 9, http://www.ndu.edu .pk/issra/issra_pub/articles/ndu-journal/NDU-Journal-2011/01-Ballistic-Missile -Defence.pdf.

168. Maleeha Lodhi, "Pakistan's Nuclear Compulsions," *The News*, November 6, 2012, https://web.archive.org/web/20121106152952/http://www.thenews.com.pk /Todays-News-9-141314-Pakistan%E2%80%99s-nuclear-compulsions.

169. Xia Liping, "On China's Nuclear Doctrine," *Journal of China and International Relations* 3, no. 1 (2015): 169–70; Hans M. Kristensen, "Pentagon Report: China Deploys MIRV Missile," *Strategic Security* (blog), May 11, 2015, https://fas.org/blogs/security /2015/05/china-mirv/; Zhao Tong and David Logan, "What If China Develops MIRVs?" *Bulletin of the Atomic Scientists*, March 24, 2015, http://thebulletin.org /what-if-china-develops-mirvs8133.

2

PAKISTAN'S NUCLEAR THOUGHT AND POSTURE

Implications for India

India faces two principal strategic adversaries—Pakistan and China—that present combined security challenges to India experienced by few other states. While idiosyncratic in their traditions of nuclear thought and the type of challenges they pose, China and Pakistan have colluded in bilateral projects to enhance nuclear-deterrent platforms and supportive infrastructure. The ultimate strategic intentions of Pakistan and India, from each other's point of view, are clouded in threatening ambiguity. New Delhi also worries about growing Chinese projection in the Indian Ocean and China's apparent new wave of nuclear technology support to Pakistan. The scale of mistrust in the India-Pakistan and India-China bilateral relationships is often difficult to fully capture; indeed, a book has recently been devoted to documenting the neuralgic fears of China that often radiate through the Indian strategic community.[1]

Inequitable power differentials further complicate this triad. Pakistan's history of several wars fought against India, including suffering permanent territorial amputation in the 1971 war, has led its policymakers and analysts to view India as the principal external threat to its survival as a state. To asymmetrically compensate for the disparities in the comparative sizes of population, economy, and perceived conventional power projection capabilities between India and Pakistan, Pakistan increasingly emphasizes the role of its nuclear force in its general defense. Unlike India, Pakistan refuses to adopt an NFU posture; this means Rawalpindi envisions a lower threshold of nuclear use than India does. Pakistan's nuclear force, in terms of warhead numbers and production rate, is believed by many analysts today to exceed that of India.

To underline this emphasis on its nuclear force against India, Pakistan has recently introduced a 60-kilometer (37-mile) range nuclear missile, the Nasr, which is widely viewed as intended for nuclear first use against an Indian cross-border conventional advance. No peaceful long-term resolution to the India-Pakistan standoff—involving an end to Pakistan-sponsored terrorism and a mutually satisfactory solution to the Kashmir issue—appears in sight. As the disparity between the economic and conventional military capacities of the two states continues to grow and as their nuclear forces continue to diversify, the task of ensuring stable bilateral relations will grow ever more challenging. Indeed, the coming years will witness the likely entry of this rivalry into a new dimension: naval nuclear-armed deterrence.

This chapter and the next will explore in more detail the nuclear thought and posture of Pakistan and China, the way these countries interact with India, and the security challenges all three states will face in the coming years. This chapter will examine Pakistan, and the next will focus on China. We will argue that while the India-Pakistan-China nuclear triad is already complex, managing stable relations will be further complicated by two developments: (1) the blurring of conventional and nuclear capabilities and thresholds by Pakistan and China and (2) the advent of nuclear-armed naval fleets fielded by all three states. A lack of doctrinal clarity in this context will prove ever more costly for each state in the triad, as the state may find itself plunged into a scenario that it is unprepared for and in which it must decide its nuclear stance in the heat of a crisis, rather than through clear prior planning and communication in peacetime.

These potential complications underline the need for greater doctrinal clarity and a trilateral nuclear dialogue among India, China, and Pakistan to clarify strategic intentions and mutual conceptions regarding the use of nuclear force. While there are bilateral strategic dialogues between India and China, India and Pakistan, and Pakistan and China, there is still no institutionalized trilateral nuclear dialogue. As strategic competition increases among the three states, a dialogue could help to reduce the demand for nuclear weapons and the risk of a miscommunication or misperception during a crisis leading to further escalation.

OVERVIEW

Pakistan's nuclear force has been developed to address long-standing insecurities within the country regarding India's conventional superiority. The permanent loss of East Pakistan (now Bangladesh), engineered by India during its 1971 war with Pakistan, was a direct trigger for the Pakistani nuclear weapon program.[2] Ensuring Pakistan's territorial integrity against another conventional Indian invasion became the program's raison d'être. Because the nuclear program is linked to continuing pervasive fears of Indian subjugation among

Pakistan's security community and because Pakistan's powerful defense establishment has a bureaucratic interest in expanding its aegis, there is little constituency in favor of restraint in nuclear force production in Pakistan. Indeed, Pakistan today has one of the fastest-growing nuclear arsenals in the world, and it is India-specific in its conception and targeting.

This chapter will first explore the tradition of nuclear thought that has characterized Pakistan's nuclear force development from 1998 to the present. It will next outline Pakistan's current nuclear force posture and potential changes in this posture given emerging platforms. The chapter will conclude by exploring the consequences of these shifts for Indian security.

PAKISTAN THREAT PERCEPTIONS AND EFFECTS ON NUCLEAR DOCTRINE

In the 1971 war, India forcibly amputated East Pakistan from West Pakistan. This humiliating and chilling experience—and the subsequent worry that India would return to dissolve the remainder of Pakistan—drove the early Pakistani nuclear weapon program. During the 1980s and 1990s, several flash points further fueled the core insecurity propelling the program. Islamabad perceived India's Operation Brasstacks military exercise in 1986–87, a massive military mobilization, as preparation for a major cross-border invasion with Pakistan's military nuclear facilities as likely targets. The Indian architect of the mobilization, Gen. K. Sundarji, later confirmed that this was its intention, admitting that the operation "was the last chance India had to dominate a non-nuclear Pakistan."[3] The 1998 Indian nuclear tests also triggered fears in Pakistan that India, now shielded by a nuclear deterrent, would immediately attempt to destroy Pakistan's nuclear capabilities. Pakistan's armed forces were placed on the highest alert, and its nuclear establishment raced to conduct nuclear tests and emphasize its overt nuclear deterrent.[4]

Since the 1998 nuclear tests, Pakistan-sponsored militant groups operating from Pakistani territory have conducted increasingly bold strikes in India. These include the Lashkar-e-Taiba attack on the Indian Parliament in December 2001, during which the militants at one point came within twenty-five yards of the minister of external affairs before they were put down by Indian security forces.[5] In November 2008 a group of Lashkar-e-Taiba militants, arriving in Mumbai by boat from Karachi, launched a multiday killing spree throughout the city. Targets included the Chhatrapati Shivaji Terminus central train station, the Taj Mahal Palace and Oberoi Trident Hotels, and the Nariman House Jewish Center. Using gunfire and planting bombs for nearly sixty hours, the terrorists killed 166 people before they were stopped by Indian security forces.[6]

These increasingly audacious strikes have led to Indian frustrations, as its policymakers and defense community perceive that Pakistan's nuclear force and the fear of escalation prohibit India from sufficiently punishing Pakistan and its militant groups in the wake of attacks.[7] These frustrations led the Indian Army to develop a Cold Start doctrine in 2004. Premised on the notion that there is space for limited conventional war with Pakistan before a conflict approaches the nuclear threshold, the doctrine intends the rapid mobilization of Indian mechanized forces, from a "standing cold start" to quickly seizing and holding shallow tracts of Pakistani territory as leverage to coerce Pakistan to end its support for subconventional strikes on India.[8] In developing the doctrine, the military recognized that the Revolution in Military Affairs and India's force modernization plans may provide opportunities to effectuate the strategy.[9] In Pakistan's view Cold Start is the newest face of the continuing Indian threat to invade and dismantle Pakistani sovereignty. Pakistani official and semiofficial statements regularly invoke Cold Start as a core reason why Pakistan needs a nuclear force and continues to develop new delivery platforms. While the doctrine has never been formally adopted by the Indian armed forces or supported by its political leadership, India regularly conducts military exercises that appear to feature operations related to Cold Start. An example is the Drad Sankalp exercise that concluded in December 2015. This involved 45,000 soldiers and emphasized "swift, high-intensity attacks into enemy territory," including "hundreds of T-90 and T-72 main battle tanks, artillery guns and multiple-launch rocket systems."[10]

The perceived threat of an Indian conventional attack has further been underlined by a successful Indian operation conducted in Myanmar in June 2015 to eradicate militant groups hosted there that operate within India.[11] In the wake of the Myanmar raid, an Indian minister said, "We will carry out surgical strikes at the place and time of our own choosing." He added, in a clear reference to India's western border with Pakistan, "Western disturbances will also be equally dealt with."[12] In response, a Pakistani minister drew attention to Pakistan's nuclear force as the shield against such plans: "We are not Myanmar. Don't you know our military strength? Pakistan is a nuclear nation. India should stop day dreaming."[13] Pakistani concerns about a conventional Indian attack were further amplified by the "surgical strike" India conducted against militants on the Pakistan side of the Line of Control (LOC) following the Pakistan-sponsored attack on the Uri Indian Army base in September 2016.

Because Pakistan's nuclear force evolved as an asymmetric defense against Indian conventional dominance, Pakistan has not articulated an NFU policy. It has not issued an official public nuclear doctrine, but the broad outlines of its doctrine have been made clear in semiofficial statements by serving and retired defense officials. Lt. Gen. Khalid Kidwai, who from 2000 to 2013 headed the Strategic Plans Division (SPD), which directs Pakistan's nuclear force complex, has provided the most comprehensive explanation.[14] In an interview with scholars in 2002, he outlined four principal dimensions of vulnerability for Pakistan that could trigger nuclear use:

> Nuclear weapons are aimed solely at India. In case that deterrence fails, they will be used if
>
> a. India attacks Pakistan and conquers a large part of its territory (space threshold)
>
> b. India destroys a large part either of its land or air forces (military threshold)
>
> c. India proceeds to the economic strangling of Pakistan (economic strangling)
>
> d. India pushes Pakistan into political destabilization or creates a large scale internal subversion in Pakistan (domestic destabilization)[15]

The latter two thresholds—the economic and domestic political—are an addition to the traditional focus of state nuclear thresholds on territorial and conventional military integrity, as represented by the first two thresholds in this list. Analysts often hold the economic threshold to refer primarily to the threat of Indian naval blockade, which could immobilize Pakistan's naval forces and substantially reduce its commercial activity and oil imports.[16] These four thresholds, in illustrating multiple perceived avenues by which India could engineer Pakistan's collapse, reveal the depth of concern within Pakistan's security establishment regarding Indian strategic intentions. The perceived relevance of nuclear weapons as a bulwark against each category of Indian aggressive action helps explain the mushrooming growth and diversification of Pakistan's nuclear arsenal.

Having surveyed the threat perceptions that underpin Pakistan's nuclear thought, we will now explore the nuclear posture that flows from these influences.

PAKISTAN'S NUCLEAR POSTURE

The concept for Pakistan's nuclear doctrine at the time of the 1998 tests has been described by Kidwai as "credible minimum deterrence." This was the same phrase then used by Indian officials to describe their nuclear force. This posture implies that the state will seek the smallest nuclear force able to deter its adversaries and that this force will change as those of its adversaries do to ensure continued deterrence. Pakistan agreed to a ten-year nuclear force development plan after the 1998 tests, and Kidwai has implied that this plan included a certain targeted number of warheads and delivery vehicles.[17]

In 2005 Pakistani president Pervez Musharraf said that Pakistan had attained a minimum deterrent capability.[18] However, in April 2006 a meeting of the National Command Authority (NCA), the Pakistani government body that makes nuclear policy, reviewed the implications of the Indo-US civil nuclear agreement for India's military fissile material production potential. A former American intelligence official claims that this meeting likely took into account analyses by the agreement's critics who estimated that Indian fissile material production could dramatically increase. This projected increase was based on a theory that India's new international access to nuclear fuel for civilian energy could permit the state to devote its entire domestic uranium resources to its military nuclear program.[19] Following the April 2006 meeting, the NCA issued a press release that said, "In view of the fact that the [Indo-US nuclear] agreement would enable India to produce significant quantities of fissile material and nuclear weapons from unsafeguarded nuclear reactors, the NCA expressed firm resolve that our credible minimum deterrence requirements will be met."[20] This strongly suggests that Pakistan increased its nuclear force production efforts as a result of this review.

The revelation of the Cold Start doctrine has also influenced Pakistan's nuclear thought. Speaking in 2015, Kidwai said that Cold Start had compelled Pakistan to discard credible minimum deterrence and adopt a new posture, now organized around the concept of "full spectrum deterrence." Full spectrum deterrence means that Pakistan is willing and able to use nuclear force at every level of conflict. As Kidwai emphasized, "And we hope, therefore, that the complete spectrum that we say, the full spectrum, strategic, operational, tactical, all three levels of nuclear weapons have been covered, and therefore we have now deterred—in our thinking—the tactical level operations under the Cold Start Doctrine as well."[21]

Full spectrum deterrence indeed closely aligns conceptually with Pakistan's posture of asymmetric escalation, which intends to advance a credible nuclear counterthreat against conventional or nuclear challenges to ensure escalation dominance at each level of conflict. However, current and former Pakistani officials have not entirely discarded credible minimum deterrence; it is still rhetorically referred to in their official statements and analyses.[22]

Nevertheless, Pakistan's emerging nuclear posture, best encapsulated by the introduction of the Nasr missile and the fast rate of arsenal production, is better characterized by the doctrine of full spectrum deterrence; indeed, it is difficult to see where "minimum" would now be an accurate adjective to describe its developments.

PAKISTAN NUCLEAR CAPABILITIES

Pakistan has one of the fastest-growing nuclear forces in the world. It is diversifying its delivery vehicles with intentions to build land-based long- and short-range ballistic missile platforms and sea-based nuclear platforms. Furthermore, it is investing in its already considerable fissile material infrastructure. Pakistan opened two new heavy water plutonium production reactors, Khushab-III and Khushab-IV, in 2013 and 2015. These reactors complemented the two reactors already present at the Khushab complex in Punjab province.[23] A Pakistani official has reportedly stated that plutonium produced at the Khushab site will be allocated to a new generation of "smaller, shorter range nuclear weapons, including tactical nuclear-tipped missiles" under development.[24]

This marks a transition in the fissile basis of Pakistan's nuclear arsenal, which has historically relied on weapons-grade HEU. Pakistan has operated an enrichment plant at Kahuta in Punjab since the early 1980s. There are also reports of a second enrichment facility in service at Gadwal near Islamabad, built in the late 1990s.[25] Pakistan's combined plutonium and HEU production rate is estimated to be sufficient to generate 10–27 new warheads annually.[26] This is on top of an estimated HEU stockpile of up to 3.29 tons and a plutonium stockpile of up to 230 kilograms (507 pounds).[27] Analysts estimate that Pakistan has 110–70 warheads, a larger number than India (estimated 90–120 warheads).[28]

Warheads are stored separately from delivery vehicles in peacetime, a practice that reduces the risk of accidental use and that Pakistani officials highlight as an example of their responsible stewardship of nuclear weapons.[29] However, maintaining this separation will prove more difficult with some of Pakistan's new and future delivery vehicles, especially submarine-launched cruise missiles and the Nasr short-range missile. Both delivery vehicles will need to be deployed to the field fully armed in order to be usable. This could increase the chances of accidental use based on misperception or miscommunication.

Pakistan's current nuclear delivery platforms allow it to hold all Indian territorial targets at risk. However, it is still diversifying these platforms, with notable projects including the Nasr; the Shaheen-3, a 2,750-kilometer (1,709-mile) range ballistic missile; and the Ababeel, a 2,200-kilometer (1,367-mile) range ballistic missile designed to host multiple warheads.[30]

As Pakistan intends to field a naval nuclear deterrent force in the coming years, new sea-launched missiles or naval variants of existing missiles will join the list of delivery vehicles in table 2.1. Indeed, Rawalpindi recently tested a 450-kilometer (280-mile) range Babur-III nuclear submarine-launched cruise missile (SLCM).[31]

TABLE 2.1
Pakistani Nuclear Forces, 2018

Type	Range	Current status
Aircraft		
F-16 A/B	1,600 km (994.2 mi)	Inducted
Mirage V	2,100 km (1,304.8 mi)	Inducted
Ballistic missiles		
Nasr (Hatf-9)	60 km (37.3 mi)	Inducted
Ghaznavi (Hatf-3)	400 km (248.5 mi)	Inducted
Ghauri (Hatf-5)	1,200 km (745.6 mi)	Inducted
Abdali (Hatf-2)	180 km (111.8 mi)	In development
Shaheen-1 (Hatf-4)	750 km (466 mi)	In development
Shaheen-2 (Hatf-6)	2,000 km (1,242.7 mi)	In development
Ababeel	2,200 km (1,367 mi)	In development
Shaheen-3	2,750 km (1,708.7 mi)	In development
Cruise missiles		
Babur (Hatf-7)	350–750 km (217.5–466 mi)	In development
Ra'ad (Hatf-8)	350 km (217.5 mi)	In development

Sources: Data from Franz-Stefan Gady, "Pakistan Tests New Ballistic Missile Capable of Carrying Multiple Warheads," *The Diplomat*, January 25, 2017, http://thediplomat.com/2017/01/pakistan-tests -new-ballistic-missile-capable-of-carrying-multiple-nuclear-warheads/; Interservices Public Relations, "Shaheen 3 Missile Test," news release, March 9, 2015, https://www.ispr.gov.pk/front/main.asp?o "=t-press_release&date=2015/3/9#pr_link2804; Tim Craig, "Pakistan Tests Missile That Could Carry Nuclear Warhead to Every Part of India," *Washington Post*, March 9, 2015, https://www.washingtonpost .com/world/asia_pacific/pakistan-tests-missile-that-could-carry-nuclear-warhead-to-every-part-of-india /2015/03/09/920f4f42-c65c-11e4-bea5-b893e7ac3fb3_story.html; Zia Mian, "Pakistan," in *Assuring Destruction Forever*, 2015 ed., ed. Ray Acheson (Geneva: Reaching Critical Will, 2015), 54–63; Hans M. Kristensen and Robert S. Norris, "Pakistani Nuclear Forces, 2016," *Bulletin of the Atomic Scientists* 72, no. 6 (2016): 368–76; Khalid Kidwai, "Conversation with Gen. Khalid Kidwai," interview by Peter Lavoy (Carnegie International Nuclear Policy Conference, Washington, DC, March 23, 2015), http://carnegie endowment.org/files/03-230315carnegieKIDWAI.pdf.

Like several other nuclear weapon states, Pakistan relied on air-delivered gravity bombs early in its nuclear history. However, it is now transitioning toward greater use of land-based ballistic missiles and preparing for a sea-based nuclear deterrent.[32] The range of the Shaheen-2 missile gives Pakistan the ability to target the entirety of Indian territory and thus might be expected to be the capstone of Pakistan's land-based missile force. However, in 2015 Pakistan tested the Shaheen-3, which has a range that extends beyond Indian territory to include Iran, Israel, Myanmar, Saudi Arabia, and Sri Lanka. Asked in 2015 why Pakistan developed a missile with this longer range, Kidwai noted the growing strategic importance of the Indian Andaman and Nicobar Islands in the Bay of Bengal and strongly suggested that no farther-reaching missiles would be forthcoming:

> The Nicobar, and the Andaman Islands are very much part of India, not in main landmass, but their islands. I'm sure you know where they are, but they are being developed as strategic bases, and therefore Pakistan cannot afford to let any landmass, whether it's an island, or it's a mainland, to be out of its range. And therefore, 2,750 is a very well calculated range. And I don't particularly expect us to go beyond that, because it is now a comprehensive coverage of any particular land area that India might think of putting its weapons.[33]

The Shaheen-3 thus appears intended to hold at risk Indian offshore bases and platforms and to erode any advantage for India's second-strike capability gained by moving some of its nuclear forces out of the Indian mainland.

Whereas the Shaheen-3 is meant to deter long-range nuclear threats, another prominent new missile, the Nasr, is designed for use on or near Pakistani territory. The Nasr is directed at the threat of a Cold Start Indian conventional advance. More theoretically, it is aimed at the underlying logic of Cold Start: that India can use a certain dimension of solely conventional warfare without escalating to nuclear exchanges. As Kidwai has remarked, "Nasr, specifically, was born out of a compulsion of this thing that I mentioned about some people on the other side toying with the idea of finding space for conventional war, despite Pakistan nuclear weapons. . . . And Pakistan would not pick up the courage, in that kind of a scenario, to use its strategic weapons, or the operational level nuclear weapons. So it was this particular gap that we felt needed to be plugged at the lowest rung."[34]

The Ababeel, a 2,200-kilometer (1,367-mile) range ballistic missile, represents another new dimension of Pakistan's diversifying nuclear force. First tested and announced in January 2017, the missile is described by Rawalpindi as the first able to host multiple warheads, including potentially MIRVs. The official press statement justified its development as providing Pakistan a nuclear strike option that can penetrate India's BMD systems. Although Pakistan's present ability to develop MIRV technology is unclear, language in the press statement strongly suggests that this technology is an ongoing effort for Pakistan's defense scientists.[35]

In addition, cruise missiles, such as the ground-launched Babur and air-launched Ra'ad platforms, also appear set to assume a greater role in Pakistan's nuclear posture. Pakistani officials have indicated that cruise missiles would ensure a sustained, credible nuclear strike capacity given India's emerging BMD capabilities.[36] The Babur model is additionally likely to be assigned conventional missions, reflecting the rising importance of cruise missiles to general offensive strike planning.[37]

Concluding this brief overview of the major trends of Pakistan nuclear force development, we will now explore in detail the trends' implications for the evolving deterrent relationship with India. We will first focus on the naval domain and then turn to the land theater.

IMPLICATIONS FOR NUCLEAR INTERACTIONS WITH INDIA: THE NAVAL DOMAIN

Pakistan's rapidly growing nuclear arsenal, plus the capabilities emerging to meet perceived long-range nuclear and tactical conventional threats, seems to address the substantive conventional and nuclear threats that India poses on land. However, the "economic" threshold—the threat of naval blockade—is still an area of vulnerability for Pakistan. India's navy outmatches Pakistan's, and Pakistan likely has no current naval nuclear deterrent platforms in service.[38]

Pakistan is endeavoring to develop this capability. Speaking in 2008, Pakistan's then chief of Naval Staff said that Pakistan was "fully capable of deploying strategic weapons on the sea, if and when the government takes such a decision."[39] The Naval Strategic Force Command was established in 2012, creating the logistical base for assigning future operational nuclear forces to the Navy in line with the already existing Army and Air Force Strategic Force Commands.

Indeed, serving and retired officials have made clear the naval dimension's importance to Pakistan's nuclear future. The press statement announcing the Naval Strategic Force Command described it as "the custodian of the nation's second strike capability."[40] Kidwai has further implied that Pakistan will not have a functioning second-strike capability until a naval nuclear force is operational, even though Pakistan has a bigger nuclear arsenal than India and can reach all Indian targets with the land-based Shaheen-3.[41]

Experts think that the first wave of Pakistan's sea-based nuclear force will consist of nuclear cruise missiles, such as the Babur-III, carried by its current diesel-powered conventional submarine fleet.[42] Pakistan's existing submarine fleet, consisting of two Agosta-70 and three Agosta-90B submarines, is reaching the end of its life span.[43] A retired Pakistani naval commander wrote in 2010 that Pakistan's Agosta-90Bs could potentially host nuclear cruise missiles "within five years" if several technical issues were addressed: "Missile installation and subsequent integration with the onboard combat system, as well as with the nuclear command and control infrastructure (C4I network), could be daunting tasks. The combat system, meant for conventional weapons, may require major changes to accommodate nonconventional weapons."[44]

In April 2015 Prime Minister Nawaz Sharif approved the purchase of eight diesel-electric submarines from China; the deal was finalized in October 2015. A retired Pakistani officer familiar with the negotiations estimated the total cost of the deal to be $4–5 billion.[45] While the submarine model details have not been confirmed, a Pakistani official who attended a navy parliamentary briefing in March 2015 and external analysts believe the S-20 export variant of the Chinese Type-039A/Type-041 model diesel-electric submarine is the most likely model. A Chinese Type-041 boat visited Karachi's commercial port, close to Pakistan's principal naval base, in May 2015, while negotiations were presumably ongoing.[46]

The Type-041 can feature an air-independent propulsion system, a capability already present on one of Pakistan's current Agosta 90-B submarines.[47] This system, which has not been integrated into current Indian boats, extends the submarine's possible undersea operational period. As one scholar notes, this "would give them [Pakistan's submarines] a notable tactical edge over India's submarines."[48] The Type-041 boats are also reportedly less noisy than India's *Arihant* SSBN, which would provide another operational advantage.[49]

Pakistani and external experts anticipate that this Chinese-origin submarine fleet will host nuclear cruise missiles in the future.[50] To successfully mate the nuclear missiles to the submarines, China may quietly assist in modification of the Type-041 conventional torpedo tubes.[51]

Although the thrust of Pakistan's seaborne nuclear deterrence creation currently appears based on ship-launched or sub-launched naval Baburs, other options are technically available. Pakistan currently operates seven P-3B/C Orion maritime patrol aircraft.[52] This aircraft model can carry US AGM-84 standoff land attack missiles armed with Tomahawk nuclear warheads and Mk 101 "Lulu" nuclear depth charges. Orions in American service were assigned a nuclear mission and carried nuclear depth charges during the Cold War.[53] A retired Pakistani naval commander has suggested that "a suitably equipped P-3C could serve as a powerful backup to an undersea second strike on board Agosta 90Bs."[54]

There are nevertheless certain vulnerabilities to using Orions as a nuclear platform. First, adversaries can more easily locate and destroy aircraft than they can submarines. Second, the fact that the Orion is US technology creates additional headaches for Pakistani defense planners. Converting Orions to nuclear strike platforms would likely constitute a violation of the US Arms Export Control Act (AECA), under which the planes were sold. Washington confronted Islamabad in 2009 with reports that Orions were being assigned conventional land attack roles that were illegal under the AECA.[55]

Certainly, the US reaction to reports of Pakistan's using Orions for nuclear purposes would be even more hostile. This interaction would worsen the already tense US-Pakistan political and military relationship, highlighted in 2016 by Pakistan's ill-fated negotiations with Washington to buy eight new F-16 Block-52 fighters. These negotiations, like other Pakistani purchases of US arms, were subjected to a tortuous and public political process complicated by Pakistan's status as a nuclear weapon state and the general mistrust in the US-Pakistan relationship.[56] For example, the chair of the US Senate Foreign Relations Committee criticized the proposed 2016 arms agreement, arguing that Pakistanis "continue to support the Taliban, the Haqqani network and give safe haven to al Qaeda."[57]

Congressional opposition in 2016 reached such a level that the US government informed Pakistan that no Foreign Military Financing program subsidies would be made available for the deal, elevating the price from $270 million to $700 million. Islamabad cancelled negotiations following this development, switching its focus to an offer from Jordan to sell fourteen of its less sophisticated F-16A/B fighters. Because these fighters are also US technology, this second agreement would still require US approval and end-use monitoring provisions. The negotiations have so far been inconclusive.[58]

By contrast, relying on Chinese nuclear technology, by way of the Chinese-origin Type-041 submarine fleet, avoids these political difficulties. China and Pakistan have a robust, "all-weather" defense relationship.[59] Plus, the Chinese technology tree extends to a third potential option for Pakistan's naval nuclear force involving the Chinese *Xia*-class SSBN, commissioned in the late 1980s.[60] This boat has reportedly not sailed from the North Sea Fleet base near Qingdao since at least 2006.[61] China is instead focusing its SSBN projection on the more modern *Jin*-class fleet. Pakistan could use the Chinese *Xia* to train "a pool of selected Pakistan Navy officers . . . with theoretical/academic work ashore followed by operational training at sea and finally a strategic deployment."[62] There is regional precedent for such activity: India has leased a *Charlie*-class SSBN and an *Akula*-class SSN from Russia to train its navy to operate a nuclear-powered submarine, and Indian sailors have also been hosted aboard USS *Annapolis*, a *Los Angeles*–class SSN, for the same reason.[63]

However, if anyone discovers that China transferred *Xia* to the Pakistan navy, it would attract international condemnation. If *Xia* was handed over armed with nuclear weapons, it would constitute a clear Chinese violation of Article I of the NPT. The Russian submarine leases to India have included strict conditions against hosting nuclear weapons on board. Similar Chinese transfer terms might reduce the furor of the international reaction to a *Xia* transfer but would also undermine the main original purpose of the transfer: generating Pakistan seaborne nuclear deterrence.

Still, the current Chinese approach of selling dual-use submarines enables both parties to quietly work on the nuclear deterrence task under the pretense of conventional naval force development. An outright transfer of *Xia* therefore looks unlikely at the time of this writing. However, both states are likely to pursue the less controversial element of this approach—Chinese training of Pakistani sailors in nuclear submarine operation—because training can build Pakistani naval deterrence without attracting publicity for their nuclear force cooperation.

Pakistan's fourth option is to build its own indigenous nuclear-armed submarine fleet. However, SSBNs are some of the most complex machines invented, as indicated by the thirty-year period that India required to indigenously develop and field *Arihant*. Pakistan's development of a nuclear submarine is further complicated by the lack of budgetary resources allocated to its navy as compared to its air force and especially its army.[64]

There are conflicting accounts of whether an indigenous Pakistani SSBN program has ever been initiated. One report in 2013, from a think tank specializing in Pakistani defense issues, claimed that the Pakistan Atomic Energy Commission had been engaged since 2001 in a "KPC-3" project to develop a naval nuclear reactor.[65] However, a retired naval commander claimed in 2010 that "no efforts to develop a sea-based nuclear capability and thus expand the survivability of nuclear forces have ever surfaced in Pakistan's policy making" and based his subsequent exploration of seaborne nuclear deterrence options for Pakistan on the premise that there was no extant indigenous program.[66]

The technical difficulty, financial cost, and long project life span of developing an indigenous SSBN are in tension with Pakistan's urgent determination to field seaborne nuclear deterrence. This again suggests that the purchase of eight Chinese Type-041 boats represents the main route through which Pakistani policymakers currently intend to deliver a naval nuclear force. The particular perceived strategic importance of this purchase to Pakistani defense planners is underlined by the colossal expense—an estimated $4–5 billion—especially compared to the reported full 2014 budget for the Pakistan navy: $725 million.[67] The Type-041 purchase agreement has been structured to develop Pakistan's technical expertise of indigenous submarine construction. Four of the eight boats will be built in Pakistan with an associated technology transfer agreement.[68] While the first generation of Pakistani naval nuclear deterrence will involve dual-use Chinese-origin diesel-electric submarines, the experience gained constructing these boats in Pakistan will support a future indigenous SSBN program.

A final option at this point is for Pakistan to field nuclear weapons aboard surface ships as opposed to submarines. The successful launch test of a naval nuclear missile from a "warship" in December 2012 suggests that surface ship nuclear capability is more imminently deployable than submarine nuclear capability. Potential candidate platforms for this surface nuclear force, carrying a Babur naval variant or nuclear-armed C-802 antiship missile, include *Alamgir*, Pakistan's single US-origin *Oliver Hazard Perry*–class guided missile frigate (acquired in 2011); four Chinese-origin *Zulfiquar*-class F-22P frigates (commissioned from 2009 to 2013); two Chinese-origin *Azmat*-class missile patrol boats; four indigenous *Jalalat*-class and *Jurrat*-class missile craft; and two Turkish-origin *Zarrar*-class multirole fast attack boats.[69]

The platforms that are not of US origin appear more likely to host nuclear weapons, again because of the greater political difficulty of converting US, as opposed to Chinese, technology to serve nuclear roles. In its notification to Congress of the proposed sale of the *Oliver Hazard Perry*–class boat to Pakistan in 2010, the Pentagon detailed its approved Pakistan navy role as limited to "counter-narcotics and counter-piracy operations and to assist[ing] with Pakistan's efforts to secure its maritime border."[70] Pakistan's subsequent effort to purchase additional *Perry*-class frigates failed because of Congress's hostile views toward Islamabad.[71] Given this context, the US political reaction to Pakistan's arming its sole *Perry*-class frigate with nuclear weapons, in violation of AECA conditions, would render its inclusion in a surface nuclear fleet unlikely.

Hosting nuclear weapons aboard recently commissioned non-US-origin surface ships, therefore, appears to be the most feasible immediate option for Pakistan in fielding naval nuclear deterrence, with Chinese-origin submarines to be later integrated into the naval nuclear force as they are built and commissioned. The submarines will form a stronger eventual backbone of the seaborne deterrent owing to their increased stealth compared to surface ships.

What are the implications of such a Pakistan naval nuclear force for regional security? The previously mentioned nuclear-capable vessels, including the Type-041, F-22P, and *Azmat*-class boats, are the main elements of Pakistan's current naval force modernization. As these boats are commissioned and extend Pakistani naval projection, the fact that they may have nuclear missions will greatly complicate Indian responses to their incursions and general strategic planning. This generates a risk of Indian self-deterrence; Indian naval commanders may hesitate to confront a Pakistan vessel out of concern for immediate nuclear escalatory consequences. This risk of self-deterrence could become associated with most of the new Pakistan navy because multiple new Pakistan naval platforms are capable of nuclear roles. Alternatively, Indian commanders could refuse to be self-deterred and respond aggressively to perceived Pakistani incursions, generating the kind of fast-moving escalatory scenario that those who are self-deterred are deterred by. While not all Pakistan vessel classes or vessels within each class may be nuclear-armed, simply the potential for a few to have nuclear missions produces these new strategic concerns. This nuclear potential could extend Pakistan's full spectrum deterrence nuclear posture and, consequently, India's strategic dilemma to the naval domain. Threatening a seaborne nuclear incident in response to an Indian operation against most of Pakistan's new navy vessels would indeed substantially reduce the nuclear threshold to lower levels of conventional naval conflict and subsequently limit Indian conventional operational flexibility.

Indeed, these concerns are heightened by the Pakistan navy's bold intentions. First, it is planning to field antiaccess/area-denial capabilities. This intention is best reflected in Pakistan's acquisition of Harpoon and C-802 antiship missiles, which asymmetrically threaten the larger and carrier-based Indian naval fleet.[72] As of 2012 Pakistan had obtained over 120 C-802s and had plans to base these on land littoral areas to enhance antiaccess/area-denial capabilities.[73] One Pakistan nuclear expert suggests that Pakistan may assign small plutonium-based warheads to some C-802s, and the potential for this modification overlays nuclear risk onto an already concerning antiaccess/area-denial challenge for Indian strategists.[74] Like other dual-use platforms, potentially dual-use C-802s can blur the nuclear threshold.

Second, Pakistan has a propensity for risk-taking behavior, including a tendency for Pakistani maritime aircraft to speed close to Indian boats and deliberately risk collision with them.[75] This practice could potentially have nuclear implications given the ambiguous conventional/nuclear role of the Pakistani craft involved and could, in turn, maximize the effect of full spectrum deterrence in limiting India's ability to respond. These implications of Pakistan's efforts to develop a naval nuclear force should be carefully considered by the Indian navy and NCA and should be integrated into the official defense review that this book recommends India conduct.

We can discern here the two major trends involved in the blurring of nuclear thresholds in the India-Pakistan-China strategic rivalry. First, this blurring manifests itself in the increasing use of dual-use platforms and delivery vehicles. When dual-use platforms are involved, any confrontation with an adversary unit wrongly assumed to have a solely conventional mission can threaten in nuclear escalation. Alternatively, instances of nuclear brinkmanship may increase if an adversary encourages the incorrect belief that a unit is nuclear-armed.

Both situations in effect could lower the nuclear threshold as interference with a new generation of regional conventional naval units, through their potential nuclear armament, could produce nuclear implications.

The second trend is this broader extension of largely land-based nuclear deterrence into the naval domain. This generates the prospect of merging seaborne nuclear deterrence with Indian Ocean conventional naval competition. The potential here is for the intermingling of conventional and nuclear naval missions and strategic perceptions in a tense maritime environment with increasingly ambiguous boundaries.

In responding to these trends, Indian defense planners should focus on enhancing surveillance and intelligence capabilities in order to monitor armament loading and deployment patterns for new Pakistani vessels and thus better discern their nuclear or conventional missions on the basis of certain recurring tendencies in these areas. They should also develop a naval dialogue mechanism with Pakistan to deconflict potential patrol routes and manage standoffs that could have nuclear escalatory implications.

The challenges of seaborne nuclear deterrence in the India-Pakistan relationship are complemented by those in the land domain, where they have fought several wars and where most of their nuclear competition is conducted. It is this context to which we now turn.

IMPLICATIONS FOR NUCLEAR INTERACTIONS WITH INDIA: THE LAND DOMAIN

In the last twenty years, Pakistan has faced three major crises with India: the 1999 Kargil War, the 2001–2 massive twin military mobilizations following the December 2001 attack on the Indian Parliament, and the 2008 Mumbai attacks crisis. The stimulus for each of these crises was an attack on Indian forces or territory by a militant group operating from within Pakistan's borders, aided covertly or overtly by Pakistan's defense establishment. This situation remains the most likely immediate trigger to another bilateral crisis. The frustration that drove the Indian Army to develop the Cold Start concept and that overwhelms Indian television news during each crisis is rooted in India's inability to halt militant group activities and their support by Pakistan in a way that does not threaten major war with potentially nuclear consequences.

The Indian discourse in the 1999 Kargil War, which occurred soon after the 1998 South Asian nuclear tests, concentrated on the necessity of removing the Pakistani militants and regular forces at the lowest possible level of conventional escalation. Any discussion of the war that even alluded to nuclear weapons' relevance to the crisis was rendered mostly taboo. The Indian government feared nuclear escalation and the consequences of even signaling with its nuclear weapons in support of the offensive for its image as a responsible nuclear state. Indian broadsheet newspaper editorial boards and commentators excoriated a rare newspaper comment calling for use of nuclear weapons to be considered in the crisis. Crossing the LOC—the de facto border—to ease Indian conventional operations was also seen as too dangerous to contemplate publicly.[76]

The Kargil War shattered the assumption among Indian analysts immediately following the 1998 nuclear tests that a nuclear South Asia could be a more conducive environment for negotiating a final India-Pakistan peace. Echoing the "nuclear optimist" arguments of Kenneth Waltz, Indian analysts argued that both New Delhi and Islamabad would rationally realize that the potential for another war to threaten nuclear devastation meant that major conventional wars were no longer feasible as an option and that differences would best be resolved through peaceful summitry.[77]

Instead of validating Waltz's thinking, the early histories of India and Pakistan as overt nuclear weapon states have developed a new nuclear concept in academic literature and policy experience: the "instability-stability" paradox. This paradox accepts Waltz's point that the mutual possession of nuclear weapons renders major conventional war a more dangerous prospect for states to contemplate. However, mutual possession of weapons can also prevent states from launching a major conventional war or escalating a smaller conflict to the nuclear level. A state's confidence that its adversary will be self-deterred from nuclear escalation can increase its proclivity for launching lower-scale conventional operations. These lower-scale conventional operations might not have been launched in a nuclear-free context, where the threat and costs of escalation could outweigh any initial gains from smaller offensives. Nuclear weapons can thus generate stability at the level of major conventional war but instability at the level of lower-scale conventional and subconventional conflict.

Pakistan continues to permit militant groups to shelter on its territory, launch attacks on India, and even receive training from elements of its defense establishment because Pakistan's leadership believes India can be destabilized through the militant groups' actions. The attacks are small enough that India will avoid a major conventional response for fear of opening the door to nuclear war. The Indian Army developed the Cold Start concept in 2004 as a credible response to the next Pakistani subconventional attack. Cold Start involves subconventional and limited conventional warfare that delivers real tactical, and even strategic, gains but that is still several rungs down the escalation ladder from major war. It is essentially in the same sphere of thought as Pakistan's interest in subconventional operations.[78]

Pakistani officials often describe the Nasr as being a direct response to India's military interest in Cold Start and accordant development of rapid limited war options.[79] The Nasr's deployment means India could not plan a conventional cross-border attack that would be "safe" from nuclear escalation. Framing Nasr as a consequence of Cold Start invites the Nasr's critics to blame Indian military adventurism for the missile's emergence as a defensive measure. However, Pakistan may have been developing tactical nuclear weapons before the Indian Army developed Cold Start in 2004. In 2014 Pakistan's permanent UN representative (who is also a former member of the Pakistan National Defence University's governing body) confirmed that Pakistan's "capacity for a tactical response was already under development" before it made "the decision to develop delivery systems for Full Spectrum Deterrence" in response to "the emerging Indian military posture" of a "proactive doctrine aimed at a rapid deployment war-fighting strategy."[80]

A second, less common, rationale for the Nasr has also been advanced, and it involves India's short-range Prahaar missile. Discussing the Nasr in 2012, an SPD official drew attention to the Prahaar, claiming that the Prahaar was a tactical nuclear weapon that predated Pakistan's development of a tactical nuclear weapon capability. This official intended to suggest that India "might have been the first in line, pulling Pakistan unnecessarily into an unending arms race."[81] While this is a less frequent justification for the existence of the Nasr, it similarly attempts to originate the Nasr in a response to destabilizing Indian behavior that should be the ultimate target of international condemnation.

The idea that Pakistan can and should issue a nuclear response to even low-level Indian conventional operations has been a consistent thread in Pakistani strategic messaging in recent years. In addition to the verbal exchange in the wake of India's 2015 Myanmar operation mentioned earlier, Chief of Army Staff Ashfaq Parvez Kayani remarked in 2009, "Proponents of conventional application of military forces in a nuclear overhang are chartering an adventurous and dangerous path, the consequences of which could be both unintended and uncontrollable."[82]

Analysts have estimated that the 60-kilometer (37-mile) range Nasr is based on the Chinese AR1A/A100-E multiple-launch rocket system (MLRS), although it has also been compared to the Chinese WS-2 and M30/M31 MLRS.[83] The Nasr is estimated to have a length of 5.4–6 meters (17.7–19.7 feet) and a diameter of 30–40 centimeters (11.8–15.7 inches). These dimensions would require a miniaturized warhead.[84] Pakistan's historical use of HEU for its nuclear weapons extends to its 1998 test devices, which were all HEU-based. This means it has no plutonium warhead test data or experience developing and testing specifically miniaturized warheads to use in assembling a Nasr-specific warhead. This challenge could, however, be partly eased with Chinese technical cooperation.[85]

An alternative is for Pakistan to develop a small HEU-based warhead. While experts have identified at least ten US warhead models as hostable by the Nasr, they have particularly focused on the example of the US W-33 HEU gun-type warhead, "simpler variants of which Pakistan has already tested," as particularly suited to the Nasr's dimensions.[86] Using the US W-33 may be a marginally easier technical pathway to obtaining a Nasr warhead because Pakistan has at least some related test data in its possession, but taking this route leaves unaddressed the challenge of proving successful miniaturization without actual tests.[87]

Assuming Pakistan can overcome these challenges and deploy a credible Nasr, its limited yield will have an insignificant military (but not political) effect on the major Indian conventional assault that would merit its use. One calculation estimates a requirement of between 257 and 436 fifteen-kiloton nuclear weapons to destroy around 250 vehicles in such an assault. By comparison, the Indian Army has conducted exercises moving 1,000 armored vehicles and trained for retaining cohesion and fighting through a postnuclear environment, most recently in April 2016.[88] Plus, India has made a doctrinal promise of massive retaliation—threatening the potential extinction of Pakistan—to even one Nasr nuclear strike.

The military case for developing a Nasr or other short-range nuclear artillery or munitions is founded on a felt need within Pakistan to establish asymmetric deterrence against perceived Indian conventional superiority that is further bolstered by Cold Start. However, recent studies of comparative conventional force postures have estimated a much closer balance between Pakistan and India, contrasting with Pakistani claims of substantial conventional inferiority.[89] Indeed, some experts have suggested that Pakistan enjoys some advantages over India, especially in the land theater. Four-fifths of Pakistan army divisions are located close to the border with India, and a policy introduced in 2012 further requires deployment of a quarter of battalion reserves immediately following a major terrorist attack in India.[90]

This reserve deployment would occur before any Indian government decision to mobilize its own forces against Pakistan, and the Indian decision would likely be made only following a time-consuming process of correctly identifying the perpetrators and acquiring and confirming solid evidence of their connections to Pakistan. Evidence of actual subsequent Indian mobilization would only flood additional Pakistan forces and reserves toward the border, continuing Pakistan's geographic and temporal advantage in the ground balance against India through this next stage.

In addition to these advantages, Pakistan has been conducting major tri-service conventional field and planning exercises to train specifically to resist a Cold Start attack. Four Azm-e-Nau (New Resolve) exercises were conducted from 2009 to 2013. The first stage of each exercise constituted scenario development and related contingency planning. The second stage involved testing these planned contingency responses in the field. Using performance data from the early exercises, the military reportedly revised its doctrinal approach to this challenge in 2011, adopting the aforementioned rule requiring early deployment of a quarter of battalion reserves.[91] The final exercise, Azm-e-Nau IV, was conducted in late 2013 and integrated armor, artillery, air defense, and civil aviation capabilities, alongside deployment of F-7P, F-16, JF-17, and Mirage aircraft.[92]

Upon conclusion of the series, Pakistan officials claimed that the armed forces had demonstrated successful mobilization in a shorter time frame than was achievable by Indian forces.[93] An assessment published on the Pakistan military website, titled "From Cold Start to Cold Storage!" said the series had proved that the armed forces were "equally effective and vigilant along the Eastern front despite being heavily committed in their fight against the terrorism along the Western borders," with "massive firepower available with Pakistan Army to meet any future challenge."[94] Given that the conventional doctrinal redesign of 2011 appears to have been successfully validated, thereby assuring Pakistan's conventional deterrence, why is a Nasr-like battlefield nuclear capability still required?

Use of the Nasr would indeed complicate Pakistan's response to an Indian attack in several ways. First, deployment of the Nasr to the field would raise the question of pre-delegating launch authority to field commanders. If the Nasr is tasked to respond to a fast-moving conventional attack, delays in launch authorization could reduce its utility. However, assigning such authority to local commanders could lead to a decision to launch based on incomplete information and extreme local pressure, in a context where the relevance of the conflict for Pakistan's overall future is still unclear.[95] Second, owing to their limited range, Nasr missiles will need to be deployed close to the fighting. The proximity of the missiles to enemy forces means that the risk of their capture or destruction could be very high; indeed, a retired Indian Army brigadier has noted that for Nasr systems to target an Indian armed offensive, they will have to be placed within range of Indian MLRS such as the Pinaka.[96]

This generates a third dilemma for local commanders described as the "use them or lose them" problem. Should the Nasrs' imminent destruction appear to be a growing risk during the conflict, field commanders may feel pressure to fire the missiles to prevent their loss and to attempt to turn the tide. Perceived risk of the Nasrs' imminent destruction would also require the missiles' frequent movement and relocation, heightening the risk of their interception and requiring a protection detail that would remove Pakistani forces from the total available for actual conventional fighting. Finally, the context in which the Nasr would be used—a limited Indian cross-border operation—would already signify its failure to deter, as Indian forces would have entered Pakistan territory aware of the missile's existence.

Despite these issues, no signs indicate that Pakistan has reconsidered its plans to develop tactical nuclear weapons. As the centerpiece of Pakistan's full spectrum deterrence nuclear posture, the Nasr is intended to lower the nuclear threshold with India. However, India refuses to accept that this threshold has been lowered, and the Indian Army continues to conduct exercises to fight through a nuclear strike and to emphasize India's refusal to countenance tactical nuclear warfare.

This interaction—or lack of interaction—between Pakistani and Indian conceptions of the bilateral nuclear threshold makes this threshold increasingly ambiguous. Indeed, the general stage in a conventional conflict at which Pakistan would consider nuclear first use remains unclear even to well-connected Pakistani analysts and nuclear experts.[97] Plus, the nuclearized Nasr is another example of the increasing popularity of dual-use platforms in regional nuclear force development that further blurs nuclear thresholds.

The multiple-warhead Ababeel missile is another challenge for South Asian deterrence. The Ababeel places a greater number of Indian targets at risk, and its emergence will generate additional pressure on India to expand its nuclear force to ensure continued reliability and to enhance readiness. If India makes moves to further expand its nuclear force, this could in turn stimulate efforts by Rawalpindi to further augment its nuclear forces.

Any of the potential developments discussed in this chapter would render the India-Pakistan strategic rivalry more complex and could lead to accidental and inadvertent escalation. Inadvertent escalation in particular could occur if an operational movement of Nasr missiles is interpreted as a nuclear threat, if the movement of major Indian conventional units is interpreted as preparing for a Cold Start attack, or if one state attempts to interdict an adversary naval vessel that is nuclear-armed or is escorting another nuclear-armed vessel. Accidental escalation could be delivered through political crisis decisions based on the current readings of adversary territorial red lines (on land or at sea), conventional damage tolerances, and nuclear threshold locations that vary from those declared by the adversary.

Indeed, these new concerns join a previous track record of misperception conducive to accidental and inadvertent escalation. During the 2001–2 crisis, the commander of India's 2 Corps reportedly directed a third of his total forces to within twenty-five miles of the border with Pakistan from their previous location around ninety miles away. A defense analyst claims this was an operational misinterpretation of ambiguous rules of engagement set by the Cabinet Committee on Security (CCS). This movement could have appeared to Pakistan as preparation for an imminent strike and generated an escalatory response.[98] The Chief of Army Staff and Chief of Naval Staff later said that the rules of engagement as set by the CCS were far from clear during the crisis.[99]

At the height of the crisis, India's Chief of Army Staff told journalists that if Pakistan were to use nuclear weapons, the Indian nuclear response would ensure Pakistan was "punished so severely that [its] continuation thereafter in any form of fray will be doubtful" and also remarked in the same press engagement, "If we go to war, jolly good!" These statements were not authorized by Indian political decision makers and again could have been interpreted by Pakistan as containing escalatory significance.[100] Another example of risk of unplanned escalation based on adversary misperception was provided in the Kargil War, when Prime Minister Sharif was unaware that the military was preparing nuclear weapons, a development that could have stimulated an escalatory Indian response.[101]

Another recent example has also been provided in the Mumbai attacks crisis starting in late November 2008 and continuing into early 2009. While bilateral strategic tensions were high immediately following the attacks, an Indian surveillance plane flew near the LOC and was perceived by Pakistan as entering its airspace. Pakistan responded by launching F-16 aircraft to intercept the Indian plane. The IAF conducted an internal inquiry to determine what had happened and found that the Indian aircraft involved had been operated by the Research and Analysis Wing intelligence agency and not the air force.[102]

Pakistan's evolving nuclear doctrine and posture as it interacts with India's on the land vector, therefore, offers little optimism for greater stability in strategic relations in the years to come. The blurring of conventional and nuclear thresholds, as both states harbor different ideas about where the threshold should be, is particularly concerning. This blurring is compounded by the growing prominence of dual-use platforms and the resultant difficulty of discerning the conventional or nuclear mission of an adversary force concentration. Indeed, as we will see, the blurring of conventional and nuclear thresholds and platforms is a broad emerging theme of the India-Pakistan-China nuclear triad.

CONCLUSION

The challenges discussed in this chapter emphasize the need for broadening nuclear strategic dialogue between India and Pakistan to determine the implications of the Nasr missile, to develop an understanding of comparative naval conventional and nuclear perceptions, and to develop procedures to manage potential contingencies. A dialogue will help reduce tensions and render resolution of a standoff more achievable as compared to improvising responses entirely in situ.

However, for such a dialogue to be effective, it must also fully include China as the third member of this triad. Moreover, potential Pakistani developments must be incorporated into a public Indian official defense review that conducts a threat assessment, evaluates the feasibility and credibility of conventional and nuclear force development and deployment programs to meet the specific threats identified, and reiterates that the only credible military role of nuclear weapons is as a tool to prevent the dissolution of India as a territorial entity; all other threat responses should be assigned to conventional forces.

We will now turn to China's historical and evolving role in regional nuclear dynamics. As we will see, the central trends of the India-Pakistan-China triad in the early twenty-first century—the blurring of perceived doctrinal thresholds and of operational thresholds through rising use of dual-use platforms—resurface in recent Chinese nuclear behavior and its effects in the region.

NOTES

1. Harsh V. Pant, *The China Syndrome: Grappling with an Uneasy Relationship* (New Delhi: HarperCollins India, 2010).
2. Sumit Ganguly and Devin T. Hagerty, *Fearful Symmetry: India-Pakistan Crises in the Shadow of Nuclear Weapons* (Seattle: University of Washington Press, 2006), 123.
3. Stephen P. Cohen and Sunil Dasgupta, "The Drag on India's Military Growth," Brookings Policy Brief No. 176, Brookings Institution, September 2010, http://www.brookings.edu/research/papers/2010/09/india-cohen-dasgupta.
4. Peter R. Lavoy, "Islamabad's Nuclear Posture: Its Premises and Implementation," in *Pakistan's Nuclear Future: Worries Beyond War*, ed. Henry D. Sokolski (Carlisle, PA: US Army War College Strategic Studies Institute, 2008), 143–45.
5. Steve Coll, "The Stand-Off," *New Yorker*, February 13, 2008, https://www.newyorker.com/magazine/2006/02/13/the-stand-off.
6. Sadanand Dhume, "When Bombay Came Under Siege," *Wall Street Journal*, November 26, 2013, https://www.wsj.com/articles/when-bombay-came-under-siege-1385480039; IISS, "Terror in Mumbai," *IISS Strategic Comments* 14, no. 10 (December 2008): 1–2.
7. V. P. Malik, "Challenges of Limited War: Parameters and Options" (closing address at a national seminar, "The Challenges of Limited War: Parameters and Options,"

Institute of Defence Studies and Analyses, New Delhi, January 6, 2000), http://www.idsa-india.org/chief6-2000.html.

8. Walter C. Ladwig III, "A Cold Start for Hot Wars? The Indian Army's New Limited War Doctrine," *International Security* 32, no. 3 (Winter 2007–8): 158–90.

9. Yogesh Joshi and Harsh V. Pant, "India and the Changing Nature of War: Gradual Incrementalism?" in *Handbook of Indian Defence Policy*, ed. Harsh V. Pant (London: Routledge, 2015), 74–93.

10. PTI, "Army Chief General Dalbir Singh Reviews Training Exercise 'Drad Sankalp,'" *Economic Times*, December 5, 2015, https://economictimes.indiatimes.com/news/defence/army-chief-general-dalbir-singh-reviews-training-exercise-drad-sankalp/articleshow/50054839.cms; Rajat Pandit, "India Eyes Swift Attacks into Enemy Land in Upcoming Drill on Pak Front," *Times of India*, September 22, 2015, https://timesofindia.indiatimes.com/india/India-eyes-swift-attacks-into-enemy-land-in-upcoming-drill-on-Pak-front/articleshow/49053262.cms.

11. Nitin Gokhale, "Myanmar Operation Sends a Larger Political Message: India Will Pay Back, if Provoked," *Economic Times*, June 14, 2015, https://economictimes.indiatimes.com/news/defence/myanmar-operation-sends-a-larger-political-message-india-will-pay-back-if-provoked/articleshow/47657355.cms.

12. PTI, "Rajyavardhan Singh Rathore Lauds Army Operation in Myanmar, Says It Is Beginning," *Economic Times*, June 10, 2015, https://economictimes.indiatimes.com/news/defence/rajyavardhan-singh-rathore-lauds-army-operation-in-myanmar-says-it-is-beginning/articleshow/47606435.cms.

13. Harinder Baweja, "Pak Isn't Myanmar, We Are a Nuclear Nation, Minister from Neighbouring Country Tells India," *Hindustan Times*, June 11, 2015, http://www.hindustantimes.com/india/pak-isn-t-myanmar-we-are-a-nuclear-nation-minister-from-neighbouring-country-tells-india/story-q0fF95PhYa87Bmf7jTvGmM.html.

14. Ankit Panda, "Pakistan's Longest-Serving Strategic Nuclear Weapons Head Retires," *The Diplomat*, December 21, 2013, http://thediplomat.com/2013/12/pakistans-longest-serving-strategic-nuclear-weapons-head-retires/.

15. Paolo Cotta-Ramusino and Maurizio Martellini, *Nuclear Safety, Nuclear Stability and Nuclear Strategy in Pakistan: A Concise Report of a Visit by Landau Network–Centro Volta* (Como, Italy: Landau Network–Centro Volta, 2002), 5, http://web.archive.org/web/20020406023646/https://pugwash.org/september11/pakistan-nuclear.htm.

16. Rodney W. Jones, "Conventional Military Imbalance and Strategic Stability in South Asia," South Asian Strategic Stability Unit Research Paper No. 1 (Bradford, UK: South Asian Strategic Stability Unit, Department of Peace Studies, University of Bradford, March 2005), http://www.policyarchitects.org/pdf/Conventional_imbalance_RJones.pdf; Lavoy, "Islamabad's Nuclear Posture," 133–34.

17. Khalid Kidwai, "Conversation with Gen. Khalid Kidwai," interview by Peter Lavoy (Carnegie International Nuclear Policy Conference, Washington, DC, March 23, 2015), 12, http://carnegieendowment.org/files/03-230315carnegieKIDWAI.pdf; Bruno Tertrais, "Pakistan's Nuclear and WMD Programmes: Status, Evolution and Risks," Non-Proliferation Papers No. 19, EU Non-Proliferation Consortium, July 2012, 2, http://www.sipri.org/research/disarmament/eu-consortium/publications/Nonproliferation-paper-19.

18. Tertrais, "Pakistan's Nuclear and WMD Programmes," 2.

19. Lavoy, "Islamabad's Nuclear Posture," 155–56. See also Daniel S. Markey, *No Exit from Pakistan: America's Tortured Relationship with Islamabad* (Cambridge: Cambridge University Press, 2013), 44.

20. Tertrais, "Pakistan's Nuclear and WMD Programmes," 2–3.

21. Kidwai, interview, 9.

22. Inter Services Public Relations (ISPR), "22nd Meeting of the National Command Authority," news release, February 24, 2016, https://www.ispr.gov.pk/front/main.asp?o=t-press_release&id=3211#pr_link3211; ISPR, "Meeting of the National Command Authority," news release, September 9, 2015, https://www.ispr.gov.pk/front/main.asp?o=t-press_release&id=3026#pr_link3026; Kidwai interview, 19.

23. International Panel on Fissile Materials, "Countries: Pakistan," last modified January 15, 2016, http://fissilematerials.org/countries/pakistan.html.

24. David Albright and Serena Kelleher-Vergantini, "Construction Continues at Pakistan's Khushab Site," Imagery Brief, Institute for Science and International Security, August 12, 2015, 1, http://isis-online.org/uploads/isis-reports/documents/Construction_Continues_at_Khushab_August12_2015_Final.pdf.

25. Rajesh Rajagopalan and Atul Mishra, *Nuclear South Asia: Keywords and Concepts* (New Delhi: Routledge India, 2014), 132.

26. Hans M. Kristensen and Robert S. Norris, "Pakistani Nuclear Forces, 2015," *Bulletin of the Atomic Scientists* 71, no. 6 (November–December 2015): 3; Toby Dalton and Michael Krepon, *A Normal Nuclear Pakistan* (Washington, DC: Stimson Center and Carnegie Endowment for International Peace, 2015), 19, http://carnegieendowment.org/files/NormalNuclearPakistan.pdf.

27. David Albright, "Pakistan's Inventory of Weapon-Grade Uranium and Weapon-Grade Plutonium Dedicated to Nuclear Weapons," Institute for Science and International Security, October 19, 2015, 3, http://isis-online.org/uploads/isis-reports/documents/Pakistan_WGU_and_WGPu_inventory_Oct_16_2015_final_1.pdf.

28. Ibid.; Dalton and Krepon, *Normal Nuclear Pakistan*, 19; Kristensen and Norris, "Pakistani Nuclear Forces, 2015," 1.

29. Tertrais, "Pakistan's Nuclear and WMD Programmes," 6.

30. ISPR, Press Release No PR-34/2017-ISPR, January 24, 2017, https://www.ispr.gov.pk/front/main.asp?o=t-press_release&id=3705&search=1; Hans M. Kristensen and Robert S. Norris, "Pakistani Nuclear Forces, 2016," *Bulletin of the Atomic Scientists* 72, no. 6 (October 2016): 369.

31. ISPR, Press Release No PR-10/2017-ISPR, January 9, 2017, https://www.ispr.gov.pk/front/t-press_release.asp?id=3671&print=1#pr_link3672.

32. Zia Mian, "Pakistan," *Assuring Destruction Forever*, 2015 ed., ed. Ray Acheson (Geneva: Reaching Critical Will, 2015), 54–63.

33. Kidwai, interview, 10.

34. Ibid., 8.

35. ISPR, Press Release No. PR-34/2017-ISPR, January 24, 2017, https://www.ispr.gov.pk/front/main.asp?o=t-press_release&id=3705.

36. George Perkovich, "The Non-Unitary Model and Deterrence Stability in South Asia," in *Deterrence Stability and Escalation Control in South Asia*, ed. Michael Krepon and Julia Thompson (Washington, DC: Stimson Center, 2013), 37.

37. Kristensen and Norris, "Pakistani Nuclear Forces, 2016," 369.

38. IISS, *The Military Balance 2016* (London: IISS, 2016), 252–54, 281.
39. "Navy Capable of Deploying Strategic Weapons," *Dawn*, October 15, 2008, https://www.dawn.com/news/325371.
40. ISPR, "Naval Chief Inaugurates Naval Strategic Force Headquarters," news release, May 19, 2012, https://www.ispr.gov.pk/front/main.asp?o=t-press_release&id=2067&search=1.
41. Kidwai, interview, 14–15.
42. Muhammad Azam Khan, "S-2: Options for the Pakistan Navy," *Naval War College Review* 63, no. 3 (Summer 2010): 96; Rehman, *Murky Waters*, 17–20.
43. Usman Ansari, "Pakistan to Buy 8 Submarines from China," *Defense News*, April 3, 2015, https://www.defensenews.com/naval/2015/04/03/pakistan-to-buy-8-submarines-from-china/.
44. Khan, "Options for the Pakistan Navy," 96.
45. Reuters, "Pakistan PM Approves Deal to Buy Eight Chinese Submarines: Official," April 2, 2015, https://www.reuters.com/article/us-china-pakistan/pakistan-pm-approves-deal-to-buy-eight-chinese-submarines-official-idUSKBN0MT05M20150402.
46. Ibid.; James Hardy and Sean O'Connor, "IMINT Confirms Type 041 Visit to Karachi," *Jane's Defence Weekly*, July 8, 2015, http://www.janes.com.
47. Usman Ansari, "Pakistan, China Finalize 8-Sub Construction Plan," *Defense News*, October 11, 2015, https://www.defensenews.com/naval/2015/10/11/pakistan-china-finalize-8-sub-construction-plan/; IISS, *Military Balance, 2016*, 281.
48. Iskander Rehman, "Tomorrow or Yesterday's Fleet? The Indian Navy's Operational Challenges," in *India's Naval Strategy and Asian Security*, ed. Anit Mukherjee and C. Raja Mohan (Oxford: Routledge, 2016), 43; Usman Ansari, "Pakistani Naval Modernization Appears Stalled," *Defense News*, January 15, 2016, https://www.defensenews.com/global/asia-pacific/2016/01/15/pakistani-naval-modernization-appears-stalled/; Ansari, "Pakistan, China Finalize 8-Sub Construction Plan."
49. Ansari, "Pakistan, China Finalize 8-Sub Construction Plan."
50. David Tweed, "Xi's Submarine Sale Raises Indian Ocean Nuclear Clash Risk," *Bloomberg Business*, April 16, 2015, https://www.bloomberg.com/news/articles/2015-04-16/xi-s-submarine-sale-raises-risk-of-nuclear-clash-in-indian-ocean; Ansari, "Pakistan, China Finalize 8-Sub Construction Plan."
51. Tweed, "Xi's Submarine Sale."
52. IISS, *Military Balance, 2016*, 281.
53. Federation of American Scientists, "AGM-84 Harpoon SLAM [Stand-Off Land Attack Missile]," February 18, 2015, http://fas.org/man/dod-101/sys/smart/agm-84.htm; Walter J. Boyne, "P-3 Orion," *Air Force Magazine*, August 2014, 88.
54. Khan, "Options for the Pakistan Navy," 98.
55. Eric Schmitt and David E. Sanger, "U.S. Says Pakistan Made Changes to Missiles Sold for Defense," *New York Times*, August 29, 2009, http://www.nytimes.com/2009/08/30/world/asia/30missile.html; Richard F. Grimmett, *U.S. Arms Sales to Pakistan*, RS22757 (Washington, DC: Congressional Research Service, 2009), https://fas.org/sgp/crs/weapons/RS22757.pdf; Richard F. Grimmett, *U.S. Defense Articles and Services Supplied to Foreign Recipients: Restrictions on Their Use*, RL30982 (Washington, DC: Congressional Research Service, 2005), https://fas.org/sgp/crs/natsec/RL30982.pdf.
56. Grimmett, *U.S. Arms Sales to Pakistan*.
57. Andrea Shalal, "U.S. Senator Wants Hearing on Possible F-16 Sale to Pakistan,"

Reuters, February 26, 2016, https://in.reuters.com/article/usa-pakistan-f16-deal/u-s
-senator-wants-hearing-on-possible-f-16-sale-to-pakistan-idINKCN0VY237; Reuters,
"U.S. Senate Committee Chairman Questions Pakistan F-16 Deal," February 23, 2016,
https://www.reuters.com/article/usa-pakistan-aircraft/u-s-senate-committee-chair
man-questions-pakistan-f-16-deal-idUSKCN0VW1X0.

58. Ryan Maass, "Pakistan Ambassador to U.S. Pushes for F-16 Sale," UPI, January 18,
    2017, http://www.upi.com/Defense-News/2017/01/18/Pakistan-ambassador-to
    -US-pushes-for-F-16-sale/1961484763759/; PTI, "Pak Bid to Buy F-16s from Jordan
    Would Require US Approval," *The Hindu*, June 16, 2016, http://www.thehindu.com
    /news/international/Pak-bid-to-buy-F-16s-from-Jordan-would-require-US-approval
    /article14425891.ece; Franz-Stefan Gady, "US-Pakistan F-16 Deal Is Dead: Islamabad
    Mulling Jordan F-16 Fighter Jets Instead," *The Diplomat*, June 15, 2016, http://the
    diplomat.com/2016/06/us-pakistan-f-16-deal-is-dead-islamabad-mulling-jordan-f
    -16-fighter-jets-instead/.

59. For a comprehensive history of this defense relationship, see Andrew Small, *The
    China-Pakistan Axis: Asia's New Geopolitics* (Gurgaon: Random House India, 2015).

60. Hans M. Kristensen and Robert S. Norris, "Chinese Nuclear Forces, 2015," *Bulletin of
    the Atomic Scientists* 71, no. 4 (July–August 2015): 81; Nuclear Threat Initiative, "China
    Submarine Capabilities," July 30, 2015, http://www.nti.org/analysis/articles/china
    -submarine-capabilities/; Khan, "Options for the Pakistan Navy," 99.

61. Federation of American Scientists, "Type 92 Xia," June 10, 1998, http://fas.org/nuke
    /guide/china/slbm/type_92.htm; Kristensen and Norris, "Chinese Nuclear Forces,
    2015," 81.

62. Khan, "Options for the Pakistan Navy," 99.

63. O'Donnell and Joshi, "Lost at Sea," 477.

64. Usman Ansari, "Pakistan Wraps Up Major Naval Exercise," *Defense News*, November 13,
    2015, https://www.defensenews.com/naval/2015/11/13/pakistan-wraps-up-major
    -naval-exercise/; Usman Ansari, "Pakistan Seeks to Energize Naval Modernization,"
    Defense News, June 17, 2015, https://www.defensenews.com/naval/2015/06/17/pak
    istan-seeks-to-energize-naval-modernization/; "Navy Capable of Deploying Strategic
    Weapons."

65. Andrew Detsch, "Pakistan's Oversized Submarine Ambitions," *The Diplomat*, Octo-
    ber 9, 2013, http://thediplomat.com/2013/10/pakistans-oversized-submarine-ambi
    tions/; Jake Thompson, "The Growth of an Indian Nuclear Navy," in *Project on Nuclear
    Issues: A Collection of Papers from the 2012 Conference Series*, ed. Stephanie Spies and Sarah
    Weiner (Washington, DC: CSIS, 2013): 144, https://csis-prod.s3.amazonaws.com
    /s3fs-public/legacy_files/files/publication/130702_Spies_PONI2012Conf_WEB
    .pdf; Albright, "Pakistan's Inventory," 10.

66. Khan, "Options for the Pakistan Navy," 90.

67. Jack Detsch, "Debt Strangles Pakistan's Naval Ambitions," *National Interest*, February
    19, 2015, http://nationalinterest.org/print/feature/debt-strangles-pakistan%E2%80
    %99s-naval-ambitions-12282.

68. Ansari, "Pakistan, China Finalize 8-Sub Construction Plan."

69. *Jane's Fighting Ships*, "Azmat Class," "Kaan 33 Class," "Oliver Hazard Perry Class,"
    "Sword (F-22P) Class," February 9, 2016, http://www.janes.com; *Jane's Navy Interna-
    tional*, "Interview: Captain Mirza Foad Amin Baig, Commanding Officer, PNS Zul-
    fiquar," April 22, 2010, http://www.janes.com; IISS, *Military Balance, 2016*, 281.

70. Defense Security Cooperation Agency, "Pakistan—Refurbishment of Oliver Hazard Perry Class Frigate," news release, February 19, 2010, http://www.dsca.mil/sites /default/files/mas/pakistan_09-28_0.pdf.

71. Usman Ansari, "US Congress Stymies Pakistani Naval Modernization Efforts," *Defense News*, April 17, 2014, https://defence.pk/pdf/threads/us-congress-stymies-pakistani -naval-modernization-efforts.309880/.

72. Farhan Bokhari, "Pakistan to Build Half of Type 041 Submarine Fleet in Country," *Jane's Defence Weekly*, October 6, 2015, http://www.janes.com; Ansari, "Pakistani Naval Modernization"; *Jane's Fighting Ships*, "Azmat Class," "Sword (F-22P) Class."

73. M. K. Narayanan, "Lurking Dangers," Seminar 665 (January 2015), http://india-semi nar.com/2015/665/665_m_k_narayanan.htm; Rehman, "Drowning Stability," 73–74.

74. Usman Ansari, "Pakistan Navy Test-Fires Land Attack Missile," *Defense News*, December 21, 2012, http://defenceforumindia.com/forum/threads/pakistan-navy-test -fired-missiles.45465/#post-640848.

75. Rehman, "Drowning Stability," 79.

76. Tavleen Singh, "Nuke Nuts in the RSS," *India Today*, July 12, 1999, http://indiato day.intoday.in/story/just-when-the-world-backs-india-sangh-loonies-talk-of-nuclear -war/1/255823.html; "Saffron Bombshell (Editorial)," *Times of India*, June 23, 1999, http://www.global.factiva.com; "United We Stand (Editorial)," *Indian Express*, June 12, 1999, http://archive.indianexpress.com/Storyold/103252/.

77. Siddharth Varadarajan, "The Bus Must Return with No-War Pact," *Times of India*, February 18, 1999, http://www.global.factiva.com; K. Subrahmanyam, "Peace at N-Point," *Times of India*, May 31, 1998, http://www.global.factiva.com; Kenneth Waltz, *The Spread of Nuclear Weapons: More May Be Better*, Adelphi Paper No. 171 (London: International Institute for Strategic Studies, 1981).

78. Ladwig, "Cold Start."

79. Feroz Hassan Khan, *Eating Grass: The Making of the Pakistani Bomb* (Stanford, CA: Stanford University Press, 2012), 395–96; Kidwai, interview, 9.

80. Kapil Kak, "Rationale and Implications," in *Pakistan's Tactical Nuclear Weapons: Conflict Redux*, ed. Gurmeet Kanwal and Monika Chansoria (New Delhi: KW Publishers, 2014), 73; Mateen Haider, "PM Nawaz Appoints Dr Maleeha Lodhi as Permanent Representative to UN," *Dawn*, December 15, 2014, https://www.dawn.com/news/1151028; Lodhi, "Pakistan's Nuclear Compulsions."

81. Zafar Khan, "Emerging Shifts in India's Nuclear Policy: Implications for Minimum Deterrence in South Asia," *Strategic Studies* 34, no. 1 (Spring 2014): 100, 111; Zafar Khan and Rizwana Abbasi, *Pakistan in the Global Nuclear Order*, Nuclear Paper Series No. 1 (Islamabad: Institute of Strategic Studies Islamabad, February 2016), 18, http:// issi.org.pk/wp-content/uploads/2016/02/Nuclear-Paper-Series-No.-1.pdf.

82. "Tough Kayani Warning to Proponents of 'Adventurism,'" *Dawn*, January 2, 2010, https://www.dawn.com/news/847867/tough-kayani-warning-to-proponents-of -adventurism; Kak, "Rationale and Implications," 67–68.

83. Rajaram Nagappa, Arun Vishwanathan, and Aditi Malhotra, *Hatf-IX/Nasr—Pakistan's Tactical Nuclear Weapon: Implications for Indo-Pak Deterrence* (Bangalore: National Institute of Advanced Studies, 2013), 16, http://isssp.in/wp-content/uploads/2013/07 /R17-2013_NASR_Final.pdf; Jeffrey Lewis, "Pakistan's Nuclear Artillery?" *Arms Control Wonk*, December 12, 2011, http://www.armscontrolwonk.com/archive/204866

/pakistans-nuclear-artillery/; "Nasr Tactical Ballistic Missile," *Military Today*, accessed December 16, 2017, http://www.military-today.com/missiles/nasr.htm.

84. Kak, "Rationale and Implications," 67–70.

85. Ibid., 72; Christopher Clary, "The Future of Pakistan's Nuclear Weapons Program," in Tellis, Denmark, and Turner, *Strategic Asia 2013–14*, 146.

86. Rajaram Nagappa, "Technical Aspects of Hatf-9/Nasr Missile," in Kanwal and Chansoria, *Pakistan's Tactical Nuclear Weapons*, 163–65; Clary, "Pakistan's Nuclear Weapons Program," 145–46; Kak, "Rationale and Implications," 70; Nagappa, Vishwanathan, and Malhotra, *Hatf-IX/Nasr*, 20–21.

87. Clary, "Pakistan's Nuclear Weapons Program," 146.

88. Rajat Pandit, "Army Hones Proactive Strategy with Massive Exercise in Thar," *Times of India*, April 15, 2016, https://timesofindia.indiatimes.com/india/Army-hones-proactive-strategy-with-massive-exercise-in-Thar/articleshow/51834944.cms; Shashank Joshi, "New Year, New Problem? Pakistan's Tactical Nukes," *The Diplomat*, January 2, 2013, http://thediplomat.com/2013/01/pakistans-new-nuclear-problem/; A. H. Nayyar and Zia Mian, "The Limited Military Utility of Pakistan's Battlefield Use of Nuclear Weapons in Response to Large Scale Indian Conventional Attack," Pakistan Security Research Unit Brief No. 61, Pakistan Security Research Unit, Department of Peace Studies, University of Bradford, November 11, 2010, 4–9, https://www.princeton.edu/sgs/faculty-staff/zia-mian/Limited-Military-Utility-of-Pakistans.pdf; John Cherian, "An Exercise in Anticipation," *Frontline* 18, no. 11 (May 26–June 8, 2001), http://www.frontline.in/static/html/fl1811/18110990.htm; Ashley J. Tellis, "India's Emerging Nuclear Doctrine: Exemplifying the Lessons of the Nuclear Revolution," *NBR Analysis* 12, no. 2 (May 2001): 96.

89. Walter C. Ladwig III, "Indian Military Modernization and Conventional Deterrence in South Asia," *Journal of Strategic Studies* 38, no. 5 (2015): 729–72; Christopher Clary, "What Might an India-Pakistan War Look Like?" *Précis* (Spring 2012), http://web.mit.edu/cis/precis/2012spring/india_pakistan.html#.Vt1q0ZxkjDd.

90. Pranab Dhal Samanta, "New Pak Doctrine: Deploy at Border If Terror Strike in India," *Indian Express*, January 8, 2012, http://indianexpress.com/article/news-archive/web/new-pak-doctrine-deploy-at-border-if-terror-strike-in-india/; Ladwig, "Conventional Deterrence," 18.

91. Samanta, "New Pak Doctrine."

92. Muhammad Khan, "From Cold Start to Cold Storage!" ISPR, November 2013, https://www.ispr.gov.pk/front/t-article.asp?id=87.

93. "Pakistan Develops New War Doctrine to Counter India," *India Today*, June 17, 2013, http://indiatoday.intoday.in/story/pakistan-develops-new-war-doctrine-to-counter-india/1/280569.html.

94. Khan, "Cold Start to Cold Storage!"

95. Shashank Joshi, "Pakistan's Tactical Nuclear Nightmare: Déjà Vu?" *Washington Quarterly* 36, no. 3 (Summer 2013): 165–66.

96. Arun Sahgal, "Logic and Options for Use," in Kanwal and Chansoria, *Pakistan's Tactical Nuclear Weapons*, 104.

97. Zafar Khan, "Pakistan's Nuclear First Use Doctrine: Obsessions and Obstacles," *Contemporary Security Policy* 36, no. 1 (2015): 149–70.

98. Prasun K. Sengupta, "Travesties of National Security," *Tris* (blog), September 2, 2012,

http://trishul-trident.blogspot.co.uk/2012/09/travesty-of-national-security.html; Ladwig, "Cold Start," 173–74.

99. "Operation Parakram after Parliament Attack Lacked Clear Objectives: Ex-Navy Chief Sushil Kumar," *Times of India*, November 6, 2011, https://timesofindia.indiatimes.com/india/Operation-Parakram-after-Parliament-attack-lacked-clear-objectives-Ex-Navy-chief-Sushil-Kumar/articleshow/10625959.cms; Praveen Swami, "Gen. Padmanabhan Mulls over Lessons of Operation Parakram," *The Hindu*, February 6, 2004, http://www.thehindu.com/2004/02/06/stories/2004020604461200.htm; Sengupta, "Travesties of National Security."

100. Celia W. Dugger, "A Blunt-Speaking General Says India Is Ready for War," *New York Times*, January 11, 2002, http://www.nytimes.com/2002/01/11/international/a-bluntspeaking-general-says-india-is-ready-for-war.html.

101. Bruce Riedel, "American Diplomacy and the 1999 Kargil Summit at Blair House" (Philadelphia: Center for the Advanced Study of India, University of Pennsylvania, 2002), 11–12, http://citeseerx.ist.psu.edu/viewdoc/download?doi=10.1.1.473.251&rep=rep1&type=pdf; Ladwig, "Cold Start," 173–74.

102. Pranab Dhal Samanta, "26/11: How India Debated a War with Pakistan That November," *Indian Express*, November 26, 2010, http://indianexpress.com/article/news-archive/web/26-11-how-india-debated-a-war-with-pakistan-that-november/.

3

CHINA'S NUCLEAR THOUGHT AND POSTURE

Implications for India

Like the India-Pakistan relationship, the India-China relationship is characterized by implications of power differentials. However, in relation to China, India is the inferior. Although India and China have similar population sizes, China's economy and military technological sophistication are much greater. Whereas the lacerating experience of the 1971 war infuses Pakistani anxieties about India today, India suffered a humiliating defeat to China in a short bilateral war in 1962. China claims most of a whole state of India—Arunachal Pradesh—as its own and upholds other disputed territorial claims in the Ladakh and Aksai Chin regions. India has only recently begun upgrading roads on its side of the border, overcoming a previous concern that good roads could only ease the southward path of another Chinese invasion.

As India presently holds the entirety of Pakistan's territory at nuclear risk, substantive energies within India's nuclear thought and planning today are directed toward achieving a similar goal against China. In a leaked letter to President Bill Clinton explaining the 1998 nuclear tests, Indian prime minister Atal Bihari Vajpayee referred to the threat posed by "an overt nuclear weapon state on our borders, a state which committed armed aggression against India in 1962" as a primary cause of the Indian decision to develop an overt nuclear force.[1] India's most recent missile, the Agni-V, has been developed with Chinese east coast targets in mind.[2] India's emerging *Arihant*-class nuclear-armed submarine fleet is designed to ensure second-strike capacity but is also often spoken about in India as an additional signal of general naval resolve against Chinese conventional projection into the Indian Ocean.[3]

Chinese nuclear threat perceptions primarily revolve around the challenge of deterring its more powerful geopolitical rival—the United States—rather than its inferior rival, India. This tendency forms a regional pattern, with Pakistan principally concerned with deterring India as the superior rival, and India similarly concerned with deterring China. China practices an NFU policy and a nuclear posture that relies substantially on deception and mobility for a limited number of weapons to ensure deterrence, rather than numerical strength as in the American and Russian traditions.

To address its anxieties about the potential for American BMD systems to block Chinese nuclear retaliation, China is reportedly developing MIRV technology for its missiles and antisatellite strike capabilities to degrade supportive infrastructure for adversary BMD systems. China is also fielding a nuclear-armed submarine fleet and emphasizing the use of conventional nuclear-capable ballistic and cruise missiles in its power projection. While the United States is still the greatest external influence on China's nuclear force development, a 2015 Pentagon report noted that India's nuclear force advancements are an "additional driver" for those of China.[4]

This chapter will first explore China's tradition of nuclear thought. It will then investigate Chinese conventional force advancements in the land and naval domains of competition with India and the way these developments are affecting Indian nuclear threat perceptions. It will conclude by examining Chinese efforts to build Pakistan's nuclear and general national infrastructure relevant to military mobilization.

CHINESE THREAT PERCEPTIONS AND EFFECTS ON NUCLEAR DOCTRINE

The history of China's nuclear weapon program has not been principally influenced by insecurities in its relationship with India. Instead, China's interest in nuclear weapons originated in a desire to attain great-power status and to deter the United States. The United States and, to a lesser degree, the Soviet Union / Russia have occupied the majority of China's nuclear threat perceptions and have shaped its nuclear force.[5]

The early Chinese nuclear weapon program was characterized by the belief that China's leaders, even without nuclear weapons, were less afraid of their use than US leaders were. This attitude—that nuclear weapons were less consequential in actual war than assumed by American policymakers—created better cognitive and political flexibility for Chinese policymakers and domestic propaganda to withstand American nuclear threats and even use in a conflict. Attaining a Chinese nuclear weapon capability would escalate the anxiety in Washington attendant to any serious discussion of nuclear use and would further strengthen China's defenses against the bomb. This initial approach has been described as "counter-nuclear blackmail," rather than as deterrence based on nuclear retaliation, which was the goal for early nuclear weapon programs in other states.[6]

Following from this belief that the United States is more prone to self-deterrence by the threat or use of nuclear weapons than China is, China's nuclear force development has more recently been focused on generating not first-strike primacy but a nuclear force adequate to create enough uncertainty in the minds of adversary policymakers regarding their ability to conduct a first strike that obliterates any prospect of Chinese nuclear retaliation. As a Chinese analyst has described this thinking, "What's the threshold of first strike uncertainty to deter? The basic question . . . is: 'how uncertain is enough?' as opposed to the classical question in the Cold War: 'how much is enough?'"[7]

China's nuclear force, conceptually built on generating just enough uncertainty in the minds of adversary leaderships, is a fraction of the numerical size of its two primary nuclear targets—the United States and Russia. China has the technological and economic capacity to field a much larger nuclear force. Thus, this comparatively small size of China's nuclear force, plus its reliance on mobility and deception, is truly determined by doctrinal thinking rather than by the technological or economic limits to nuclear force capabilities often faced by young nuclear weapon programs.

China's nuclear doctrine was most recently concisely outlined in a 2015 defense white paper: "China has always pursued the policy of no first use of nuclear weapons and adhered to a self-defensive nuclear strategy that is defensive in nature. China will unconditionally not use or threaten to use nuclear weapons against non-nuclear-weapon states or in nuclear-weapon-free zones, and will never enter into a nuclear arms race with any other country. China has always kept its nuclear capabilities at the minimum level required for maintaining its national security."[8] Compared to India's and Pakistan's doctrines, China's doctrine is notable in that it is described as "minimum" without the careful qualifier "credible," as in the Indian doctrine of "credible minimum deterrence" and in contrast to Pakistan's march in the other direction, toward "full spectrum deterrence." China is also the only state of the three to regularly issue public official statements of its nuclear doctrine in white papers.

However, China's nuclear thinking is not universally as minimalist as the doctrinal statement suggests. Since the 1980s the Chinese military has debated whether nuclear force planning should continue to adhere to a minimum deterrence posture or transit to a more flexible limited deterrence. The essence of the *minimum* deterrence posture is ensuring sufficient retaliatory capacity with the lowest warhead count and quantum of destructive capability possible. This also involves countervalue (adversary population center) target selection, an option that the 2013 iteration of the authoritative Chinese Academy of

Military Sciences *Science of Military Strategy* manual identifies as requiring numerically smaller, less precise, and lower-yield nuclear forces as compared to counterforce (adversary military) targeting.[9] The posture of *limited* deterrence would entail constructing this counterforce nuclear war-fighting capacity with comparatively larger, more precise, and higher-yield nuclear forces. It would also involve greater diversification of nuclear platforms to build different nuclear force options for each domain (land, air, and sea) and for escalation of nuclear conflict. The manual rejects this latter approach, suggesting that minimum deterrence remains the organizing concept of China's nuclear posture.[10]

However, pressures for adopting a form of limited deterrence still exist in China. As we will see, a new generation of Chinese ballistic missiles that are MIRV-capable and more precise than those currently deployed is being developed. More focused targeting options are also being delivered through advancements in Chinese space-based surveillance, communications, and geolocation capabilities.[11] These improvements create new counterforce options for China that could render a limited deterrence approach more technically feasible and thus less of a distant concept than it was in the past.[12]

The Chinese efforts to develop more precise, multiple-warhead nuclear forces primarily emanate not from a perceived Indian threat but from a perceived US capability to successfully conduct a nuclear first strike. This capability is generated by the numerical superiority of US nuclear forces; the increasingly sophisticated BMD technology being deployed by the US and its allies around China's periphery, potentially blocking Chinese nuclear retaliation; a high degree of adversary targeting precision delivered by the unparalleled sophistication of US missile and space-based global positioning technologies; and growing US interest in developing conventional precision strike options, such as Prompt Global Strike conventional ballistic missile packages. The latter development, in particular, should not be overlooked in understanding Chinese nuclear threat perception; the *Science of Military Strategy* warns, "The 'rapid global strike' plan currently being put into effect by the United States, as soon as it takes shape as an actual combat capability, will, when used to carry out a conventional attack against our nuclear missile forces, put us into a passive position, greatly influencing our capability for nuclear retaliation, weakening the efficacy of our nuclear deterrence."[13]

Another area of Chinese minimum deterrence nuclear practice under discussion concerns alert procedures. Chinese nuclear forces, like Indian nuclear forces, have traditionally been stored in "de-alerted" format, with warheads and missiles held separately. This practice has been viewed as an element of the minimum deterrence philosophy of eschewing policies implying a high degree of military readiness that would resemble a nuclear war-fighting approach.

The Chinese anxiety regarding a US first strike, however, is driving discussion on this practice. The *Science of Military Strategy* suggests that nuclear forces could be held on a higher alert level, ready to launch upon receipt of intelligence of an incoming nuclear strike: "When conditions are prepared and when necessary, we can, under conditions confirming the enemy has launched nuclear missiles against us, before the enemy nuclear warheads have reached their targets and effectively exploded, before they have caused us actual nuclear damage, quickly launch a nuclear missile retaliatory strike."[14]

Launching a nuclear attack before China has suffered one would appear to contravene China's NFU commitment, but the manual guarantees that this launch would occur only following receipt of irrefutable intelligence "confirming the enemy has launched nuclear missiles against us." As an American expert has noted, such a degree of technical confidence that an incoming missile is nuclear-armed may not ever be attainable before impact.[15] Nevertheless, military interest in effecting a shift toward launch-on-warning persists. This interest extends to developing a study on options for building an attack warning network in 2014, planning to explore space-based early warning sensors, and in the 2015 defense white paper, making a commitment to "improve strategic early warning."[16]

CHINESE PERSPECTIVES ON NUCLEAR INDIA

Chinese officials and members of China's strategic community rank India substantially below the United States and Russia in the nuclear threat hierarchy facing the country. This is primarily due to the limited technical capabilities of India's nuclear force and the absence in New Delhi of any intentions to launch an attack against China.[17] However, the Chinese nuclear discourse on India is starting to shift, driven by the increasing credibility of Indian nuclear and nuclear-capable delivery vehicles and India's deepening strategic partnership with the United States. Particular areas of focus include the significance of India's emerging delivery vehicles, such as the Agni-V and *Arihant*, for China's strategic environment; the prospect of India's enhanced abilities to expand fissile material stockpiles; and potential benefits from close US military cooperation following the conclusion of the civil nuclear agreement. While these recent reassessments of Indian strategic capabilities have not yet been translated into new Chinese nuclear diplomatic and military approaches toward South Asia, they nevertheless could compel a revision in the future.

The emergence of new Indian nuclear and nuclear-capable platforms has drawn interest from Chinese analysts. A survey of Chinese literature about Indian military posturing has turned up substantial commentary on the *Arihant* and Brahmos platforms, including on their positive effects for India's defense projection.[18] The range, destructive capacity, and meaning of new force developments for India's military rise have also been evaluated in recent People's Liberation Army (PLA) Academy of Military Sciences commentaries. One study has remarked on the multiple-warhead potential and testing progress of the Agni-V and prospective Agni-VI missiles, noted their ability to reach major Chinese east coast population centers, and highlighted the importance of these developments for India's military rise. The commentary drew attention to the prospect of multiple miniaturized warheads being hosted aboard an 8,000-kilometer-range Agni-VI as a substantive landmark in India's strategic force posturing. This article also concluded that these new platforms would contribute to pressures within India for a strategic nuclear dialogue with China.[19] Another Academy of Military Sciences report has surveyed the Agni-IV, Agni-V, and *Arihant* programs, illustrating their contributions to developing a more credible Indian nuclear force and predicting that they would influence a greater boldness by New Delhi in pursuing its Indian Ocean and broader national interests.[20]

Chinese experts have also studied the implications of the Indo-US nuclear deal for China's strategic context. Significant concerns include the risk that India may now be able to increase its fissile material production, including that for military purposes.[21] New Delhi will also now benefit from greater access to global military technologies than China has and from a deepening defense partnership with the United States. These developments could further complicate China's regional environment and narrow its military edge against India.[22]

The Chinese discourse on India has also evidenced debate regarding New Delhi's continued commitment to its NFU policy. National Security Advisor Shivshankar Menon's 2010 description of the NFU pledge as "no first use against non-nuclear weapon states" was quickly dismissed as an incorrect mischaracterization of the policy within India, and some descriptions of the pledge refrain from mentioning this caveated version.[23] Still, a Chinese expert has described the 2010 iteration of the NFU policy as continuing to inform perceptions of India's nuclear doctrine in China.[24] Threat assessments based on this conditional NFU pledge would entail an Indian interest in first use against China and Pakistan and, accordingly, a larger and longer-range nuclear arsenal held at a higher degree of readiness. As discussed in chapter 1, recent Indian force developments could be interpreted to conform with a conditional NFU policy. The combination of canisterized Agni-V and prospective Agni-VI missiles, the *Arihant*-class SSBN fleet, and the continuing absence of visible political limits to Indian nuclear force development could indicate the emergence of a posture characterized by increased permanent readiness.

The evolving India-Pakistan strategic rivalry and its implications for regional nuclear stability have also attracted comment in China. One Chinese scholar, again reflecting on the 2010 version of India's NFU pledge, suggested that India would probably seek to retain the option of nuclear first use against Pakistan, including striking nuclear targets, in a conventional conflict.[25] Recent discussions in India regarding the potential existence of a preemptive nuclear counterforce strike policy against Pakistan (discussed in chapter 5) reinforce this perception. A RAND investigation of Chinese strategic opinion noted that India's development of limited nuclear war capabilities and concepts could motivate Chinese security planners to develop similar capabilities, even if both states continue to formally adhere to their stated NFU doctrines. It continued, "Should India deploy a broad range of warfighting capabilities, Chinese military planners might fear that China could potentially face an Indian foe capable of using nuclear weapons to win battlefield victories."[26]

A related concern is the possibility of India attaining nuclear numerical parity with China, as the former continues warhead production and the development of longer-range delivery vehicles. The recent RAND analysis of Chinese strategic opinion found that multiple sources thought China would not permit India to reach this benchmark and would expand its arsenal as a reactive measure to this situation.[27] This outcome would represent the emergence of a closer interactive sensitivity between Chinese and Indian nuclear planners to their mutual posturing intentions and could threaten arms race dynamics.

These facets of Chinese strategic thought toward India all align with the more challenging nuclear strategic environment identified in the *Science of Military Strategy* manual.[28] Several Chinese experts, including a retired general, have noted the emergence of a strand of opinion within China that favors revoking the NFU pledge and assigning nuclear forces a broader role in general deterrence. While this is still a comparatively small segment of opinion, it is shared by sections of the military.[29] The retired general noted that these arguments are partly based on views that "nuclear weapons continue to spread among China's neighbors" despite the NFU policy and that "the situation involving China's neighbors seems to be deteriorating."[30]

A continuation of this negative trendline in China's evaluation of its regional security could therefore stimulate further support for the hawkish school of Chinese nuclear strategy. Further Indian strategic force advancements and evidence of new defense cooperation initiatives with the United States could enhance pressures in China for doctrinal and posturing changes in the direction of flexible response and associated new war-fighting options. These perceptions, and their accordant recommendations for Chinese policy responses, could be further amplified by transitions in China's strategic policymaking structures. As noted earlier, the military forms a notable element of the constellation of support for a Chinese flexible response doctrine and options. Structural empowerment of the military within China's nuclear policy complex could therefore enhance the weight of these perceptions and voices within policy deliberations. Indeed, "the day-to-day supervision of top leaders has declined since the 1960s and 1970s, and the role of the military in nuclear policymaking has grown," while the "elevation of the Second Artillery from branch to service (with its name change to PLA Rocket Force) will strengthen nuclear advocacy within the PLA."[31]

This overview of Chinese perceptions of India illuminates the increasing incompatibility of the evolving threat that India poses to China and China's strategic responses to this threat. Despite the transitions in the Chinese discourse, Chinese security managers still publicly and privately prioritize India as a minor concern in their strategic evaluations at the policy level. Beijing continues to refuse New Delhi's entreaties for a bilateral strategic nuclear dialogue, as this would reflect an official recognition of India as a de facto nuclear power.[32] Chinese diplomats continue other efforts to delegitimize India's nuclear status, such as hindering its campaign for NSG membership. Another recent initiative has been to claim that the emergence of the Agni-V violates UN Security Council Resolution 1172, passed in 1998 to condemn the South Asian nuclear tests and demand that India and Pakistan desist from further weaponization and ballistic missile development.[33]

Indeed, a close analysis of China's reactions to the December 2016 Agni-V test highlights the extent to which this policy approach toward India is counterproductive for China's regional security interests. The Ministry of Foreign Affairs paired the aforementioned UN Security Council violation claim with a call for "strategic balance" between India and Pakistan.[34] This "balance" framing justifies China's continuing efforts to bolster Pakistan's nuclear force capabilities, including the sharing of submarine and multiple-launch rocket system technologies (see chapter 2). Indeed, a retired Second Artillery Corps officer claimed that China would begin new ballistic missile cooperation initiatives with Pakistan following the Agni-V test. A Chinese foreign affairs spokesperson denied this claim, but it was nevertheless reported in Indian media.[35]

Although Chinese defense publications and discourse suggest that the developments in Indian force modernization and US-India relations significantly complicate China's threat environment, Beijing's current policy attitude toward India can serve only to maintain, if not accelerate, these trends. Refusing to diplomatically engage India on nuclear strategic stability and simultaneously enabling Pakistan's arsenal growth will further propel India toward fielding a nuclear force that is closer to parity with China.

Recognizing this dilemma, some Chinese scholars have begun to call for a revision of China's approach toward India. One expert proposed a strategic nuclear dialogue with India because "to no small extent, India's distrust of China's nuclear policies has driven India's nuclear weapons development. A regular bilateral dialogue is the only way to gradually reduce misunderstanding and build confidence." This dialogue could include discussion of mutual nuclear threat perceptions, doctrinal and posturing principles, and delivery vehicle development, as well as broader topics such as the nuclear nonproliferation regime.[36]

Another Chinese academic recommended a new approach toward nuclear force transparency. As China has traditionally hosted a nuclear arsenal smaller than that of the United States, the arsenal's survivability has partly relied on opacity, deception, and mobility regarding the precise constitutions and locations of its forces. Beijing has accordingly refrained from outlining details of its nuclear force size and shape in multilateral dialogue with NPT nuclear weapon states, a tendency also reflected in its bilateral engagements with Washington.[37] A diplomatic statement of China's approach toward nuclear transparency asserts that more advanced military powers should have greater transparency obligations than rising powers.[38] However, the academic argued that Beijing should nevertheless adopt new unilateral transparency measures because "the lack of transparency is damaging to China's national image. In the context of China's rising strength, a good national image is very important for promoting mutual trust among nations and achieving a peaceful rise." This recommendation entails the issuance of a defense white paper with the following details:

> This white paper should at least contain an upper limit to the number of nuclear warheads that China possesses—that is, no more than 300 or 500. This document should also announce that China has stopped producing fissile materials for use in nuclear weapons, and that China has no tactical nuclear weapons. It also should release the names of all of China's nuclear weapons, clarify that the country's short-range ballistic missiles are not being used for nuclear purposes, clarify whether the country's cruise missiles are only being used for conventional purposes or if they could also be used for nuclear purposes, and clarify whether it still has bombers carrying active nuclear weapons.

Further measures, as outlined under this proposal, could also involve public notification of missile tests, including the missile model, launch and landing locations, scheduled date and time of the test, and outcome.[39] These recommendations could certainly reduce Indian threat perceptions of China; they could help to build mutual trust and correct New Delhi's worst-case scenario projections for Chinese nuclear intentions and capabilities. Moreover, since China is the superior power in relation to India, these efforts would model China's own expressed principle that more militarily capable states should take the lead in establishing transparency initiatives.

Nevertheless, there are few signs that these recommendations for a nuclear dialogue with India and greater transparency will become official policy in the near term. Chinese strategic discourse is increasingly cognizant of India's military nuclear capabilities, but assessments of the threat posed by India have not yet compelled Chinese officials to revise the current policy approach toward South Asia. Each element of this policy framework—including assisting Pakistan's nuclear force expansion, delegitimizing India's nuclear status, and resisting strategic dialogue with India or transparency measures—motivates Indian development of a larger, more sophisticated, and longer-range nuclear force and closer strategic ties with the United States.

These Indian responses could amplify existing pressures in China for a larger nuclear force and more flexible doctrine. Such Chinese policy outcomes would further elevate Indian threat perceptions and potentially stimulate similar doctrinal and posturing transitions in India. The interactive effects of shifts in Indian and Chinese strategic thought and policy behavior are growing evidence of conditions conducive to more heightened nuclear competition, including an increased interest in flexible response and limited nuclear war strategies.

As the Chinese debates progress, Beijing is building a new generation of potentially higher-yield nuclear weapons with more accurate targeting, and military analysts are exploring the possibility of raising the permanent alert level to launch-on-warning. The next section will explore the present Chinese nuclear posture in this context, focusing particularly on specific implications for India.

CHINA'S NUCLEAR POSTURE

China was estimated to hold around 260 nuclear warheads in 2018. China's nuclear posture relies heavily on land-based ballistic missiles, although the country is presently developing a nuclear-armed submarine fleet (see table 3.1). Like India and Pakistan, China still stores warheads separately from delivery vehicles in peacetime. However, China's intention to field a nuclear-armed submarine fleet will require sea-launched missiles to be fully armed before deployment. In the coming years, China, India, and Pakistan will all face the policy challenge of managing the civil-military and operational issues that arise from deploying fully-armed nuclear weapons and the accordant delegation of authority to launch.

TABLE 3.1
Chinese Nuclear Forces, 2018

Type	Range	Current status
Aircraft		
H-6	3,100 km (1,926 mi)	Inducted
Land-based ballistic missiles		
DF-5A	13,000+ km (8,077.8+ mi)	Inducted
DF-5B	12,000 km (7,456+ mi)	Inducted
DF-31A	11,200+ km (6,960+ mi)	Inducted
DF-4	5,400+ km (3,355+ mi)	Inducted
DF-31	7,200+ km (4,473.8+ mi)	Inducted
DF-3A	3,000+ km (1,864+ mi)	Inducted
DF-21	1,750+ km (1,087.4+ mi)	Inducted
Cruise missiles		
DH-10	1,500 km (932 mi)	Inducted
DH-20	Unknown	Unknown
Sea-based ballistic missiles		
JL-1	1,000+ km (621.4+ mi)	Inducted
JL-2	7,400 km (4,598 mi)	Inducted

Sources: Data from Hans M. Kristensen and Robert S. Norris, "Chinese Nuclear Forces, 2016," *Bulletin of the Atomic Scientists* 72, no. 4 (October 2016): 205–11; Hans M. Kristensen and Robert S. Norris, "Chinese Nuclear Forces, 2015," *Bulletin of the Atomic Scientists* 71, no. 4 (July–August 2015): 77–84; Zhang Hui, "China," in *Assuring Destruction Forever*, 2015 ed., ed. Ray Acheson (Geneva: Reaching Critical Will, 2015), 22–28.

IMPLICATIONS FOR NUCLEAR INTERACTIONS WITH INDIA: THE LAND DOMAIN

Although China's land-based nuclear missiles have long been able to target the Indian mainland, these missiles are being replaced with a new generation of more accurate and potentially more destructive weapons. Chinese land-based nuclear forces are divided into six missile bases, also known as units. Analysts suggest that Chinese nuclear missiles intended for Indian targets are principally located at sites under the aegis of the Fifty-Third Base in Yunnan Province in southwestern China and the Fifty-Sixth Base in Qinghai Province in the northwest.[40] The Fifty-Third Base reportedly holds nuclear-capable 1,750-kilometer (1,087-mile) range DF-21 ballistic missiles. Experts have observed that India is the only nuclear-armed state that DF-21s stationed at Kunming under the Fifty-Third Base can reach. DF-31A missiles, with a range of over 11,200 kilometers (over 6,960 miles), and DF-21s have been assigned to the Fifty-Sixth

Base. In addition, 13,000-kilometer (8,078-mile) range DF-5A and 5,400-kilo-meter (3,355-mile) range DF-4 missiles are stationed at the Fifty-Fourth Base in Henan Province and Fifty-Fifth Base in Hunan Province.[41]

Adjustments to this nuclear missile force emphasize improvements in accuracy, mobility, and destructive capability. China is increasing the number of warheads carried aboard its nuclear missiles, reportedly equipping around ten of its twenty DF-5A missiles with MIRV warheads.[42] There may be a prospect for further advancements in this direction. One analysis suggests that the DF-31 has successfully been tested carrying multiple warheads in the past and that DF-31 missile variants could be replaced with MIRV-capable versions in the future.[43] China is also experimenting with potentially nuclear-capable hypersonic glide vehicles designed to evade BMD systems; a successor to the DF-21 is a likely candidate missile to carry this new vehicle.[44]

DF-4 rockets, which are reportedly stationed in relatively fixed sheltered locations, are being gradually replaced with road-mobile DF-31 missiles. China is increasing its number of DF-21 road-mobile missiles and introducing conventionally armed DF-21s that blur the line between nuclear and conventional missile strike missions for analysts outside China.[45] These advancements are underpinned by China's growing communications, targeting, and geolocation capabilities, which will improve accuracy. India appears set to face in the coming years a Chinese nuclear missile threat that is increasingly road mobile, MIRV capable, precise, and ambiguous in constitution, with growing potential for nuclear-capable ballistic missiles to be assigned conventional missions and vice versa.

The announcement on December 31, 2015, of the most far-reaching Chinese military reforms in generations generated additional ambiguity regarding China's nuclear future. One specific reform replaced the Second Artillery Corps, hitherto responsible for China's nuclear and conventional ballistic missile operations, with the new Rocket Force. The Rocket Force has been formally elevated to the status of a full military service on the same level as the army, navy, air force, and the new Strategic Support Force, reportedly responsible for reconnaissance and cyber and space war.[46] This adjustment formalizes the de facto treatment of the Second Artillery Corps as an "independent branch treated as a service" but entails more than a name change.[47] The Ministry of National Defense explained the formation of the Rocket Force as "representing the core strength of the Chinese military to provide strategic deterrence and strategic support on a par with China's status as a great power." In addition, the new service was intended to "build a stronger and modern missile force in line with its functions and missions."[48]

Indeed, alongside advancing the missile modernization programs outlined previously, the Rocket Force has appeared to be tasked in its early life with new measures to improve missile reliability. Reports published on a PLA website claimed that in February 2016 the Rocket Force conducted tests of short-range ballistic missiles in a desert area in northwest China and in a tropical forest in the south. The northwest desert tests were conducted at a temperature reaching −30 degrees Celsius (−22 degrees Fahrenheit) and potentially included the 600-kilometer (373-mile) range nuclear-capable DF-15 missile.[49] External analysts believe most DF-15s are currently assigned conventional strike missions.[50] An IAF group captain has claimed that conventionally armed DF-15s are stationed at Chengdu and targeted against India, although this has not been confirmed by other experts.[51] An earlier series of tests, also emphasizing low-temperature launch conditions, was conducted in January 2016. This selection of launch conditions is notable given that Qinghai Province, where the Fifty-Sixth Base is located, is mostly on the Tibetan plateau. The official China Central Television (CCTV) network reported that the tests "developed over 10 new tactics for snowfield combat, including rapid mobility methods and tactics to avoid airstrikes."[52]

The Rocket Force also has a new missile training facility, announced in February 2016. The PLA claims that this facility can simulate launch conditions of "rain, snow, galeforce winds, fog and lightning, as well as electronic warfare situations."[53] The Rocket Force is therefore dedicating itself to improving the usability and technical sophistication of its missile forces, with a particular early focus on tests under environmental conditions similar to those of its bases likely to be assigned India targeting missions.

It remains unclear whether the Rocket Force will receive more responsibilities than its Second Artillery Corps predecessor. The Second Artillery Corps controlled land-based nuclear and conventional ballistic missiles, while the air force and navy managed air-based and sea-based nuclear forces, respectively. It is uncertain whether the Rocket Force will assume responsibility for air- and sea-based assets as well.[54] What service controls sea-based assets is especially pertinent given the emergence of the *Jin*-class SSBN fleet and the question SSBNs raise regarding operational responsibility for the SLBMs on board.

Reported answers to this question vary. *Global Times*, an official newspaper of the Chinese Communist Party, in a report dated January 5, 2016, cited a former Second Artillery Corps officer: "The most important function shift is that the new rocket force will be a commanding unit for land-, air- and sea-based nuclear power, while the previous force was only responsible for land-based nuclear power."[55] A Chinese military website reported additional remarks by the same officer in a January 8 report, stating that it was a "matter of time" before the Rocket Force assumed air and sea nuclear strike responsibilities. The officer also suggested that the army could assume control of short-range ballistic missiles from the Rocket Force in order to enable the latter to focus on long-range nuclear and conventional strike missions.[56] However, a PLA newspaper affirmed on January 10, 2016, that no reorganization of individual Rocket Force units would be included as part of the reforms, suggesting that the service's responsibilities would remain confined for now to land-based nuclear and conventional ballistic missiles.[57] This question of the potential extension of Rocket Force responsibilities to airborne and seaborne nuclear forces remains unresolved at the time of writing in 2018.

A second potential area of difference between the Second Artillery Corps and the Rocket Force is in conventional missile strike autonomy. Recent Second Artillery Corps doctrine had outlined the branch's intentions to develop autonomous conventional missile attack capabilities alongside its existing missile support to the other services.[58] The creation of the Rocket Force as a full independent service suggests these intentions are unlikely to have been revised.

India therefore faces in 2018 a Chinese land-based nuclear force featuring a newly elevated official status, an ongoing program introducing a new generation of road-mobile and MIRV-capable nuclear missiles in range of Indian targets, a dedicated testing program simulating conditions like those anticipated in a Chinese attack against India, and growing ambiguity in conventional and nuclear missions of Rocket Force units, as conventional ballistic missiles continue to attain greater prominence in Chinese strategy.

Broader Chinese military reforms, alongside the specific formation of the Rocket Force, also have relevance for India-China nuclear stability. The overarching headline reform was replacing the seven PLA military regions (with the northwest Lanzhou region and southwest Chengdu region closest and most relevant to India) with five joint service "theater commands."[59] The PLA was divided into eighteen group armies, each including around 30,000–65,000 personnel, across the seven military regions. Two group armies (the Twenty-First and Forty-Seventh) were stationed in Lanzhou, and another two (the Thirteenth and Fourteenth) were located in Chengdu.[60] As a retired Indian Army brigadier has noted, the formal division of China's ground forces nearest to India into the two separate Chengdu and Lanzhou organizational structures would complicate Chinese logistics and operations in a conflict with India.[61] A commentary published on a PLA website in February 2016 agreed with this point: "Both Lanzhou and Chengdu MACs [military area commands, or military regions] face India and Pakistan. If a war broke out in that direction, the two MACs would have to implement wartime organizational adjustment."[62]

This website commentary also claimed that, in comparison with the more offensively oriented Shenyang and Beijing military regions close to Russia, the India-facing regions were more defensive in outlook and were organized around holding ground in the event of an attack while reserves were mobilized from the Chinese interior. The new theater commands, however, brought with them a new operational approach that would be universally applied: "In terms of strategic planning, the five Theater Commands is no longer positioned for regional defense, but head-on and proactive defense. . . . The new Theater Commands will attack proactively once a war broke out instead of passively waiting for defending the enemy at home."[63]

This thinking aligns with the official Chinese strategic concept of "active defense," a concept the PLA confirmed had remained unchanged through the military reforms.[64] The concept emphasizes a philosophy of not attacking unless attacked first, with this underpinning a strategically defensive general posture. However, in the event of an attack, forces must be quickly able to "seize the initiative" at an operational level and conduct maneuvers that are "operationally offensive" (and thus potentially escalatory) in order to meet overall objectives that are viewed by Chinese decision makers as generally strategically defensive.[65]

Some PLA writings have interpreted this concept to permit preemptive attacks on an adversary if China is perceived to be facing substantial threat at the strategic level. For example, PLA experts at the Shijiazhuang Army Command Academy have argued, "Gaining mastery through counterattacks [i.e., striking only after being attacked] . . . is not an effective way to seize initiative on the informatized battlefield." This study recommended that the PLA consider attacking first upon perceived adversary force mobilizations. Alternatively, once "signs of enemy invasion are clear" (thus, again before any adversary attack has taken place), the PLA should be prepared to "boldly conduct cross-border combat operations, directing the fighting to the enemy side and inflicting heavy strikes on the enemy." This implies potentially attacking adversary areas and targets outside where adversary force mobilization is taking place.[66]

While not all PLA commentaries argue in favor of these two specific options, a 2008 study of PLA thinking identified a common theme of seizing the initiative as early as possible, including initiating rapid escalation at the outset of a conflict in order to quickly gain and retain the initiative and compel adversary submission.[67] If the creation of theater commands is intended to encourage capability development in favor of operations to "attack proactively once a war broke out instead of passively waiting for defending the enemy at home," per the PLA commentary, then the aggressive thinking of these PLA commentators may assume greater prominence in Chinese military planning and structuring.[68]

Indeed, reforms relevant to India thus far have focused on streamlining structures to render them conducive to more rapid operations intended to seize the initiative early. The Lanzhou and Chengdu military regions have been replaced with the new Western Theater Command, headquartered in Chengdu, which significantly unifies oversight of significant India border areas.[69] The overall army headcount will be cut by 300,000 and focus will be shifted to mechanization and "informatization," defined as making full use of communications and geolocation capabilities alongside other current information technologies.[70] The reforms will produce a numerically smaller Chinese army, but one that is more precise and fast acting.

Logistical advancements before the military reorganization were also intended to develop rapid army mobilization capabilities, including in areas close to India. These advancements did not focus on stationing new Chinese forces along the India border but on improving transport links to the border from existing military bases in China's interior and alongside the border. In 2011 Indian defense minister A. K. Antony determined that these efforts included construction of a 58,000-kilometer road system and development of five airfields.[71] The China Study Group policy body of the Indian government, estimating the effect of these advancements, calculated that China can now transport over 10,000 troops to the Indian border in about three weeks, a task that would have taken up to eight times as long ten years before.[72]

The PLA Air Force has also in recent years been bolstering its presence in areas close to India. It has, for example, established new airfields in Tibet. According to one estimate, the new Western Theater Command contains nine airfields capable of supporting a conventional attack on India, and this number could potentially increase to twelve by 2025.[73] An authoritative external assessment has found that the IAF has the air advantage against China for now, primarily because of the greater number (and thus redundancy) of IAF local airfields and poor Chinese bomber capabilities against Indian air defenses. However, this balance may shift as Chinese Western Theater Command infrastructural developments continue to advance in the coming years and if IAF modernization continues to stall.[74]

A more crucial challenge for India against China in the land domain is the Chinese military focus on conventional ballistic missile strikes to bridge several of the doctrinal and operational disadvantages it faces against India and other adversaries. Chinese views regarding uses of conventional missiles represent perhaps the most aggressive strand of strategic thinking under the "active defense" concept, and American experts have suggested that China is "pursuing what is arguably the world's most missile-centric approach to warfare today."[75] Conventional missile strikes are the centerpiece of Chinese operational plans to seize the initiative at the earliest possible stage in the conflict and quickly settle it on Chinese terms. In PLA thinking heavy conventional ballistic missile strikes are at the forefront of initial operations both to degrade adversary capabilities before perceived adversary offensive operations and even potentially to end the adversary campaign before it begins. A Chinese summary of Second Artillery Corps campaign theory regarding conventional missile use detailed targets of "political and economic centers, important military bases, command centers, communication hubs, massive force groups, and rear-area targets in the enemy's strategic and campaign depth."[76]

China has compensated for its disadvantages in the land and air domains against India by bolstering its conventional missile forces.[77] Along with conventionally armed nuclear-capable missiles of the types held by the Rocket Force missile bases near India, an IAF group captain has claimed that Chinese DF-11 short-range ballistic and DH-10 cruise missiles have relevance in a potential conflict with India.[78]

A 2015 study of Chinese strategic planning highlighted the exploration by military analysts of potential conflict scenarios in "high plateau frigid border regions," a description that would well characterize Tibet. These military commentaries have emphasized counterdeterrence operations in these scenarios, which "include unmasking weapons and moving them in ways the enemy can observe, conducting nuclear weapons exercises, and conducting conventional ballistic missile strikes."[79] Chinese interest in using conventional missile attacks for nuclear signaling poses significant inadvertent escalation risks for India given that such strikes also remain prominent in China's conventional order of battle. Because of China's potential dual use of missile movements or attacks for both nuclear signaling and standoff conventional strike purposes, New Delhi could interpret Chinese conventional missile attacks, or related preparations, as a nuclear threat and launch responsive nuclear and conventional missile mobilizations. And even if India began only conventional missile movements in response, Chinese decision makers, according to their own perception of the movements' potential nuclear significance, could view Indian action as representing an escalatory nuclear counterthreat.

Furthermore, a 2017 report indicated that the Forty-Seventh Army Corps, headquartered in Lintong, Shaanxi Province, would be specifically dissolved as part of the military restructuring.[80] This will leave the remaining Seventy-Sixth (formerly Twenty-First) Group Army, based in Chongqing, and Seventy-Seventh (formally Thirteenth) Group Army, located in Baoji, as the major regional army concentrations, while there remain smaller divisions within the new Tibet and Xinjiang Military Districts, overseen directly by the army rather than through the Western Theater Command joint command structure.[81] The 2017 report quoted a Chinese defense source, saying, "Two army corps in the Western military area is enough because China's most powerful missile troops in the Rocket Force are all stationed there."[82]

Indeed, Chinese use of conventional ballistic missiles, and even the prominence they are being assigned in Chinese military planning without being fired, could elevate Indian strategic anxieties. Indian decision makers, facing the launch of any conventional ballistic missiles toward India, would be forced to consider whether the incoming missiles were nuclear and whether the missile attacks were intended as the first step of a wider Chinese invasion. The risk of misperception and responsive alert or use of Indian conventional ballistic or nuclear forces would be high.

The dual-use nature of many of these Chinese conventional ballistic missiles, plus the variety of missions that a Chinese missile strike may be part of, is further complicated by a vagueness in some Chinese thinking as to what constitutes a nuclear attack. For example, some PLA commentary suggests that a major conventional strike on Chinese nuclear facilities could be viewed as nuclear first use and legitimate a Chinese nuclear counterattack without violating the NFU policy.[83] Similarly, if India suffers a Chinese conventional missile or other strike on a facility that could contain nuclear weapons or related materials, such as the IAF Ambala base, should this attack be considered Chinese nuclear first use given how China might view the same attack on its own soil?

Indian strategists are currently grappling with these concerns. An expert at an Indian think tank warned that the PLA is "capable of inundating the region around China's vicinity and beyond with hundreds, if not thousands of conventional and nuclear armed missiles."[84] Balraj Nagal, former head of the Indian SFC and SPS nuclear planning cell, identified the risks of nuclear misperception caused by Chinese dual-use missile operational intentions but also commented on how these developments should inform Indian nuclear arsenal sizing plans: "China's superiority will create a strategic imbalance, and India will be forced to obtain matching or counter capabilities. The balance is not easily restorable unless India boosts the growth of the deterrent."[85]

Indian decision makers therefore face multiple and increasing pressures in the land and air domains from China. Among these threats are a new generation of more accurate, road-mobile, and MIRV-capable nuclear forces; a growing conventional ballistic missile strike capability that threatens inadvertent nuclear escalation; Chinese military thinking that prioritizes conventional missile strikes on adversaries but that can potentially view a similar attack visited on Chinese forces as nuclear first use; reorganization of Chinese conventional force structures to pose a more unified and precise threat against India; and logistical improvements near India border areas in order to mobilize Chinese troops more quickly and to bolster the PLA Air Force presence.

Indian Responses

These challenges inflame Indian worries about Chinese military intentions and capabilities and motivate Indian efforts to build its presence in the land and air theaters relevant to China. They are also opening a discussion regarding revision of India's nuclear doctrine. We will now explore these developments in Indian nuclear and conventional threat perceptions regarding China.

Chinese conventional forces in areas near to India are estimated to number about 400,000, although this will decline to 300,000 as the planned cuts to the PLA are implemented.[86] By comparison, total Indian forces under the Eastern Command facing China are estimated at over 300,000, although the bulk of these are reported to focus on domestic counterinsurgency operations in the northeast.[87] Indian Army formations in this category are divided into the Third Corps headquartered at Dimapur in Nagaland, the Fourth Corps at Tezpur in Assam, and the Thirty-Third Corps at Siliguri in West Bengal. The Fourteenth Corps under the Northern Command, headquartered in Ladakh, could add another estimated 30,000 to this total.[88]

Indian Army corps have been largely traditionally structured into "strike" and "holding/pivot" formats. The offensively orientated strike corps are intended to penetrate adversary territory and tend to include an armored division and mechanized infantry. The holding/pivot corps also have limited offensive capabilities but "are largely designed to operate in a defensive role" and are not allocated "armored formations larger than brigades and the armored regiments attached to the infantry regiments."[89] Only three army formations—the First, Second, and Twenty-First Corps, all directed against Pakistan—have historically been strike corps.[90] All the corps relevant to China have been built as holding/pivot corps.

Indian defense planners have observed the Chinese military advancements detailed previously and assessed their likely impacts on the ground force balance. Seeking to address a perceived risk of growing Indian disadvantage, the army is raising new China-specific conventional forces. Two new divisions—the Fifty-Sixth and Seventy-First Mountain Divisions—including about 35,000 troops, are being raised in Arunachal Pradesh. The divisions will be equipped with artillery and T-90 tanks, normally used for penetrating assault.[91] The Indian Army is also creating the Mountain Strike Corps, originally designed to possess a total troop strength of around 90,000. This new Seventeenth Corps would be the first China-specific strike corps built to launch penetrating offensives into Chinese territory and would include two armor brigades, two infantry divisions, and an artillery division.[92]

However, progress in raising the Seventeenth Corps has been hindered by insufficient funding. While the Indian government initially approved a sum of $13.8 billion for the formation of the corps in 2013, no new funds were actually provided to the armed services; they have been forced to locate resources for the corps in their existing budgets. The army has been compelled to arm this new corps from war wastage reserves crucial for resupplying forces with equipment and fuel in the event of a conflict. This has contributed to the army as a whole now having only enough war wastage reserves for 125 out of a total of 170 ammunition types to sustain three weeks of heavy fighting, violating an MoD rule that stocks sufficient to last six weeks be kept.[93] The army is also under strength by 24,000 soldiers and is severely lacking in 155-millimeter howitzers and attack helicopters, which are particularly crucial to establishing the Seventeenth Corps.[94] These difficulties forced Defence Minister Manohar Parrikar to reduce the corps's planned strength to 35,000 soldiers and the planned budget to $6.1 billion in April 2015. It is uncertain if even this reduced corps will be ready by the targeted deadline of 2021–22, and in fact, a senior army officer has predicted that it "will be yet another immobile, inadequately equipped formation."[95]

Additional challenges are posed by the quality of infrastructure and IAF capabilities. In managing its border with China, India had previously permitted its border infrastructure to remain deliberately undeveloped, guided by the notion that poor roads would slow the pace of a major Chinese invasion and buy time for Indian reinforcements to arrive. However, the difficulty of organizing Indian patrols and logistical support in these border areas, compared with China's substantive border infrastructure development program, compelled the Indian government to rethink its position. India has now launched a road-building program in its border areas. And yet this infrastructure development is being hindered by continuing dysfunctions within the Indian defense policy-making system. The Indian government has allocated sixty-one new planned roads along the China border, totaling 3,410 kilometers, to the Border Roads Organisation for construction. As of September 2017, only twenty-seven of these roads had been completed. Slow progress in this area will limit the mobility of the Seventeenth Corps.[96]

The IAF upgraded three airfields at Along, Pashigat, and Ziro in 2016 and is modernizing its other five airfields in the state, located at Mechuka, Tawang, Tuting, Vijaynagar, and Walong. This is part of a larger program of airfield development in the northeast, with thirty-five sites in total targeted by the IAF for improvement programs.[97] However, IAF Vice Chief Air Marshal B. S. Dhanoa admitted in March 2016 that India could no longer sustain simultaneous air force operations against China and Pakistan, owing to their improving capabilities, the retirement of the ten IAF MiG-21 and MiG-27 squadrons in 2016–17, and the complexity of Indian defense procurement processes in addressing the shortfall.[98]

Despite these difficulties, it is important to note the underlying Indian intention to field credible capabilities for striking into Chinese territory. Until the shortcomings in bolstering the general theater army and air force presence are addressed, this penetrating strike objective may compel a greater reliance on nuclear-capable platforms that form one of the few bright spots of force modernization to help generate forward strike capabilities. In addition to the Agni nuclear missiles already described in chapter 1, relevant platforms that are nuclear-capable or reportedly so include the Brahmos and Nirbhay missiles and the Sukhoi Su-30MKI, Jaguar, and Mirage aircraft.

The army is inducting at least five Brahmos Block-III regiments, each consisting of thirty-six missiles. Three of these regiments have already been inducted.[99] The Block-III variant is designed with a "steep-dive" capability that can reach targets on the rear side of a mountain, and at least one of the Block-III regiments will be stationed in Arunachal Pradesh.[100]

Sukhois are being stationed at Tezpur and Chabua air bases in Assam in the northeast and at Bareilly in Uttar Pradesh, near the central border region with China.[101] While the prospective nuclear role of Sukhois is still unclear, these plans for the aircraft again underline Indian intentions to field potentially nuclear-capable platforms to strike into Tibet in a conflict with China.[102] The newly upgraded Pasighat airfield, which is located just 120 kilometers (74.5 miles) from the Chinese border, can host Sukhois, Jaguars, and Mirages.[103]

Given the uncertain nuclear status of the Brahmos and Nirbhay missiles (the latter either independently launched or fired from a Sukhoi), their potential heavy use early in a conflict with China could further blur the line between conventional and nuclear operations. The Indian Army intends to rely on Prahaar strikes rather than on the IAF in the earliest stages of a conflict (see chapter 1; note that this strategy echoes the Chinese strategy of early missile barrages), and the missiles' nuclear or conventional role will be difficult to discern until the moment of impact. This intention further elevates the theater risks of nuclear misperception and thus inadvertent escalation.

India's potentially weak theater conventional deterrence against China could tempt the Indian government to bolster general deterrence by shrouding the nuclear status of its forward-deployed units in ambiguity. Without violating India's NFU policy, creating this ambiguity would nevertheless pose an escalatory risk if China unwittingly launches a conventional strike on Indian nuclear platforms.

The deployment of farther-reaching Indian strike platforms along the China border will bring a greater number of Chinese targets into reach. Having followed the PLA commentaries, Indian strategists expect that a Chinese attack will involve an early blitzkrieg including overwhelming use of conventional ballistic missiles. Thus, Indian military commanders will feel pressure to identify and destroy Chinese military concentrations and facilities in the earliest stages of a conflict. In this scenario distinguishing the potential nuclear missions attached to certain Chinese units may become a task of secondary importance. Indian conventional force commanders reportedly categorize all adversary stationary or mobile missile launchers as "legitimate targets" regardless of their potential nuclear missions and do not feel obliged to seek prior political authorization to strike these targets.[104] An Indian attack on Chinese nuclear facilities or units—whether Indian forces originally intended to strike a specifically nuclear target or not—could prove dangerously escalatory and could further cloud the position of both states on the conventional-nuclear threshold.

Indian capability development and nuclear doctrinal discussion also includes a growing interest in preemption, as does Chinese discourse. This could have further implications for escalation control and management of the conventional nuclear threshold. An expert has pointed out the potential of India's "legitimate target" policy to empower voices within the Indian defense establishment favoring a preemptive approach.[105] A former SFC chief has indeed called for the development of "select conventional hardware that tracks and targets nuclear forces," arguing that this would "provide the pre-emptive teeth to a deterrent relationship that leans so heavily on NFU."[106] The officer later developed this thinking, albeit with reference primarily to the Pakistan Nasr challenge, and recommended "building a specialised force that continuously tracks and marks all tactical nuclear missiles and incorporates an airborne conventional capability to neutralise them through preemptive action" before the launch of an Indian Army ground offensive.[107]

The intention of both Indian and Chinese defense planners to strike into adversary territory, including targeting potential nuclear facilities or nuclear-armed units, creates substantial challenges for determining adversary nuclear thresholds and managing escalation control. Escalatory pressures are likely to beset both India and China early in a conflict as both sides seek early dominance through missile and air strikes and a fast-moving ground offensive. In this new context, where are the vertical limiting points that will mark mutually recognized firebreaks between small and major conventional conflict or between conventional and nuclear conflict?[108] Indeed, a retired Indian Army officer has argued that the army must "build in suitable 'exit points' in the unfolding of its operation, such as prior to launch of pivot corps offensive resources, prior to launch of strike corps, prior to break out of enemy operational depth and prior to developing a threat to terminal objectives. . . . These would act as cues to maximising diplomatic pressures on the enemy leadership to concede legitimate and reasonable aims."[109]

The lack of strategic dialogue between India and China on these topics, combined with the poor record of border settlement talks, further hinders the possibility of either state gaining a clear picture of the adversary's limiting points to inform their operations planning. Also, given their ambiguity regarding the nuclear threshold, substantial use of potentially nuclear-capable platforms can cloud an adversary's reading of which escalation stage the conflict has entered.

Doctrinal Tensions

This blurring of conventional and nuclear platforms and missions, with negative consequences for understanding adversary nuclear thresholds, is one challenge in India's nuclear thinking regarding China in the land domain. This first, capability-led challenge is joined by a second doctrinal concern: a debate within India's strategic community regarding potential nuclear doctrinal adjustments to meet the growing China threat.

The Indian nuclear doctrine formally remains no first use and massive retaliation in the event of a nuclear attack. However, the slow pace of Indian conventional force development along the Line of Actual Control—illustrated by the difficulties that have beset the Mountain Strike Corps and border roads construction—and a widespread perception that the conventional and nuclear disparity between China and India is increasing are generating pressure in India's strategic community to revise India's nuclear doctrine to compensate for these deterrence capability gaps. While a full discussion of the Indian doctrinal debate is in chapters 4 and 5, China-specific doctrinal recommendations have been made and will be discussed here.

First, Indian experts question the validity of China's NFU policy for scenarios involving India. China's NFU formulation is silent on the use of nuclear weapons on its own territory, and Indian analysts suggest this exemption could extend to Arunachal Pradesh and other areas claimed by China as its own territory. A 1995 formulation of China's NFU pledge also applied the policy only to NPT member states or members of nuclear-weapon-free zones, and India belongs to neither category.[110] These doubts regarding the applicability of China's NFU pledge vis-à-vis India also fuel calls for reviewing India's NFU policy.[111]

Second, the perceived growing difficulty of maintaining credible conventional deterrence against China has led to Indian suggestions regarding doctrinal adjustment tailored to this challenge. Balraj Nagal has noted that while the NFU commitments of both India and China formally rule out nuclear war between them, "nuclear coercion as a possibility remains high." He also raises the possibility that either state may dispense with its NFU policy under extreme pressure in a bilateral conventional conflict: "In severe conditions during war, the option of nuclear use may be the only one to seek victory rather than accept defeat, notwithstanding the consequences."[112]

Col. Ali Ahmed, a retired army officer, has argued that in the event of a perceived looming major Chinese conventional offensive against India—but before such an offensive has actually begun—Indian decision makers could publicly verbally repeal the NFU policy to warn and deter China. The scenario envisioned for such an adjustment would be Chinese offensive preparations in the Siliguri Passage and around Arunachal Pradesh. Ahmed argues that this verbal repeal would have the effect of establishing the clear, mutually recognized natural limiting point in an India-China conflict that is presently lacking: "Retracting from NFU itself would be a significant move to indicate that thresholds are being crossed in a conventional war."[113]

The effect of new Chinese and Indian nuclear and conventional capabilities and the continuing dissatisfaction within the Indian strategic community regarding the perceived effectiveness of its general deterrence against China are therefore substantially clouding bilateral perceptions of nuclear thresholds. As we have seen, these new capabilities and Indian dissatisfaction are also placing pressure on the NFU policies of India and China. These developments threaten India's ability to establish clear intra-conventional and conventional-nuclear escalation thresholds in the event of a conflict with China. The use of potentially dual-use platforms can erode the distinction between conventional and nuclear conflict, and more so if they are deployed to eradicate Chinese nuclear units, significant conventional force concentrations, and command centers. This becomes especially salient given India's intentions to field Brahmos-II (K) missiles, specifically intended to destroy these latter targets. Calls to revise India's NFU doctrine immediately in the face of China's perceived growing military superiority or to hold this option as a card to be played during a conflict further highlight temptations within Indian strategic discourse to use nuclear weapons, even if only for signaling purposes, to solve a challenge better addressed by building strong conventional defenses.

Implications for Nuclear Interactions with India: The Naval Domain

A similarly rapidly changing domain of Sino-Indian strategic competition is the naval sphere. China has held a long-standing technical and political interest in fielding a nuclear-armed submarine fleet. A 2007 analysis of Chinese naval discourse found a recurring perception that developing a nuclear-armed submarine fleet was essential to general naval projection and a core long-term objective of the PLA Navy.[114] Despite this political commitment, however, a viable SSBN fleet is emerging only today. China has possessed a solitary *Xia*-class submarine since the late 1980s, and it is not viewed by analysts and foreign government reports as a core element of the Chinese nuclear posture. However, a new fleet of *Jin*-class SSBNs is presently entering service. Up to five *Jin*-class boats are planned.[115] The PLA Navy dream of an SSBN fleet as the symbolic flagship of credible Chinese maritime projection is finally coming to fruition.

Beijing previously justified its growing naval projection with a narrative of limited Indian Ocean antipiracy missions. Now it is complementing this justification with a greater emphasis on the need to guarantee Chinese access to sea lines of communication (SLOCs). This new narrative is paving the way to a more expansive and permanent Chinese Indian Ocean presence.

The perceived vulnerability of China to blockade and the necessity for sufficient SLOC force protection animate recent Chinese maritime discourse.[116] The 2015 Chinese defense white paper specified, "The PLA Navy will gradually shift its focus from 'offshore waters defense' to the combination of 'offshore waters defense' with 'open seas protection.'"[117] The director of the PLA Naval Research Institute has estimated that four-fifths of the total value of Chinese foreign commerce is transported by sea, and another Chinese expert calculates that over a third of Chinese oil imports must travel through the Strait of Hormuz alone, concluding, "To sustain development, China needs secure sea-lanes and unfettered freedom of navigation."[118]

The linkage of Chinese nuclear-armed submarines to a broader mission of growing maritime projection in Chinese strategic thought is also reflected in conventional naval developments. The US Department of Defense observed in 2015 that China fielded the largest naval force by number of vessels in Asia. Chinese submarines have also docked in Colombo and Gwadar; the US Department of Defense commented that these types of forays were likely "area familiarization" missions designed to support and regularize further visits and patrols to expand Chinese naval reach.[119]

The Andaman and Nicobar Islands, the site of an Indian tri-service command in the Indian Ocean, seem to be an area of interest for these Chinese operations. Chinese submarines are reportedly identified around the "Ten

Degree Channel," a 150-kilometer-wide passage separating the Andaman from the Nicobar Islands, an average of four times every twelve weeks.[120] The true volume of submarine traffic may be higher; in one encounter reported in February 2016, the Indian navy could locate only a Chinese submarine support boat and was unable to determine whether this boat was accompanied by submarines.[121]

The impact of these developments in Indian security discourse echoes the fear of naval blockade raised by Indian maritime expansion in Pakistani discourse. Indian newspapers regularly print maps showing recent Chinese port visits and port development projects surrounding India alongside technical details about the Chinese ships involved. The "string of pearls" concept, first pioneered by an American defense contracting firm, has become a principal frame through which Indian analysts view Chinese maritime nuclear and conventional projection.[122] The "string of pearls" is China's virtual chain of patrolling naval forces at friendly foreign bases and ports surrounding India. Successfully creating this chain would prevent India's navy from traveling far beyond its littoral.

But whether China is actually trying to create a "string of pearls" is disputed; analysts argue that the sheer logistical difficulty of managing an array of foreign bases and the accordant diplomatic relations is reason enough to doubt the "string of pearls" policy would ever be implemented. Nevertheless, China is exploring options for establishing a network of facilities, or "places," in the Indian Ocean that could permit permanent access for refueling and replenishment without being formally declared a Chinese military base. The first node in this network could perhaps be the Chinese naval "logistical facility" in Djibouti, announced in February 2016.[123] Djibouti's foreign minister has estimated that thousands of Chinese military and civilian staff will staff this base.[124] The Indian concern is that future nodes will be set up in locations surrounding India, such as Gwadar, Colombo, and the Coco Islands in the Indian Ocean.[125]

This fear of Chinese nuclear and naval projection affects Indian perceptions of the role of *Arihant*. While India's nuclear doctrine refers to the triad of land-, air-, and sea-launched nuclear forces as fulfilling a second-strike posture guided by an NFU policy, Indian naval and nuclear discourse frequently suggests that *Arihant* can serve an additional role and deter general Chinese naval projection. This suggestion overlooks the fact that *Arihant* will likely initially patrol only around Indian littorals because of its technological novelty, is technically designed and politically intended to serve only as a last-resort deterrent, and is not suited to be the spear of a blockade-breaking Indian conventional naval offensive.[126]

A further challenge—linked to a core theme of this book—is the rising risk of nuclear misperception in this context.[127] The growing naval projection of India and China, especially in the form of potentially nuclear-armed ships and submarines, threatens to combine tensions arising from the regional competition for Indian Ocean access with tensions arising from nuclear force growth and diversification. As well as the dedicated SSBN fleets, Chinese naval force modernization includes a new generation of potentially dual-use platforms, such as the Chinese Type-041 attack submarine (see chapter 2). Determining the class and potential nuclear mission of these vessels will be difficult—even more so because they will operate with conventional escorts.

These challenges generate multiple potential scenarios for inadvertent introduction of a nuclear dimension into conventional naval tensions. One situation could be an attempt to block the route of an enemy boat, not knowing that the enemy boat has a nuclear mission. Alternatively, as discussed in the land theater section, both states may have an incentive to create the incorrect impression that far-reaching vessels have a nuclear mission in order to deter adversary efforts to deny access.

Despite these challenges, there is very little institutionalized naval dialogue between India and China to reduce misperceptions about the other's intentions and to discuss mechanisms to resolve a maritime standoff. India has established the Indian Ocean Naval Symposium, a wide-ranging forum of thirty-five full-member states, to discuss Indian Ocean maritime security. However, its membership includes China only as an observer.[128] For its own part, China is planning a "One Belt One Road" interstate partnership and logistics chain of land and sea routes stretching to Europe.[129] As of the time of writing, India had refused to join this project. The near-absence of dialogue regarding maritime intentions further complicates naval nuclear planning, as both states operate without a clear picture of the other's boundaries of naval nuclear projection and escalation triggers.

This exploration of Sino-Indian competition in the maritime domain highlights the same growing risk of nuclear misperception seen in the land theater. In the naval domain, this risk is based on misidentification of adversary nuclear thresholds, platform missions, and ultimate nuclear intentions.

CHALLENGES POSED BY CHINA-PAKISTAN COOPERATION

A final element of China's strategic policy that has greatly affected Indian security is its long-standing support to Pakistan in developing nuclear and defense infrastructure. China has transmitted warhead designs and missile technology to Pakistan in the past, and the two states' nuclear cooperation is entering a new stage. As discussed in chapter 2, China is assisting Pakistan in its naval nuclear ambitions and is involved in at least six nuclear reactor projects in Pakistan. China's effort to assist Pakistan in maintaining a degree of strategic nuclear parity with India also extends to endorsing Pakistan's prospective membership in the NSG, the forum of states that sets nuclear technology export rules.[130]

The China-Pakistan Economic Corridor (CPEC), announced in 2015, also threatens to complicate India's strategic environment. CPEC includes multiple projects, including the strategic Gwadar port, under the overarching One Belt One Road initiative intended to develop Pakistan's energy logistics, general logistics, and transportation infrastructure, while also easing Chinese access to Central Asia and beyond in the process.[131] The Pakistan government has estimated the total value of the projects to be $46 billion.[132] A 2017 analysis by a Pakistani financial trading and research firm, factoring in the investments and interest, concluded that the country may have to repay a total sum of $90 billion to China.[133]

Specific projects include the expansion of major Pakistani railway stations, including those in Bahawalpur, Karachi, Okara, Peshawar, Quetta, and Rawalpindi. Major motorways, such as the Multan-Sukkur Highway, running between Lahore and Karachi, will also be redeveloped.[134] A new motorway between Quetta and Gwadar was inaugurated by the prime minister and Pakistan army chief in February 2016.[135] An Indian analyst has suggested that these improvements will enhance the ability of the Pakistan military to mobilize ground forces.[136]

Planned CPEC project sites include territory in Kashmir that is claimed by India. These particular projects thus represent not just a Chinese rejection of Indian territory claims but intentions to actively develop the presence of China and Pakistan in these areas.[137] Indian intelligence agencies reportedly briefed the government in March 2016 about a forthcoming assignment of Chinese troops to Pakistan, ostensibly under CPEC project security roles. Reportedly, PLA troops have been repeatedly identified in Pakistan-governed Kashmir close to the LOC since 2015.[138] If the reports are accurate, this growing direct Chinese troop presence would complement Pakistan's separate plans to raise 10,000 new troops for CPEC project security missions.[139] Even if the Chinese forces involved are minimal, they are symbolically placed at the forefront of a likely conflict area between Pakistan and India, threatening India with China's involvement as a party to this conflict at the very outset. Indian prime minister Narendra Modi robustly criticized CPEC as "not acceptable" during a meeting with Xi Xinping in May 2015.[140]

This expansive new stage of Chinese support for Pakistan's nuclear program therefore combines with an ambitious plan to bolster Pakistani infrastructure, including many projects potentially relevant to supporting military mobilization. The links between the nuclear and conventional planning of Beijing and Islamabad illustrate the complexity of the Pakistan-India-China nuclear triad and underline the importance of institutionalizing nuclear dialogue between the three states to clarify nuclear intentions and reduce the risk of conflicts arising from misperception.

CONCLUSION

This chapter has surveyed Chinese nuclear thought, nuclear and conventional force advancements in the maritime and land theaters, and military cooperation with Pakistan. The land-based nuclear threat that China currently poses to India involves an increasingly precise, mobile, and MIRV-capable nuclear missile force; a testing program simulating environmental conditions similar to those in India-facing nuclear base locations; a higher priority given to nuclear forces in military reforms; and growing ambiguity in Rocket Force unit missions as conventional ballistic missiles obtain greater prominence in Chinese strategy. Many of these same challenges—greater precision, rising prominence of dual-use capabilities, and ambiguity of nuclear intentions—recur in the naval domain. To the naval theater challenges can also be added the significant complication of nuclear naval competition entering the tense conventional Indian Ocean naval rivalry, with a lack of clarity regarding exact intended patrol routes and maritime boundaries to be defended. Finally, a new level of Chinese nuclear and infrastructural cooperation with Pakistan threatens to further heighten Indian nuclear and general threat perceptions.

As the nuclear context changes, several issues conducive to inadvertent escalation arise. Of the issues surveyed in this chapter, inadvertent escalation could be particularly delivered by a misinterpretation of Chinese intentions in specific ballistic missile, air force, or ground force movements involved in establishing the Western Theater Command or protecting the CPEC project in Pakistan; heightened nuclear threat perceptions generated by China's high level of seemingly India-relevant missile testing; increased general threat perceptions produced by China's aggressive submarine "area familiarization" patrols close to Indian littorals, potentially including nuclear-capable vessels in the future; and with this maritime issue, the danger of conventional interdiction of a nuclear-armed vessel or its conventional escorts.

Indeed, alongside the issues identified in this chapter, China has a broader record of military activities, conducted without political decision-maker knowledge, that have elevated adversary threat perceptions. According to the Pentagon, China's 2007 antisatellite kinetic test, which generated significant strategic alarm in New Delhi and Washington, was scheduled and conducted without the prior knowledge of political leaders (although the antisatellite technology development program had been likely politically authorized).[141] The Pentagon also concluded that Chinese civilian leaders did not know about Chinese naval harassment of the US *Impeccable* surveillance vessel in 2009, which compelled the US to send a guided missile destroyer to reinforce the boat and to issue a public diplomatic protest.[142] In 2011 the Chinese military provocatively unveiled its J-20 stealth fighter, again without informing Chinese political leaders, during a visit of US defense secretary Robert Gates to Beijing and immediately before a Chinese state visit to Washington. Gates remarked that with this action "the PLA nearly wrecked both trips."[143] Poor Chinese civil-military coordination has indeed been generally identified in a recent major study as a substantial concern in Chinese defense policymaking.[144] Inadvertent escalation therefore remains a real regional danger with regard to Chinese nuclear and conventional defense approaches.

The India-Pakistan-China regional context also creates potential for accidental escalation. Politically ordered conventional missile strikes on nuclear or nuclear-capable units may not be deliberately designed to introduce the nuclear dimension to a conflict, but an adversary may perceive the attacks and their effects as nuclear escalation. In addition, if China authorizes either substantial conventional ballistic missile strikes on Indian territory or troops or aggressive general attacks by its conventional forces, this may compel an intracrisis political review of India's NFU commitment, as the former head of India's nuclear planning cell, among other Indian experts, has suggested. Risks of inadvertent and accidental escalation are further elevated by the absence of substantive nuclear and general defense dialogue.

Some recurring factors in this chapter—and throughout this book—are the growing ambiguity in nuclear thresholds arising from new debates on nuclear doctrine; the fielding of a new generation of nuclear forces; the multiple technical posturing and doctrinal options presented by new potentially dual-use ballistic missiles, naval platforms, and air platforms; and the opportunities for adversary misperception of ultimate nuclear intentions, and risk of inadvertent nuclear escalation, within this context. These points highlight the importance of convening regular nuclear dialogues among all three states to discuss and clarify nuclear and naval intentions. Dialogues would particularly support efforts to prevent the risk of misperceiving a conventional mission as a nuclear mission, or vice versa, because misperception is a core emerging challenge in both the land and sea domains. As the nuclear forces of all three states come into increasing direct contact through nuclear-armed naval fleets, institutionalizing the practice of trilateral nuclear dialogue will prove a worthy endeavor to prevent a nuclear crisis or reduce tensions if one occurs.

Admittedly, all three states can gain some strategic advantage by creating ambiguity regarding nuclear thresholds in the current context. Efforts to create ambiguity discussed in this chapter include the growing reliance of both India and China on dual-use conventional missiles; the reported intentions of Indian and Chinese military staff to target nuclear-capable adversary facilities and platforms in the early stages of a conflict; and strategic discourse that suggests the NFU commitments of India and China may be more conditional than at first sight. Indian strategists have proposed this conditioning of NFU with reference to a conventional Chinese force buildup in areas close to India, and Chinese strategists have discussed a similar flexibility in the event India launches a conventional attack on Chinese nuclear facilities.

China and India may be persuaded to formally lower their nuclear thresholds, as Pakistan is doing through full spectrum deterrence, in order to bolster general deterrence against a fast-changing threat environment. If they decide not to issue a formal declaration of a new doctrinal concept, more subtle shifts could push the threshold in the same direction. The informal method could be executed by quietly introducing potentially nuclear implications into conventional operations, such as mixing conventional and nuclear missile forces at the same bases; continuing to rely on conventional ballistic missiles, which are difficult to identify as nuclear or conventional until the moment of impact, in offensive planning; assigning dual-use naval platforms to far-reaching "area familiarization" missions in sensitive adversary areas; and having influential strategists discuss nuclear warfare, even if only in the form of intraconflict nuclear doctrinal revision, as a relevant option in resolving conventional force dilemmas.

However, deliberately increasing the opportunity for nuclear misperceptions in this way will do little to improve the national security of these states. New nuclear and naval dialogues, combined with a dedicated effort to separate rather than blend the conventional and the nuclear domains in force planning and strategic thought, will better stabilize regional security.

To fully integrate the Chinese nuclear and conventional doctrine and force developments into Indian strategic planning, a public Indian official defense review should be conducted. This review should assess these challenges and recommend a posturing response that clearly separates conventional from nuclear threats and assigns response packages to conventional and nuclear forces, respectively. As well as disaggregating and prioritizing the specific threats that China poses to Indian security and generating a more efficient use and development of defense resources in response, the review process would reduce capability-led and doctrine-led ambiguity regarding nuclear thresholds.

The next chapter will explore India's nuclear doctrinal evolution and outlook in more detail, including the relevance of the perceived Chinese and Pakistani threats in shaping India's current and future doctrinal approaches.

NOTES

1. "Nuclear Anxiety: Indian's Letter to Clinton on the Nuclear Testing," *New York Times*, May 13, 1998, http://www.nytimes.com/1998/05/13/world/nuclear-anxiety-indian -s-letter-to-clinton-on-the-nuclear-testing.html.
2. O'Donnell and Pant, "Evolution of India's Agni-V Missile," 584–86.
3. O'Donnell and Joshi, "Lost at Sea," 466–81.
4. Office of the Secretary of Defense, *Military and Security Developments Involving the People's Republic of China 2015* (Washington, DC: US Government Printing Office, 2015), 31.
5. Jeffrey Lewis, *Paper Tigers: China's Nuclear Posture*, Adelphi Paper 446 (London: International Institute for Strategic Studies, 2014), 15–22; Kampani, *China-India Nuclear Rivalry*, 11.
6. Xia, "On China's Nuclear Doctrine," 172; Lewis, *Paper Tigers*, 15–17.
7. Wu Riqiang, "Certainty of Uncertainty: Nuclear Strategy with Chinese Characteristics," *Journal of Strategic Studies* 36, no. 4 (2013): 581.
8. State Council Information Office, *China's Military Strategy* (Beijing: People's Republic of China [PRC], 2015), https://news.usni.org/2015/05/26/document-chinas-mili tary-strategy.
9. Gregory Kulacki, "The Chinese Military Updates China's Nuclear Strategy," Union of Concerned Scientists, March 2015, 2–3, https://www.ucsusa.org/sites/default/files /attach/2015/03/chinese-nuclear-strategy-full-report.pdf; M. Taylor Fravel and Evan S. Medeiros, "China's Search for Assured Retaliation: The Evolution of Chinese Nuclear Strategy and Force Structure," *International Security* 35, no. 2 (Fall 2010): 50–51; Kampani, *China-India Nuclear Rivalry*, 16.
10. Kulacki, "Chinese Military Updates," 2–3; Kampani, *China-India Nuclear Rivalry*, 16.
11. US-China Economic and Security Review Commission (USCC), *2015 Report to Congress* (Washington, DC: USCC, 2015), 299–303.
12. Sean O'Connor, "China's ICBM Modernisation Alters Threat Profile," *Jane's Intelligence Review*, October 26, 2015, http://www.janes360.com/images/assets/617/55617 /China_s_ICBM_modernisation_alters_threat_profile.pdf.
13. Gregory Kulacki, "China's Military Calls for Putting Its Nuclear Forces on Alert," Union of Concerned Scientists, January 2016, 1, 5, 7–8, http://www.ucsusa.org /sites/default/files/attach/2016/02/China-Hair-Trigger-full-report.pdf.
14. Ibid., 4.
15. Ibid., 6.
16. State Council Information Office, *China's Military Strategy*; Kulacki, "Nuclear Forces on Alert," 4.
17. Yang Xiaoping, "China's Perceptions of India as a Nuclear Weapons Power," Carnegie Endowment for International Peace, June 30, 2016, http://carnegieendowment

.org/2016/06/30/china-s-perceptions-of-india-as-nuclear-weapons-power-pub-63970; Zhao Tong, "China's Sea-Based Nuclear Deterrent," Carnegie Endowment for International Peace, June 30, 2016, http://carnegietsinghua.org/2016/06/30/china-s-sea-based-nuclear-deterrent/j2oc; Lora Saalman, "Between 'China Threat Theory' and 'Chindia': Chinese Responses to India's Military Modernization," *Chinese Journal of International Politics* 4 (2011): 91.

18. Saalman, "'China Threat Theory' and 'Chindia,'" 99–103.

19. "Specialist: India Wants to Use the Agni-5 Missile to Seek Strategic Parity Dialogue with China" (in Chinese), *China National Radio*, September 18, 2013; Eric Heginbotham et al., *China's Evolving Nuclear Deterrent: Major Drivers and Issues for the United States* (Santa Monica, CA: RAND, 2017), 85.

20. "Indian Indigenous Strategic Nuclear Submarine Has Missile Range of Only 750km" (in Chinese), *People's Daily*, June 6, 2012, http://news.cntv.cn/20120106/106723 .shtml.

21. Yang, "China's Perceptions of India."

22. Saalman, "'China Threat Theory' and 'Chindia,'" 102–3.

23. "Indian Indigenous Strategic Nuclear Submarine."

24. Yang, "China's Perceptions of India."

25. Ibid.

26. Heginbotham et al., *China's Evolving Nuclear Deterrent*, 86.

27. Ibid., 85.

28. Ibid., 53–54.

29. Xu Weidi, "China's Security Environment and the Role of Nuclear Weapons," in *Understanding Chinese Nuclear Thinking*, ed. Li Bin and Zhao Tong (Washington, DC: Carnegie Endowment for International Peace, 2016), 39–40, http://carnegieendowment.org/files/ChineseNuclearThinking_Final.pdf; Pan Zhenqiang, "China's No First Use of Nuclear Weapons," in Li and Zhao, *Understanding Chinese Nuclear Thinking*, 64–71; Sun Xiangli, "The Development of Nuclear Weapons in China," in Li and Zhao, *Understanding Chinese Nuclear Thinking*, 90.

30. Pan, "China's No First Use," 70–71.

31. Heginbotham et al., *China's Evolving Nuclear Deterrent*, 102.

32. Recent bilateral nuclear dialogues have focused on respective policy approaches to disarmament, nonproliferation, export controls, and India's prospective membership in the NSG. However, they have deliberately omitted nuclear doctrinal and posturing concerns. Reuters, "India Says Holds 'Substantive' Nuclear Talks with China," September 14, 2016, https://www.reuters.com/article/us-india-china-nuclear/india-says-holds-substantive-nuclear-talks-with-china-idUSKCN11J1NB?il=0; K. J. M. Varma, "India, China Hold First Dialogue on Disarmament, Arms Control," *Outlook*, April 17, 2015, https://www.outlookindia.com/newswire/story/india-china-hold-first-dialogue-on-disarmament-arms-control/892167; Zhao Tong, "The Time Is Ripe for a China-India Nuclear Dialogue," Carnegie-Tsinghua Center for Global Policy, March 17, 2016, http://carnegietsinghua.org/2016/03/17/time-is-ripe-for-china-indianuclear-dialogue-pub-64283.

33. "China Rakes Up 1998 UNSC Resolution in Response to India's Agni-V Test," *The Wire*, December 28, 2016, https://thewire.in/89944/china-rakes-1998-unsc-resolution-response-indias-agni-v-test/.

34. Ministry of Foreign Affairs, "Foreign Ministry Spokesperson Hua Chunying's Regular

Press Conference," December 27, 2016, http://www.fmprc.gov.cn/mfa_eng/xwfw _665399/s2510_665401/t1427046.shtml.

35. Sutirtho Patranobis, "Production of Jets, Missiles on Agenda at Pak-China Military Meetings: Experts," *Hindustan Times*, March 17, 2017, http://www.hindustantimes .com/india-news/mass-production-of-aircraft-missiles-top-of-agenda-at-pak-china -military-meet-experts/story-PMS7VvsyiPJjaDvYPzxJnL.html.

36. Zhao, "Time Is Ripe."

37. Andrea Berger, *The P-5 Nuclear Dialogue: Five Years On* (London: Royal United Services Institute, 2014), 11–12, https://rusi.org/sites/default/files/201407_op_the_p5 _nuclear_dialogue.pdf; Gregory Kulacki, "Chickens Talking with Ducks: The U.S.-Chinese Nuclear Dialogue," *Arms Control Today*, October 2011, https://www .armscontrol.org/act/2011_10/U.S._Chinese_Nuclear_Dialogue; Frank O'Donnell, *Launching an Expanded Missile Flight-Test Notification Regime* (Washington, DC: Stimson Center, 2017), https://www.stimson.org/content/launching-expanded-missile -flight-test-notification-regime.

38. Wu Riqiang, "How China Practices and Thinks about Nuclear Transparency," in Li and Zhao, *Understanding Chinese Nuclear Thinking*, 229.

39. Ibid., 242–43. There is indeed additional potential for a unified, harmonized, and deepened missile flight-test notification regime involving China, India, Pakistan, Russia, and the United States. Such a regime could include prenotification of all ballistic and cruise missile tests. See O'Donnell, *Launching an Expanded Missile Flight-Test Notification Regime*.

40. Fiona Cunningham and Rory Medcalf, "The Dangers of Denial: Nuclear Weapons in China-India Relations," Lowy Institute for International Policy, October 2011, 14 https://www.lowyinstitute.org/sites/default/files/pubfiles/Cunningham_and _Medcalf%2C_The_dangers_of_denial_web_1.pdf; Sean O'Connor, "PLA Second Artillery Corps (Technical Report APA-TR-2009-1204)," *Air Power Australia*, April 2012, http:// www.ausairpower.net/APA-PLA-Second-Artillery-Corps.html#mozTocId211040.

41. Hans M. Kristensen and Robert S. Norris, "Worldwide Deployments of Nuclear Weapons, 2014," *Bulletin of the Atomic Scientists* 70, no. 5 (September–October 2014): 98; Cunningham and Medcalf, "Dangers of Denial," 14; O'Connor, "PLA Second Artillery Corps."

42. Kristensen and Norris, "Chinese Nuclear Forces, 2015," 79.

43. O'Connor, "China's ICBM Modernisation."

44. Richard D. Fisher, "US Officials Confirm Sixth Chinese Hypersonic Manoeuvring Strike Vehicle Test," *Jane's Defence Weekly*, November 26, 2015, http:///www.janes .com.

45. Kristensen and Norris, "Chinese Nuclear Forces, 2015," 79.

46. Xinhua, "The Ministry of National Defense Expounds Defense and Military Reforms," March 16, 2016, http://news.xinhuanet.com/mil/2016-03/16/c_128804040 .htm; Zhang Hui, "New PLA Rocket Force Conducts Desert, Forest Drills," *Global Times*, January 5, 2016, http://www.globaltimes.cn/content/961840.shtml; "China Establishes Rocket Force and Strategic Support Force," *People's Liberation Army Daily* (*PLA Daily*), January 1, 2016, http://english.chinamil.com.cn/news-channels/china -military-news/2016-01/01/content_6839967.htm.

47. Kenneth Allen, Dennis J. Blasko, and John F. Corbett, "The PLA's New Organizational Structure: What Is Known, Unknown and Speculation," *Jamestown Foundation China*

Brief 16, no. 3 (February 2016), http://www.jamestown.org/uploads/media/Updated _The_PLA_s_New_Organizational_Structure_-_What_is_Known__Unknown_and _Speculation_Parts_1_and_2.pdf; Xinhua, "Ministry of National Defense Expounds."

48. Xinhua, "Ministry of National Defense Expounds."
49. "New Rocket Force Gets Facility to Acclimate Its Soldiers," *PLA Daily*, February 1, 2016, http://english.chinamil.com.cn/news-channels/pla-daily-commentary/2016-02 /01/content_6883064.htm.
50. Kristensen and Norris, "Chinese Nuclear Forces, 2015," 80.
51. Group Captain Ravinder Chhatwal, "Analysis of PLAAF Potential against India," *Air Power Journal* 8, no. 4 (Winter 2013): 66–67, http://capsindia.org/files/documents /APJ-vol-8-no-4-Oct-Dec-2013.pdf.
52. Zhang, "PLA Rocket Force Conducts."
53. "New Rocket Force Gets Facility."
54. David M. Finkelstein, *Initial Thoughts on the Reorganization and Reform of the PLA* (Arlington, VA: CNA, January 2016), 13–14, https://www.cna.org/cna_files/pdf/DOP -2016-U-012560-Final.pdf.
55. "Expert: PLA Rocket Force May Have Strategic Nuclear Submarine, Bomber," *PLA Daily*, January 8, 2016, http://english.chinamil.com.cn/news-channels/pla-daily-com mentary/2016-01/08/content_6850119.htm; Zhang, "PLA Rocket Force Conducts."
56. "Expert: PLA Rocket Force."
57. Allen, Blasko, and Corbett, "PLA's New Organizational Structure."
58. USCC, *2015 Report to Congress*, 339.
59. "Army Adjustment and Establishment Completed in Five Theater Commands," *PLA Daily*, February 4, 2016, http://english.chinamil.com.cn/news-channels/china-mili tary-news/2016-02/04/content_6890499.htm.
60. GlobalSecurity.org, "China: Group Armies/Combined Corps," April 12, 2017, http:// www.globalsecurity.org/military/world/china/ga.htm; Roy Kamphausen, "China's Land Forces: New Priorities and Capabilities," in *Strategic Asia 2012–13: China's Military Challenge*, ed. Ashley J. Tellis and Travis Tanner (Seattle: National Bureau of Asian Research, 2012), 57–58; Josef Korbel School of International Studies, "People's Republic of China Military Capabilities," April 2012, https://www.du.edu/korbel/cenex /media/documents/China_Background_Document.pdf.
61. Arun Sahgal, "The Diversified Employment of China's Armed Forces: An Indian Perspective," *CLAWS Journal*, Summer 2013, 213, http://www.claws.in/images/jour nals_doc/1394685729Arun%20Sahgal%20CJ%20Summer%202013.pdf.
62. Zhu Jiangming, "Considerations for Replacing Military Area Commands with Theater Commands," *PLA Daily*, February 3, 2016, http://english.chinamil.com.cn/news -channels/pla-daily-commentary/2016-02/03/content_6888459.htm.
63. Ibid.
64. "Experts Explain Five Key Issues on China's Military Expenditure in 2016," *PLA Daily*, March 7, 2016, http://english.chinamil.com.cn/news-channels/pla-daily-commen tary/2016-03/07/content_6946894.htm.
65. Ian E. Rinehart, *The Chinese Military: Overview and Issues for Congress*, R44196 (Washington, DC: Congressional Research Service, 2016), 7–8, https://fas.org/sgp/crs /row/R44196.pdf; Alison A. Kaufman and Daniel M. Hartnett, *Managing Conflict: Examining Recent PLA Writings on Escalation Control* (Arlington, VA: CNA, February 2016), v, https://www.cna.org/cna_files/pdf/DRM-2015-U-009963-Final3.pdf.

66. Kaufman and Hartnett, *Managing Conflict*, v, 69.

67. Morgan et al., *Dangerous Thresholds*, 57–58.

68. Zhu, "Replacing Military Area Commands."

69. Tellis, *Troubles*, 13; Rinehart, *Chinese Military*, 4; "Army Adjustment and Establishment Completed."

70. Office of Naval Intelligence, *The PLA Navy: New Capabilities and Missions for the 21st Century* (Washington, DC: US Government Printing Office, 2015), 7–8, http://www .oni.navy.mil/Portals/12/Intel%20agencies/China_Media/2015_PLA_NAVY_PUB _Print.pdf.

71. Arun Sahgal, "China's Military Modernization: Responses from India," in Tellis and Tanner, *Strategic Asia 2012–13*, 280.

72. Harsh V. Pant, "India Comes to Terms with a Rising China," in *Strategic Asia 2011–12: Asia Responds to Its Rising Powers—China and India*, ed. Ashley J. Tellis, Travis Tanner, and Jessica Keough (Seattle: National Bureau of Asian Research, 2011), 117.

73. Gurmeet Kanwal and Monika Chansoria, "China Preparing Tibet as Future War Zone," *Deccan Herald*, June 2, 2011, http://www.deccanherald.com/content/165996 /china-preparing-tibet-future-war.html; Tellis, *Troubles*, 13; Sahgal, "Diversified Employment," 215.

74. Tellis, *Troubles*, 1–2.

75. Andrew S. Erickson, Abraham M. Denmark, and Gabriel Collins, "Beijing's 'Starter Carrier' and Future Steps: Alternatives and Implications," *Naval War College Review* 65, no. 1 (Winter 2012): 41–42.

76. Morgan et al., *Dangerous Thresholds*, 70–71.

77. Tellis, *Troubles*, 8–9.

78. Chhatwal, "PLAAF Potential against India," 66.

79. Larry M. Wortzel, "PLA Contingency Planning and the Case of India," in *The People's Liberation Army and Contingency Planning in China*, ed. Andrew Scobell, Arthur S. Ding, Philip C. Saunders, and Scott W. Harold (Washington, DC: National Defense University Press, 2015), 236, http://ndupress.ndu.edu/Portals/68/Documents/Books /PLA-contingency/PLA-Contingency-Planning-China.pdf.

80. Minnie Chan, "China to Disband over a Quarter of Its Army Corps, Sources Say," *South China Morning Post*, March 18, 2017, http://www.scmp.com/news/china/diplo macy-defence/article/2080204/china-disband-over-quarter-its-army-corps-sources -say.

81. Dennis J. Blasko, "PLA Army 'Below the Neck' Reforms: Improving China's Deterrence and Joint Warfighting Posture" (paper presented to 2017 Zijin International Forum, Nanjing University, October 30–31, 2017), 10; correspondence with long-term analyst of China's military, January 2018.

82. Chan, "China to Disband."

83. Morgan et al., *Dangerous Thresholds*, 61–65, 80.

84. Temjenmeren Ao, "China's Military Regions Restructuring: Understanding Implications for India," Centre for Air Power Studies (New Delhi), January 12, 2016, 3, http:// capsindia.org/files/documents/CAPS_IB_12-JAN-2016.pdf.

85. Balraj Nagal, "Strategic Stability—Conundrum, Challenge and Dilemma: The Case of India, China and Pakistan," *CLAWS Journal*, Summer 2015, 15–16, http://www .claws.in/images/journals_doc/1190813178_BalrajNagal.pdf.

86. Srikanth Kondapalli, "The Chinese Military Eyes South Asia," in *Shaping China's*

Security Environment: The Role of the People's Liberation Army, ed. Andrew Scobell and Larry M. Wortzel (Carlisle, PA: US Army War College Strategic Studies Institute, 2006), 202.

87. GlobalSecurity.org, "Indian Army Eastern Command," June 27, 2017, http://www.globalsecurity.org/military/world/india/eastcom.htm.

88. Ibid.; GlobalSecurity.org, "Indian Army Northern Command," June 27, 2017, http://www.globalsecurity.org/military/world/india/northcom.htm; Kondapalli, "Chinese Military Eyes South Asia," 202.

89. GlobalSecurity.org, "Indian Army Corps," July 25, 2016, http://www.globalsecurity.org/military/world/india/corps.htm; Ladwig, "Cold Start," 159–60.

90. Nitin Gokhale, "So It's Going to Be 17 Mountain Corps?" November 16, 2013, http://nitinagokhale.blogspot.co.uk/2013/11/so-its-going-to-be-17-mountain-corps.html?m=1; GlobalSecurity.org, "Indian Army Corps."

91. Gokhale, "17 Mountain Corps?"

92. Rahul Bedi, "Indian Army Faces Further Issues in Creating New Mountain Strike Corps," *Jane's Defence Weekly*, March 10, 2016, http://www.janes.com; Shashank Joshi, "17 Corps: As China Rises, India Raises the Stakes," *The Interpreter* (blog), January 9, 2014, http://www.lowyinterpreter.org/post/2014/01/09/17-Corps-As-China-rises-Indias-army-raises-the-stakes.aspx; Pandit, "With Eye on China."

93. Rahul Bedi, "Arrested Development: Indian Army Modernisation Falls Short," *Jane's Defence Weekly*, February 18, 2016, http://www.janes.com.

94. Ajai Shukla, "New Strike Corps for China Border a Fiscal Minefield," *Broadsword* (blog), January 7, 2014, http://ajaishukla.blogspot.co.uk/2014/01/new-strike-corps-for-china-border.html; Bedi, "Arrested Development."

95. Rahul Bedi, "India to Halve Size of New Mountain Corps," *Jane's Defence Weekly*, April 16, 2015, http://www.janes.com; Shukla, "New Strike Corps."

96. PIB, "Road Building along China Borders," news release, May 12, 2015, http://www.pib.nic.in/newsite/PrintRelease.aspx?relid=121590; Rajeev Deshpandel, "India Speeds Up Border Road Work to Avoid Future Doklams," *Times of India*, September 10, 2017, https://timesofindia.indiatimes.com/india/more-border-roads-with-china-to-counter-future-doklams/articleshow/60444726.cms; Shukla, "New Strike Corps."

97. Anup Sharma, "IAF Gets More Teeth on Chinese Border," *Pioneer*, August 20, 2016, http://www.dailypioneer.com/todays-newspaper/iaf-gets-more-teeth--on-chinese-border.html; "IAF Reactivates Two Landing Grounds in Arunachal Pradesh," *The Hindu*, March 13, 2016, http://www.thehindu.com/news/national/iaf-reactivates-two-landing-grounds-in-arunachal-pradesh/article8346657.ece.

98. Rahul Bedi, "IAF's Depleting Assets Preclude Two-Front War Option," *Jane's Defence Weekly*, March 16, 2016, http://www.janes.com; "IAF: Don't Have the Numbers to Fully Fight Two-Front War," *Indian Express*, March 11, 2016, http://indianexpress.com/article/india/india-news-india/do-not-have-the-numbers-to-fully-fight-two-front-war-iaf.

99. "More Brahmos to Come: India Gets Two New Supersonic Cruise Missiles," *Sputnik*, April 1, 2016, https://sputniknews.com/asia/201604011037324740-russia-india-brahmos-missile/.

100. Ibid.; Ahmed, "Consideration of Sino-Indian Conflict"; Thapar, "Steep Dive Brahmos Cruise Missile."

101. Pandit, "With Eye on China."

102. Kampani, *China-India Nuclear Rivalry*, 19.

103. Ratnadip Choudhury, "Sukhoi Makes Maiden Landing Near China Border," *Deccan Herald*, August 20, 2016, http://www.deccanherald.com/content/565749/sukhoi -makes-maiden-landing-near.html; Sharma, "IAF Gets More Teeth."

104. Joshi, "Evolving Indian Nuclear Doctrine?" 80–81; Narang, "Five Myths," 151.

105. Joshi, "Evolving Indian Nuclear Doctrine?" 80–81.

106. Ibid.; Vijay Shankar, "Strategic Non-Nuclear Weapons: An Essential Consort to a Doctrine of No First Use," Institute of Peace and Conflict Studies, January 13, 2014, http://www.ipcs.org/article/nuclear/strategic-non-nuclear-weapons-an-essential -consort-to-a-doctrine-4256.html.

107. Vijay Shankar, "Tactical Nuclear Weapons: A Step Closer to the 'Abyss,'" in Kanwal and Chansoria, *Pakistan's Tactical Nuclear Weapons*, 34.

108. For background on the importance of mutually recognized limiting points in the conduct of limited war, see Thomas C. Schelling, "Bargaining, Communication and Limited War," *Conflict Resolution* 1, no. 1 (March 1957): 19–36.

109. Ali Ahmed, "Ongoing Revision of Indian Army Doctrine," Institute for Defence Studies and Analyses, January 6, 2010, http://www.idsa.in/idsacomments/OngoingRevi sionofIndianArmyDoctrine_aahmed_060110.html.

110. Ali Ahmed, "Nuclear Implications of the Two-Front Formulation," Institute for Defence Studies and Analyses, January 29, 2010, http://www.idsa.in/idsacomments /NuclearImplicationsoftheTwoFrontFormulation_aahmed_290110; Cunningham and Medcalf, "Dangers of Denial," 6.

111. Adityanjee, "No First Use Doctrine with 'Chinese Characteristics,'" Vivekananda International Foundation, May 2, 2013, http://www.vifindia.org/article/2013/may/02 /no-first-use-nuclear-doctrine-with-chinese-characteristics.

112. Nagal, "Strategic Stability," 12.

113. Ahmed, "Consideration of Sino-Indian Conflict"; and Ahmed, "Nuclear Implications."

114. Andrew S. Erickson and Lyle J. Goldstein, "China's Future Nuclear Submarine Force: Insights from Chinese Writings," *Naval War College Review* 60, no. 1 (Winter 2007): 55–79.

115. Nuclear Threat Initiative, "China Submarine Capabilities," July 30, 2015, http://www .nti.org/analysis/articles/china-submarine-capabilities/; Office of the Secretary of Defense, *Military and Security Developments*, 9; Kristensen and Norris, "Chinese Nuclear Forces, 2015," 81.

116. Linda Jakobson and Rory Medcalf, *The Perception Gap: Reading China's Maritime Strategic Objectives in Indo-Pacific Asia* (Sydney: Lowy Institute for International Policy, June 2015), 8, https://www.lowyinstitute.org/sites/default/files/the-perception-gap -reading-chinas-maritime-strategic-objectives-in-indo-pacific-asia_0.pdf.

117. State Council Information Office, *China's Military Strategy*.

118. Cai Penghong, "China's Evolving Overseas Interests and Peaceful Competition," in *Beyond the Wall: Chinese Far Seas Operations*, ed. Peter A. Dutton and Ryan D. Martinson (Newport, RI: US Naval War College, 2015), 65–66, https://usnwc2.usnwc .edu/getattachment/667e7ff9-b1e4-46cb-b709-555d151d5c3f/WEB_CMS13.pdf .aspx; Wang Xiaoxuan, "SLOC Security and International Cooperation," in Dutton and Martinson, *Beyond the Wall*, 93.

119. Office of the Secretary of Defense, *Military and Security Developments*, 8, 19.

120. Rahul Roy-Chaudhury and Arushi Kumar, "Between China, Terror and the Deep Blue Sea, India's New Naval Doctrine Takes Shape," *The Wire*, December 3, 2015, http://thewire.in/2015/12/03/between-china-terror-and-the-deep-blue-sea-indias-new-naval-doctrine-takes-shape-16665/; Jayanta Gupta, "Chinese Naval Ships Detected Near Andamans," *Times of India*, September 4, 2015, https://timesofindia.indiatimes.com/india/Chinese-naval-ships-detected-near-Andamans/articleshow/48817805.cms.

121. Jayanta Gupta, "PLAN Ships Continue to Prowl around Andamans," *Times of India*, February 26, 2016, https://timesofindia.indiatimes.com/city/kolkata/PLAN-ships-continue-to-prowl-around-Andamans/articleshow/51159533.cms.

122. Indrani Bagchi, "Now, India Gets to Tug at China's 'String of Pearls,'" *Times of India*, June 7, 2015, https://timesofindia.indiatimes.com/india/Now-India-gets-to-tug-at-Chinas-string-of-pearls/articleshow/47570510.cms; C. Raja Mohan, "Chinese Takeaway: String of Pearls," *Indian Express*, June 11, 2014, http://indianexpress.com/article/opinion/columns/chinesetakeaway-string-of-pearls/; Virginia Marantidou, "Revisiting China's 'String of Pearls' Strategy: Places 'with Chinese Characteristics' and Their Security Implications," *Pacific Forum CSIS Issues and Insights* 14, no. 7 (June 2014): 8–9, https://csis-prod.s3.amazonaws.com/s3fs-public/legacy_files/files/publication/140624_issuesinsights_vol14no7.pdf.

123. Monte Reel, "Djibouti Is Hot," *Bloomberg Businessweek*, March 23, 2016, https://www.bloomberg.com/features/2016-djibouti/; "China's Foreign Ports: The New Masters and Commanders," *The Economist*, June 8, 2013, https://www.economist.com/news/international/21579039-chinas-growing-empire-ports-abroad-mainly-about-trade-not-aggression-new-masters; Daniel J. Kostecka, "Places and Bases: The Chinese Navy's Emerging Support Network in the Indian Ocean," *Naval War College Review* 64, no. 1 (Winter 2011): 59–78.

124. Katrina Manson, "China Military to Set Up First Overseas Base in Horn of Africa," *Financial Times*, March 31, 2016, https://www.ft.com/content/59ad20d6-f74b-11e5-803c-d27c7117d132.

125. Darshana M. Baruah, "The Small Islands Holding the Key to the Indian Ocean," *The Diplomat*, February 24, 2015, http://thediplomat.com/2015/02/the-small-islands-holding-the-key-to-the-indian-ocean/.

126. O'Donnell and Joshi, "Lost at Sea."

127. Frank O'Donnell, "New Depth to Indian Ocean Nuclear Deterrence," Dartmouth Centre for Seapower and Strategy, March 3, 2016, http://blogs.plymouth.ac.uk/dcss/2016/03/03/new-depth-to-indian-ocean-nuclear-deterrance/.

128. Indian Ocean Naval Symposium, "About IONS," June 11, 2014, http://ions.gov.in/about_ions.

129. Wendell Minick, "China's 'One Belt, One Road' Strategy," *Defense News*, April 12, 2015, https://www.defensenews.com/home/2015/04/11/china-s-one-belt-one-road-strategy/.

130. World Nuclear Association, "Nuclear Power in Pakistan," December 2017, http://www.world-nuclear.org/information-library/country-profiles/countries-o-s/pakistan.aspx; Naveed Miraj, "China Assures Pakistan of Help to Join Nuclear Suppliers Club," *Express Tribune*, November 27, 2015, https://tribune.com.pk/story/999286/china-assures-pakistan-of-help-to-join-nuclear-suppliers-club/; Ananth Krishnan, "China Involved in Six Nuclear Projects in Pakistan, Reveals Official," *India Today*,

February 8, 2015, http://indiatoday.intoday.in/story/china-pakistan-nuclear-proj ects-beijing-chashma-atomic-energy/1/417661.html. For general background on the expansive China-Pakistan strategic partnership, see Small, *China-Pakistan Axis*.

131. Tim Craig and Simon Denyer, "From the Mountains to the Sea: A Chinese Vision, a Pakistan Corridor," *Washington Post*, October 23, 2015, https://www.washington post.com/world/asia_pacific/from-the-mountains-to-the-sea-a-chinese-vision-a-pak istani-corridor/2015/10/23/4e1b6d30-2a42-11e5-a5ea-cf74396e59ec_story.html.

132. Ministry of Planning, Development and Reform, "CPEC Is a National Project: Ahsan Iqbal," news release, January 5, 2016, http://pc.gov.pk/web/press/get_press/15.

133. Jawaid Bokhari, "National Debate on Game-Changer," *Dawn*, April 3, 2017, https://www.dawn.com/news/1324564.

134. Harjit Hansi, "Sino-Pak Agreements and Security Implications for India," Centre for Land Warfare Studies, April 23, 2015, http://www.claws.in/1373/sino-pak-agree ments-and-security-implications-for-india-harjit-hansi.html.

135. Syed Raza Hassan, "To Protect Chinese Investment, Pakistan Military Leaves Little to Chance," Reuters, February 8, 2016, https://uk.reuters.com/article/pakistan-china -security-gwadar/to-protect-chinese-investment-pakistan-military-leaves-little -to-chance-idUKKCN0VH06F.

136. Hansi, "Sino-Pak Agreements."

137. T. C. A. Rangachari, "China's Role in South Asia: An Indian Perspective," in *Neigh- bourhood First: Navigating Ties under Modi*, ed. Aryaman Bhatnagar and Ritika Passi (New Delhi: Observer Research Foundation, 2016), 92, http://cf.orfonline.org /wp-content/uploads/2016/03/GP-ORF_Indias-Neighbourhood1.pdf; Jeff M. Smith, "China-India Relations in the Modi-Xi Era (Testimony to the U.S.-China Economic and Security Review Commission)," USCC, March 10, 2016, http://www.uscc .gov/sites/default/files/SMITH_Remarks%2003101016.pdf; PTI, "China Defends Proj- ects in PoK, Opposes India's Oil Exploration in South China Sea," *Indian Express*, June 4, 2015, http://indianexpress.com/article/world/asia/china-justifies-projects-in-pok -objects-to-indias-oil-exploration-in-south-china-sea/.

138. Sutirtho Patranobis, "China Silent on Presence of Its Troops in Pak-Occupied Kash- mir," *Hindustan Times*, March 15, 2016, http://www.hindustantimes.com/world /china-silent-on-presence-of-its-troops-in-pak-occupied-kashmir/story-mH0DAqFX B8L2oQOl9uD76I.html; PTI, "Chinese Army Troops Spotted along Line of Con- trol in Pakistan-Occupied Kashmir," *Economic Times*, March 13, 2016, https:// economictimes.indiatimes.com/news/defence/chinese-army-troops-spotted-along -line-of-control-in-pakistan-occupied-kashmir/articleshow/51380320.cms; "Indian Se- curity Agencies Apprise Modi Government about Chinese Army's Positioning in Pakistan," *Zee News*, March 13, 2016, http://zeenews.india.com/news/india/indian -security-agencies-apprise-modi-government-about-chinese-armys-positioning-in -pakistan_1865074.html.

139. Wang Xu, "Pakistan Sets Up 10,000-Man Force to Protect Chinese Interests," *China Daily*, February 3, 2016, http://usa.chinadaily.com.cn/world/2016-02/03/content _23382836.html; Mateen Haider, "Army's Special Security Division to Protect Chinese Workers in Pakistan," *Dawn*, April 21, 2015, https://www.dawn.com/news/1177322.

140. Smith, "China-India Relations"; PTI, "China Defends Projects in PoK."

141. Robert M. Gates, *Duty: Memoirs of a Secretary at War* (London: WH Allen, 2014), 414, 527–28; Bharath Gopalaswamy and Ting Wang, "The Science and Politics of an Indian

ASAT Capability," *Space Policy* 26, no. 4 (November 2010): 229–32; Ashley J. Tellis, "China's Military Space Strategy," *Survival* 49, no. 3 (Autumn 2007): 42–44.

142. Raul Pedrozo, "Close Encounters at Sea: The USNS *Impeccable* Incident," *Naval War College Review* 62, no. 3 (Summer 2009): 101–2; Gates, *Duty*, 414, 527–28.

143. Gates, *Duty*, 527–28.

144. Michael S. Chase, Jeffrey Engstrom, Tai Ming Cheung, Kristen A. Gunness, Scott Warren Harold, Susan Puska, and Samuel K. Berkowitz, *China's Incomplete Military Transformation: Assessing the Weaknesses of the People's Liberation Army (PLA)* (Santa Monica, CA: RAND, 2015), 45–46.

4

THE DOCTRINAL BACKGROUND

Nuclear Deterrence in Indian Strategic Thought, 1964–2003

In the first three chapters, we explored India's nuclear force development and the nuclear security challenges posed by Pakistan and China. What has been the impact of India's growing nuclear profile and emerging nuclear threats on its nuclear doctrine? This chapter and the next examine the evolution of the ideational aspect of India's nuclear weapon policy: its nuclear doctrine. This chapter traces the evolution of India's nuclear doctrine after the 1998 nuclear weapon tests till the declaration of the official doctrine in 2003. Between the nuclear tests of May 1998 and the declaration of the official doctrine in January 2003, India's nuclear doctrine saw both continuities and changes. However, to fully understand the fundamentals of India's nuclear thinking, a historical background is necessary. The available literature has ignored how India's historical experiences shaped its nuclear ideology. Therefore, the discussion of India's nuclear doctrine starts from 1964, when China tested its first nuclear device and India began ruminating over a nuclear capability.

Chapter 5 reflects on India's doctrinal journey from January 2003—when India announced its official nuclear doctrine—till the current era. It underlines various internal and external factors that have generated questions about the existing nuclear doctrine and that influence the current debate. Two specific attributes of the nuclear doctrine—NFU and massive retaliation—have attracted particular attention and will be discussed in detail. Chapter 5 will conclude with an exploration of contemporary pressures, both inside and outside government, that presently affect the Indian doctrinal debate.

As this chapter and the next demonstrate, Indian strategic thought on the question of how India should exercise nuclear deterrence has traditionally been characterized by strong support for minimum deterrence. This was the dominant view of nuclear deterrence before India's nuclear tests in 1998 and was reflected in the 1999 draft nuclear doctrine. However, since the release of the 1999 doctrine, there has been increasing pressure within and outside the government to emphasize the credibility part of India's nuclear force in its doctrinal statements and nuclear force posture developments. These pressures emanate from the perception of a worsening state of rivalry with Pakistan and China and from the growing capabilities of India's technical nuclear force. An official defense review is required to establish how India intends to balance these competing imperatives to demonstrate the "credible" and "minimum" nature of its nuclear doctrine and forces within the strategic environment it faces in 2018, two decades after it declared itself a nuclear weapon state.

DOCTRINAL THINKING BEFORE THE MAY 1998 TESTS

The Chinese nuclear tests of 1964 had a singular contribution in forcing the strategic thought of nuclear weapons and nuclear deterrence on India's decision makers. Before the Chinese tests, nuclear weapons were largely considered through the lens of nuclear disarmament. China's possession of nuclear weapons brought to India's doorstep the core question of the nuclear age: How should India confront the reality of the bomb and its implications for national security?[1]

Even before China tested its nuclear weapons, Prime Minister Jawaharlal Nehru had understood that at the least Chinese possession of nuclear weapons would have a "psychological impact" on India's thinking regarding its national security.[2] Soon after China had gone nuclear, Indian decision makers confronted the inescapable insecurity vis-à-vis the Chinese nuclear arsenal and also the key question: Should India develop a nuclear deterrent of its own? This fundamental question gripped India during the latter part of the 1960s.

In response to China's nuclear threat, India first sought guarantees of extended nuclear deterrence from the major nuclear powers of the world—the United States, Soviet Union, and United Kingdom.[3] Even when India was morally against the use and existence of nuclear weapons, its own security needs merited seeking a form of nuclear deterrence. When it became apparent that India could not receive any solid security guarantees, largely because it wanted to avoid any treaty alliances with other major powers and maintain its non-aligned status, the decision makers nevertheless felt comfortable in the perception that "in case [of China attacking India], USA and USSR could not stand by and watch. The danger to both these powers from a nuclear China which has subjugated India could be tremendous for them to face."[4]

As China's nuclear capabilities grew with subsequent tests in the 1960s and development of delivery vehicles, the clamor for Indian security increased in Parliament and in the press. In April 1970, as China tested a thermonuclear weapon and launched its first satellite into orbit, indicating its ICBM capability, a vigorous domestic debate gripped India. This debate was conducted mostly in the Indian Parliament, with many members both in the ruling Congress Party and in opposition questioning the government on its policy responses to the Chinese nuclear tests.[5]

Against this background, DAE prepared a secret memo for the prime minister in April 1970. The memo was seen and approved by P. N. Haksar, Indira Gandhi's principal secretary; Vikram Sarabhai, chairman, Atomic Energy Commission (AEC); and Raja Ramanna, who played an important role in the 1974 nuclear explosion and later became AEC chairman. This notable document underlined some of Indian decision makers' earliest thinking on doctrinal issues concerning nuclear weapons. The issue that DAE seemed to dwell on was Chinese conventional superiority in a confrontation with India on the contested Himalayan border. Some noted parliamentarians had asked the government to develop tactical nukes to deter China. As the DAE memo argued, "There is today an opinion held by several military commentators and some members of parliament that tactical nuclear weapons would prove of very great advantage to our ground troops if attacked by China."[6]

The authors of the memo, however, found this argument highly fallacious. They argued that nothing seemed to distinguish the tactical use of nuclear weapons from the strategic. "Every time a tactical exchange takes place," they wrote, "it invariably escalates to a strategic exchange as soon as one of the parties starts having the worst of the tactical exchange." In this case, acquiring tactical nuclear weapons would not suffice; as the DAE memo argued, what India required was a strategic nuclear deterrent. This strategic capability, according to the memo, should be able to "inflict unacceptable damage on a second strike." Since developing this capability would require enormous resources, which India couldn't then spare, the memo concluded that the "challenge of China is most satisfactorily met by making India economically and industrially strong."[7]

Its recommendations notwithstanding, the memo is relevant for understanding the early impulses in India's doctrinal thinking. Two doctrinal precepts stand out. The first is that India would eschew nuclear war fighting involving tactical nuclear weapons. The second is that India's doctrinal impulse appears to be inspired by the logic of "deterrence via punishment": for deterrence to exist, any use of nuclear weapons against India should be met with "unacceptable damage through second strike." As we will see later, these precepts remained the fundamental guiding principles of India's doctrinal evolution when it actually began moving toward acquiring a weapon capability.

In the 1970s, thanks to India's treaty of friendship with the Soviet Union, its resounding military victory over Pakistan in the 1971 war, and the overall benign strategic environment in its neighborhood, the issue of Indian nuclear weapons remained on the back burner. India did conduct a peaceful nuclear explosion (PNE) in 1974; however, as new archival research has shown, the PNE was devoid of any military capability.[8] Serious considerations regarding a nuclear weapon capability manifested themselves only in the late 1970s, when intelligence sources confirmed Pakistan's successful development of uranium enrichment technology.[9] The existence of a covert Pakistani nuclear weapon program was first acknowledged in an April 1979 Joint Intelligence Committee (JIC) report, JIC Paper No. 4/79.[10] As K. Subrahmanyam has argued, it was the first time that India perceived a nuclear threat from Pakistan.[11]

By 1981 the Indian Ministry of External Affairs (MEA) was convinced that "Pakistan has set off on a race to go militarily nuclear."[12] China's generous aid to Pakistan's strategic program unnerved New Delhi. Equally disconcerting for India was Chinese collusion; as an August 1981 MEA memo argued, "the Chinese connection to Pakistani program was less in the realm of speculation than in the realm of reality." The memo also said that Pakistan might conduct its first nuclear explosion at Lop Nor because "it would appear to be just one more nuclear test by PRC" and would help Pakistan avoid "the range instrumentation problems."[13] Rapid advances in Pakistan's nuclear weapon program and Chinese collusion brought the nuclear threat home for India. Pakistan was going down the nuclear path with Chinese assistance, and on top of that, the US was considering selling arms, including F-16 fighter jets, to Pakistan. New Delhi called these developments a "serious aggravation in its security environment."[14]

India's response was twofold. First, Prime Minister Indira Gandhi considered preemptive strikes on Pakistan's nuclear infrastructure. As a top-secret US Central Intelligence Agency (CIA) report in September 1981 estimated, "Conditions may be ripe for a decision by Prime Minister Indira Gandhi to instigate a military confrontation with Pakistan, primarily to provide a framework for destroying Pakistan's nuclear facilities."[15] Similar assessments of Indian intentions were offered by the Soviets.[16] Second, India veered toward nuclear testing. The fear of economic sanctions, however, dissuaded Prime Minister Gandhi.[17] Even though both the preemptive strikes and the nuclear testing came to naught, this strategic context paved the way for weaponization of India's nuclear capability. By the early 1980s, DRDO had started experimenting with Jaguar deep-penetration strike aircraft for the toss bombing of nuclear weapons.[18] If aircraft provided one vector for nuclear delivery, development of ballistic missiles under the IGDMP of 1984 could provide the other.[19] India had, therefore, in the early 1980s embarked on the process of weaponizing its nuclear deterrent. Soon after, it would also start cogitating its nuclear doctrine and posture.

The formation of a committee led by Lt. Gen. K. Sundarji in 1985 was the government's first serious effort to identify requirements for establishing Indian nuclear deterrence against China and Pakistan.[20] By the early 1980s, Sundarji had already written about the problems of nuclear deterrence in the Indian context. In papers published in the College of Combat's *Combat Papers*, he suggested some requirements of an Indian nuclear deterrent that circled the idea of a minimum deterrent.[21] Likewise, the Sundarji committee in its recommendations to Prime Minister Rajiv Gandhi argued for a minimum de-terrent capability entailing a force structure of 60–130 nuclear warheads primarily mounted on aircraft. The committee operated on an assumption that India would require a second-strike capability against China; establishing this posture against India's northern neighbor would automatically generate suffi-cient deterrent capability against Pakistan. As one of the committee members noted, this was the first time the term "minimum deterrence" was used in the Indian context by any government-approved study on nuclear deterrence.[22] The committee believed that India's nuclear posture had to be retaliatory in nature; neither first use nor tactical use of nuclear weapons was considered.

The ideas of minimum deterrence and NFU remained with Indian policy-makers and analysts thereafter. After the Brasstacks crisis of 1986–87, the Rajiv Gandhi government cogitated a series of nuclear confidence building measures (CBMs) with Pakistan. One of the recommendations given by experts such as K. Subrahmanyam and Raja Ramanna was to propose an NFU agreement with Pakistan. This was indicative of India's early nuclear thinking. However, Prime Minister Gandhi considered it politically impossible. As K. Subrahmanyam re-called, since Gandhi had "talked so much about the Pakistani nuclear effort up and down the country, the offer of no-first-use at that stage would look like India backing down under the Pakistani threat."[23] Still, the idea remained em-bedded in the Indian security and foreign policy establishment.

When in the early 1990s the US pressured India to seek more nuclear CBMs with Pakistan, these ideas were rekindled by the foreign office. The Indian government not only offered an extension of the nonattack agreement for major population centers and economic facilities but, for the first time, at an official level, offered Pakistan an NFU agreement. Pakistan rejected both of these agreements.[24] Regardless, these events underlined India's basic nuclear philosophy of NFU and averseness to nuclear war fighting. In countless articles written in the 1990s, strategic experts like Sundarji, K. Subrahmanyam, and Air

Commodore Jasjit Singh advocated a minimum deterrent strategy if ever India crossed the "nuclear Rubicon" to develop an overt nuclear force.[25]

This history of Indian nuclear thought, especially during the formative years of India's nuclear weaponization in the 1980s and 1990s, in many respects established the roadmap for India's likely nuclear strategy. As India's former foreign secretary and national security advisor Shivshankar Menon argues, this "preparatory thinking" had immense consequences for formulating India's nuclear doctrine after the 1998 nuclear tests.[26] The events of May 1998 put immense domestic and international pressure on India to immediately announce its nuclear doctrine. Many of the strategic thinkers who had already advocated a policy of minimum deterrence, especially Jasjit Singh and K. Subrahmanyam, led the preparation of this post-1998 declaratory Indian nuclear strategy. Their presence on the NSAB, which prepared the nuclear doctrine, partly ensured that India would follow an approach similar to that recommended in the official studies and writings before the 1998 tests.[27]

Preparing and announcing a nuclear strategy, even with this preexisting basis for doctrinal analysis and thought, were not easy tasks. As the next section will illustrate, the government required considerable time to develop an official nuclear doctrine. Given the early focus on minimum deterrence, however, this particular doctrinal approach and posture looked the most likely choice in the immediate aftermath of the 1998 tests.

AFTER THE TESTS, BEFORE THE DOCTRINE: 1998–99

As the dust settled in the desert of Pokhran after the nuclear tests on May 11 and 13, 1998, it laid to rest one of the most highly debated and controversial subjects in India's history: its nuclear weapon status. With the tests India unambiguously declared itself a nuclear weapon state. Yet this new status brought to the fore a doctrinal issue: How would India use its newly demonstrated nuclear weapon capability? Achieving the material capability was only the first step toward nuclear deterrence; effecting deterrence on the ground required a clear articulation of intentions for how the nuclear weapons would be used and operationalized in practice. A nuclear doctrine was, therefore, necessary.

The nuclear doctrine was also important for a diplomatic reason. Soon after the nuclear tests, New Delhi initiated a nuclear dialogue with the United States. The Indian objective for the dialogue was to convince Washington, DC, to lift economic sanctions and accommodate India in the nuclear order. The Americans, in contrast, wanted to limit India's strategic capability by convincing New Delhi to sign the CTBT, negotiate the Fissile Material Cut-Off Treaty

(FMCT), and cap the country's missile capabilities.[28] Washington was equally keen on seeing New Delhi formulate a nuclear doctrine that could provide a sense of India's nuclear ambitions. Both strategically and diplomatically, therefore, there was an immediate requirement for articulation; still, New Delhi adopted a graduated response.

The first articulation of India's nuclear doctrine came as a series of statements by its political leadership spread across 1998. Just two days after the second round of tests on May 13, Prime Minister A. B. Vajpayee shared his thoughts on some of the ideas that would guide India's nuclear doctrine in an interview with *India Today*. It was clear to the prime minister that the tests had catapulted India into the ranks of the few nuclear weapon states. The 1974 PNE had shrouded India's nuclear status in "needless ambiguity," but the 1998 tests were unambiguous. However, India's weapons would never be "weapons of aggression."[29] This comment was indeed the first hint of India's stance on the use of nuclear weapons. New Delhi saw little purpose in using nuclear weapons first.

A fuller explanation of India's future nuclear weapon policy was provided in a paper tabled in the Parliament on May 27, followed by a statement by the prime minister on the same day. For the government, harnessing the power of nuclear weapons was accompanied by a sense of responsibility: "India shall not use these weapons to commit aggression or to mount threats against any country."[30] New Delhi offered an NFU pledge to Pakistan. Assuring the world that India would eschew any nuclear arms race, the prime minister declared a voluntary moratorium on further nuclear testing. For the time being, it appeared that India's nuclear policy would not "subscribe or reinvent the doctrines of the Cold War."[31]

In subsequent remarks the Indian defense minister categorically denied any movement toward developing tactical nuclear weapons meant for nuclear war fighting. India's nuclear forces had to be a purely "strategic deterrent."[32] India's nuclear command and control system would be entirely in the hands of the political leadership.[33] Influential strategic thinkers like K. Subrahmanyam and Jasjit Singh concurred. For Singh, the intention behind India's nuclear tests was not to venture into the territory of "fighting nuclear wars," a mistake that the superpowers had committed during the Cold War. Subrahmanyam, who had articulated a vision of minimum nuclear deterrence for a long time, argued against deploying, targeting, and alerting India's nuclear capability.[34]

Toward the end of 1998, the government articulated its most detailed view on nuclear weapons in India's defense posture. Addressing the Indian Parliament in December 1998, the prime minister outlined the basic principles that were to guide India's nuclear deterrent. First, he announced that New Delhi would follow a policy of NFU against nuclear weapon states and a policy of "nonuse" of nuclear weapons against non-nuclear-weapon states. Second, the shape of India's arsenal would be defined by a "minimum credible deterrent." This entailed "deployment of assets" that could ensure "survivability and capacity for an adequate response." In fact, these statements distilled to a deterrence doctrine that was entirely "retaliatory" in nature. The quantum of retaliation was also the bare minimum, defined merely by "adequate response."[35]

While the political leadership made its individual public statements about Indian nuclear intent, the process of institutionalizing an Indian nuclear policy was under way. In its election manifesto, the ruling BJP had promised to establish the National Security Council (NSC). The NSC's mandate was to produce India's first-ever strategic defense review "to study and analyse the security environment and make appropriate recommendations . . . and evaluate the country's nuclear policy and exercise the option to induct nuclear weapons."[36] Though preparations for establishing the NSC had begun in March 1998, when the newly elected government formed a three-member task force to advise the leadership on the NSC's constitution, the tests were conducted a month before the task force submitted its preliminary report in June 1998. Clearly, the BJP had jumped the gun by conducting the tests in May 1998, well before the NSC was established to undertake the strategic defense review that would presumably assess India's nuclear options.[37] India's nuclear tests, followed by Pakistan's nuclear tests later that month, rendered the idea of a prior strategic defense review redundant for defense policymakers. Thus, the first task that fell to the NSC, when it was finally established in November 1998, was to promulgate a nuclear doctrine for India. Indeed, as the prime minister announced in Parliament on December 15, the NSC was tasked with making "important contributions in elaborating the concepts" of India's nuclear deterrent.[38]

The NSC had a three-tier structure: the Strategic Policy Group, comprising civilian and military officials; the twenty-two-member NSAB, consisting of former bureaucrats, military officials, and scientists, but also a few academics and journalists; and the Secretariat, which would also include the JIC. Vajpayee's principal secretary, Brajesh Mishra, assumed the role of the national security advisor, and the veteran defense official and leading strategic thinker K. Subrahmanyam was named the convener of the NSAB. The task to promulgate a nuclear doctrine fell to a select few within the NSAB: an NSAB subcommittee including K. Subrahmanyam, M. K. Rasgotra, Raja Ramanna, Bharat Karnad, and Gen. S. F. Rodriguez.[39] For eight months following its establishment in mid-December 1998, the NSAB considered the draft framework for the nuclear doctrine prepared by this subcommittee. The Draft Nuclear Doctrine (DND), as prepared by the NSAB, was finally unveiled on August 17, 1999, by National

Security Advisor Mishra. The doctrine, as Mishra explained, was a step toward "greater transparency" in India's nuclear decision making. Mishra reiterated the path underlined by the political leadership in the spring and fall of 1998: the policy of minimum deterrence along with the pledge of NFU as "the building block of our [India's] nuclear thinking."[40]

One member of the subcommittee has argued that the NSAB doctrine was merely an exercise in institutionalizing the benchmarks of nuclear deterrence already set by the government in the various statements of 1998.[41] This observation is indeed interesting because most of the members of the NSAB were proponents of minimum deterrence and NFU, an observation made consistently in this chapter. Others, however, have argued that given that the NSAB worked on the principle of consensus, the ultimate document was an accommodation of many viewpoints.[42] It is also reported that along with the NSAB, the Indian Army and the DRDO formulated their own nuclear doctrines.[43] It is not clear what exactly the differences among these different approaches to the nuclear doctrine were.

The 1999 DND in its preamble laid out the reasons for India going nuclear: nuclear weapons bolster strategic autonomy in decision making; they provide security essential for India's development; and the nuclear weapons possessed by other states, including states with "offensive nuclear doctrines pertaining to first use of nuclear weapons" and doctrines that included nuclear use against nonnuclear states, constituted a threat to Indian security. The DND claimed that "India will pursue a policy of credible minimum nuclear deterrence." Such minimum deterrence would require "sufficient, survivable and operationally prepared nuclear forces," a "robust command and control system," "effective intelligence and early warning capabilities," "comprehensive planning and training for operations in line with the strategy," and the "will to employ nuclear forces and weapons." To fulfill the requirements of minimum deterrence, the doctrine envisaged a nuclear force structure consisting of a triad of "aircraft, mobile land-based missiles and sea-based assets." Effective deterrence also entailed a capability to convert peacetime deployment into employable forces in the shortest possible time and to survive any "significant degradation" (meaning first use) by the enemy and to retaliate effectively.[44]

The credibility of retaliatory capability, survivability of nuclear assets, and effectiveness of deterrence, as the DND argued, would guide Indian nuclear deterrence. However, three subtle changes differentiated this 1999 doctrine from what had been articulated by the government in 1998. First, nonuse of nuclear weapons against non-nuclear-weapon states, also called negative security guarantees, now kept out of its scope those nonnuclear states that were aligned with a nuclear power. This was clearly a deviation from the absolute negative security guarantees offered by Vajpayee in his December 1998 speech. The NSAB never provided the rationale for this shift. As Rajesh Rajagopalan has argued, however, this change was necessary to deter states that were not nuclear themselves but nevertheless hosted nuclear assets of other nuclear weapon states.[45] Second, the quantum of retaliation in case the deterrent failed was now deemed "punitive" in nature, replacing the earlier idea of an "adequate response." This shift again remained unexplained, but the use of punitive retaliation suggested a clear commitment to absorbing the first strike and retaliating at a time and place of India's choosing. It also guaranteed flexibility of response. Last, whereas until 1998 official statements insisted on the "minimum" nature of India's credible deterrent, by 1999 the emphasis shifted toward the "credibility" aspect of the deterrent. This was most evident in the nuclear force that the doctrine envisioned, that is, an open-ended nuclear force consisting of all possible delivery systems.

The doctrine was critically received by both domestic and international figures. Pakistan's ambassador to the Conference on Disarmament (CD), Munir Akram, ridiculed India's NFU pledge; Indian promises to use nuclear weapons only in retaliation, in his reading, were simply "incredible." The growing gap in conventional power between the two countries, according to Akram, would "intensify Pakistan's reliance on its nuclear capabilities" to deter the "threat of aggression and domination by India."[46] Clearly, while India was signaling its intent to keep nuclear weapons confined to deterrence, Pakistan was keen to link the nuclear and the conventional together.

The United States was equally rattled with India's expansive formulation of its nuclear posture. As Strobe Talbott has argued in his recollections of the United States' nuclear dialogue with India, the 1999 nuclear doctrine was "the worst possible answer to the question of how India intended to define 'credible minimum deterrence' . . . if implemented, it could give India an arsenal not just equal to but bigger than either Britain's or France's, and it would surely provoke an acceleration of China's nuclear buildup." When in December 1999, during one of the nuclear dialogue meetings, the US raised "strong objections" to the DND, India's principal interlocutor, Jaswant Singh, argued that the DND "should not be taken seriously" and the US should not "dignify it [DND] by overreacting."[47] Jaswant Singh had also promised the Americans that India would review the DND.

TOWARD THE OFFICIAL DOCTRINE: 1999–2003

Given these criticisms the Indian government was keen to review the DND or at least reshape perceptions of it. The most important challenge was to salvage the idea of minimum deterrence from the expansive articulation of India's nuclear force posture in the doctrine. In the general debate in the First Committee, India's permanent UN representative argued, "The minimum deterrent posture, based on the self-evident principle of 'more is not better when less is adequate' governs the quantum as well as operational mode of our nuclear policy."[48] The conditions the DND imposed on India's negative security guarantees—of use against non-nuclear-weapon states aligned to nuclear weapon states—were also removed.

In November 1999 Jaswant Singh formally declared such course corrections in his interview with C. Raja Mohan. Singh argued that it was a "misperception" to view the 1999 DND as India's official nuclear doctrine. Calling the NSAB a group of "nonofficial" strategic experts and policy analysts, he suggested that the doctrine was intended only to initiate a larger political debate in the country; it was, in his words, not a "policy document of the Government of India." Summarizing India's nuclear doctrine from the official statements of the political leadership a year before, he stressed the NFU pledge, which also, according to him, implicitly contained the "principle that India shall not use nuclear weapons against non-nuclear weapon states."[49]

Singh addressed two issues in the DND in detail: the idea of minimum deterrence and retaliation against nuclear use by an adversary. Emphasizing the essentially political nature of nuclear weapons, he precluded the possibility of nuclear war fighting in India's strategic view of nuclear weapons; the weapons were principally directed toward deterring nuclear weapons' "use by an adversary." However, a "retaliation only" nuclear doctrine could be credible only if nuclear forces could survive a first strike. At this point "credibility" was a function of "survivability," *not* vice versa. Insofar as survivability ensured that an adversary faced a risk of retaliation, the risk rather than the certainty of retaliation provided India with the element of deterrence. This idea was also evident in Singh's dismissal of a triadic force structure, which he considered premature in India's case: "Just as parity [of forces] is not essential for deterrence, neither is a triad, a pre-requisite for credibility."[50]

This comment on the parity of forces is important because, as Rajesh Basrur has argued, a true minimum deterrence doctrine is contingent on the "risk" rather than on the certainty of a credible second strike.[51] Given that only a small number of Indian nuclear weapons would ensure that an adversary could never fully mitigate the risk of retaliation, a minimum nuclear arsenal could provide effective deterrence.[52] However, Singh was categorical in stating that the "minimum" in India's nuclear doctrine was not a fixed entity; it was rather a "dynamic concept but firmly rooted in the strategic environment, technological imperatives and national security needs."[53] The "size, components, deployment and employment of nuclear forces" were in turn dependent on these variables. On one hand, Singh's postulations can be seen as deliberate nuclear sophistry to keep the options for expansion of India's nuclear arsenal open in the future; on the other, he was trying to balance the internal criticisms of minimum deterrence with external concerns about what appeared to be an open-ended nuclear force structure.

Insofar as India's retaliatory strategy was concerned, Singh said that it would be based on two factors: that it should be assured and effective. An "assured retaliation" strategy did not entail hair-trigger alerts. It also obviated a posture of "launch on warning" or "launch under attack"; as Singh argued, retaliation did not have to be "instantaneous."[54] The 1999 doctrine required a "shift from possible peaceful deployment to fully employable forces in the shortest possible time" and "a rapid response" if India were attacked with nuclear weapons by an adversary, and these requirements painted the picture of a prompt and rapid retaliation.[55] Achieving this kind of retaliation, in an operational sense, entailed a more militarily ready arsenal than Indian political decision makers were comfortable with at the time.[56]

Several reasons explained this preference among the political leadership. First, a ready arsenal placed onerous demands on India's material and technological capabilities. Just two years after the tests, India's nuclear forces were still in flux. Indian warheads and delivery capabilities were still rudimentary; they had not yet achieved the necessary sophistication required for a ready arsenal. Moreover, the force posture was still undecided because missile capabilities were still at a developmental stage. Even organizationally, the idea of a ready arsenal would tax India's nascent command and control structure, which at that time did not include a unified nuclear command (the SFC was established in 2002). As Tellis argues, it was "more important for India to develop a response system that guarantees successful retaliation once nuclear attacks have occurred than to focus on developing the capability for meting out 'immediate and instantaneous' reprisals."[57]

Second were political considerations. Given that NFU could not be verified by any other objective standards, a recessed weapon deployment posture was a way to operationally signal India's NFU commitment to its adversaries.[58] A ready arsenal would also militate against India's sustained efforts toward delegitimization of nuclear weapons, a policy that had gained greater official emphasis in the wake of the 1998 weapon tests. In fact, the government had made delegitimization a major plank of its disarmament diplomacy, as evident in India's introduction of a proposal titled "Reducing Nuclear Dangers" in the UN General Assembly debate in 1998. This proposal largely focused on reducing the risks posed by hair-trigger postures and related doctrines of nuclear use.[59]

Last, a rapid-response system would have meant greater incorporation of the military—which was and is the final deliverer of India's nuclear arsenal—in the body politic of nuclear decision making. Traditionally, Indian civil-military relations have veered toward absolute control of the military by the civilian decision makers, and the perennial threat of the "man on horseback" ready to overtake political authority has defined interactions between the two.[60] If this was true of civil-military relations in general, it was more so in the case of India's nuclear policy. Unlike in all other major nuclear powers, in India the involvement of the military in nuclear decision making has at best been minimal.[61] Even after overtly going nuclear, this fundamental structure of civil-military relations remained entrenched. A nuclear arsenal characterized by high readiness could have upset this balance.

Notwithstanding the various versions of the doctrine, by the end of 1999, India's nuclear thinking on the use of its newly acquired nuclear capability distilled down to three broad principles.[62] First, at the declaratory level, India articulated a vision of nuclear weapons as "more an instrument of politics rather than a military instrument of warfighting."[63] In fact, India had abjured the idea of nuclear war fighting from the very beginning. Nuclear weapons were a political tool geared toward one single objective: to avert the threat of use or actual use of nuclear weapons against it by its adversaries. A range of nuclear strategies governs the use of nuclear weapons. This range includes offensive disarming of the adversary and "bolt from the blue" nuclear strikes, defensively denying an enemy with conventional military superiority in the battlefield through demonstration shots or use of tactical nuclear weapons, and simply using the threat of assured retaliation of nuclear weapons to deter an adversary from using its nuclear weapons. India's avowed doctrine has squarely rested on this third option.[64] To this end, New Delhi rejected development of tactical nuclear weapons. India's pledge of nonuse of nuclear weapons against all non-nuclear-weapon states appeared to be absolute, despite early disruptions caused by wording in the 1999 DND that allowed use of nuclear weapons against nonnuclear states allied with nuclear states.

Second, the NFU pledge was firmly in place with hardly any conditions attached to the concept. In fact, soon after the nuclear tests, India again reiterated its intentions to sign an NFU agreement with Pakistan, which had first been mooted in 1994. Within the NSAB there was a substantial debate on the viability and effectiveness of an NFU pledge. Criticisms included the likely skeptical reception such a pledge would receive from India's nuclear adversaries, especially Pakistan, and the possibility that India might itself not adhere to an NFU commitment if facing a disastrous defeat in a conventional war with China.[65]

However, Indian decision makers viewed NFU as a risk worth taking, for both political and military reasons. First, it comported well with India's overall nuclear philosophy that nuclear weapons could never be used on the battlefield. Since nuclear weapons were only for deterrence, any first use of nuclear weapons was out of the question. Second, NFU also radiated the image of a responsible and restrained nuclear power, a perception that New Delhi was desperate to disseminate largely because, rather than remaining an outlier in the nuclear order, it wanted to be accepted into the system. From the Indian perspective, the nuclear dialogue with the United States was principally motivated by these considerations. Third, the NFU policy helped to dispel fears that India was venturing into domains of unlimited nuclear force construction, as a first-use nuclear approach would have entailed the development of massive nuclear infrastructure.

Last, the military contingencies confronting India in 1999 were still manageable through conventional means, as assessed by New Delhi. Vis-à-vis Pakistan, India had both a conventional and a nuclear edge. Even though India was conventionally weaker than China, the India-China rivalry was far more stable than the volatile India-Pakistan rivalry. Being a status quo power, India had limited but still formidable military means that translated into local military advantage along the Line of Actual Control with China. Most reassuring for India was the fact that China was the only country among the five recognized nuclear powers that adhered to an NFU doctrine. The first use of nuclear weapons, therefore, neither fit India's traditional worldview nor made political or military sense to its decision-making elites. Nuclear coercion or nuclear use by an adversary could be deterred only through a threat of counteruse or actual counteruse explicated in India's retaliatory posture.

The third ideological principle of New Delhi's nuclear doctrine in late 1999 was centered on India's response to the threat of use of nuclear weapons by its adversaries or actual use of nuclear weapons if deterrence broke down. Since New Delhi insisted that nuclear weapons were political instruments and pledged an NFU policy, it could not use nuclear weapons as elements of coercion or defense. Deterrence via punishment, therefore, was the logic behind India's nuclear posture of assured retaliation. As far as the rapidity of such punishment was concerned, Jaswant Singh's interview with C. Raja Mohan had settled the debate in favor of a delayed but certain punishment. India would absorb a first strike or first use of nuclear weapons; its response to this strike, though guaranteed, would not be immediate. On the issue of quantum of punishment, India's nuclear doctrine was moving toward a more muscular approach. From "adequate response" in December 1998 to "punitive retaliation" in August 1999 and to "assured retaliation" in November 1999, the quantum of punishment appeared to be on an ascendant trajectory.

Two factors might explain this shift. First, from the very start, Pakistan tried to link the nuclear and the conventional, suggesting that it may use nuclear weapons in a conventional war with India. Decision makers in New Delhi clearly wanted to put a stop to this linkage. Second, during the Kargil War, Islamabad had resorted to veiled nuclear blackmail, and this may have prompted India to increase the quantum of nuclear punishment. In fact, during the Kargil War, Indian decision makers suggested that India's response to any use of nuclear weapons by Pakistan would be "all out" and the effects for Pakistan would be catastrophic. India could threaten complete obliteration of Pakistan given its geography and India's nuclear arsenal, but this was simply not a credible threat to make against China, which was geographically much larger than Pakistan and also possessed a vastly superior nuclear arsenal to that of India.[66] This shift toward a more muscular retaliatory approach would reach its zenith in the later formulation of "massive retaliation," which would not be delivered until the official enunciation of nuclear doctrine in 2003.

CONCLUSION

This chapter has traced the evolution of Indian nuclear thought from initial responses to the Chinese nuclear test in 1964 to the reconsiderations of India's nuclear approach following the release of the 1999 DND and experiences in the Kargil War. It has found that minimum deterrence, and how best to operationalize it, constituted the dominant strand in Indian nuclear force thought in this period. Thinking flowing from this concept distilled into a preference for assured retaliation over nuclear war fighting, reduced arsenal readiness, and NFU. However, in response to strategic pressures India faced in the 1990s (see chapters 2 and 3), Indian decision makers and strategic analysts began revising upward the level of nuclear retaliation that an adversary could expect in response to its first strike on India. This reflected growing interest in efforts to develop the "credible" as opposed to the "minimum" nature of India's emerging nuclear force at this stage, a trend that continued from 2003 onward and that we will investigate in the next chapter.

NOTES

1. For the nuclear debate in India after the Chinese nuclear test, see Yogesh Joshi, "Waiting for the Bomb: PN Haksar and India's Nuclear Policy in 1960s," Working Paper No. 10, Nuclear Proliferation International History Project, Woodrow Wilson Center for

Scholars, September 2017, https://www.wilsoncenter.org/sites/default/files/wp11 -joshi-rc4.pdf.

2. "Summary of Records of Prime Minister's Discussion with General Maxwell Taylor, December 17, 1963 (Secret)," Subject File No. 17, B. K. Nehru Papers: 1961–63, Nehru Memorial Museum and Library (NMML), New Delhi.

3. Andrew B. Kennedy, "India's Nuclear Odyssey: Implicit Umbrellas, Diplomatic Disappointments, and the Bomb," *International Security* 36, no. 2 (Fall 2011): 120–53.

4. "Nuclear Policy (Top Secret)," May 3, 1967, Installment 3, Subject File no. 111, 1975–76, Prime Minister's Secretariat Files: Guard Files Maintained as Secretary/Principal Secretary to Prime Minister 1967–73, P. N. Haksar Papers, NMML.

5. Subramaniam Swamy, "India's Nuclear Strategy in the Nineteen Seventies," in *Nuclear Weapons: A Compilation Prepared by the Department of Atomic Energy*, ed. DAE (Bombay: GoI, 1970), 201–19.

6. "Brief for the PM for the Debate in Lok Sabha on the Motion of Shri Kanwarlal Gupta, Member, Lok Sabha on the Manufacture of an Atom Bomb (Top Secret)," April 24, 1970, File No. 56/69/70-Parl., Prime Minister Secretariat Files, National Archives of India (NAI), New Delhi.

7. Ibid.

8. Joshi, *Imagined Arsenal*, 15–18.

9. India had been keenly following the Pakistani nuclear program since 1975, but intelligence estimates underappreciated the extent of its development. See Yogesh Joshi, "Between Principles and Pragmatism: India and the Nuclear Nonproliferation Regime in the Post-PNE Era, 1974–80," *International History Review*, January 2, 2018, https:// www.tandfonline.com/doi/abs/10.1080/07075332.2017.1417322. It was only in April 1979 that the Joint Intelligence Committee first reported Pakistan's success in developing a uranium enrichment capability. See K. Subrahmanyam, "India's Nuclear Policy: 1964–1998," in *Nuclear India*, ed. Jasjit Singh (New Delhi: Knowledge World, 1998), 31.

10. In January 1982 the JIC conducted a fresh threat assessment titled "Threat to India from Pakistan." The mandate of the study was to "analyse the recent developments in Pakistan and review the threat perspective." For this task, the secretary of the JIC wrote to heads of different departments in the MEA for submission of preliminary reports. Some details of the 1979 report are available in this letter. "Letter from Commander B.L. Sharma, Member Secretary, JIC, Cabinet Secretariat to M.L. Trivedi (Deputy Secretary (MEA, PPD) (Secret)," January 19, 1982, File No. WII /104/16/82, Ministry of External Affairs Files, NAI.

11. Subrahmanyam, "India's Nuclear Policy," 31. Also see Kargil Review Committee, *Kargil Review Committee Report* (New Delhi: GoI, 1999), 187.

12. "Pakistan's Nuclear Program (Top Secret)," August 19, 1981, File No.: F/103/10/81, Ministry of External Affairs Files, NAI.

13. Ibid.

14. "US Policy Towards the Indian Sub-Continent (Secret)," February 11, 1982, File No. WII 104/16/82, Ministry of External Affairs Files, NAI.

15. "India's Reactions to Nuclear Developments in Pakistan," SNIE 32/38-I, September 1, 1981, FOIA Online Reading Room, Central Intelligence Agency, 1, https://www.cia .gov/library/readingroom/document/0005403744.

16. Balazs Szalontai, *The Elephant in the Room: The Soviet Union and India's Nuclear Program, 1967–1989*, Nuclear Proliferation International History Project Working Paper No. 1

(Washington, DC: Woodrow Wilson International Center for Scholars, 2011), https://www.wilsoncenter.org/sites/default/files/indian_nuclear_history_and_soviet_rela tions_-_ver_2.pdf.

17. PTI, "Venkataraman Speaks of an Aborted N-Test," *Indian Express*, May 27, 1998, http://archive.indianexpress.com/Storyold/34309/.

18. Kampani, "India's Long Nuclear Journey," 94.

19. Raj Chengappa, *Weapons of Peace: The Secret Story of India's Quest to Be a Nuclear Power* (New Delhi: HarperCollins, 2002), 278.

20. George Perkovich, *India's Nuclear Bomb: The Impact on Global Nuclear Nonproliferation* (Los Angeles: University of California Press, 2002), 274.

21. K. Sundarji, *Effects of Nuclear Asymmetry on Conventional Deterrence*, Combat Paper No. 1 (Mhow, India: College of Combat, 1981). K. Sundarji later explicated on this early thinking in "Imperatives of Indian Minimum Nuclear Deterrence," *Agni* 2, no. 1 (1996): 18–22; K. Sundarji, "Nuclear Deterrence: Doctrine for India—Part 1," *Trishul* 5, no. 2 (1992), 43–60; K. Sundarji, "Nuclear Deterrence: Doctrine for India—Part 2," *Trishul* 6, no. 1 (1993), 67–86.

22. Interview with a member of the Sundarji Committee, October 17, 2015.

23. Subrahmanyam, "India's Nuclear Policy," 40.

24. J. N. Dixit, *Anatomy of a Flawed Inheritance: Indo-Pak Relations, 1970–94* (New Delhi: Konark, 1995), 192.

25. K. Subrahmanyam, "Nuclear Force Design and Minimum Deterrence Strategy for India," in *Future Imperilled*, ed. Bharat Karnad (New Delhi: Viking, 1994), 177–95; K. Subrahmanyam, "Nuclear Defence Policy: Not a Numbers Game Anymore," *Times of India*, November 8, 1996; Sundarji, "Indian Minimum Nuclear Deterrence"; Jasjit Singh, "South Asian Nuclear Scene," *Times of India*, May 2, 1994.

26. Menon, *Choices*, 160.

27. Bharat Karnad (former member of NSAB), interview by the authors, November 22, 2014.

28. Strobe Talbott, *Engaging India: Diplomacy, Democracy and the Bomb* (Washington, DC: Brookings Institution Press, 2004), 96.

29. "Interview with Prime Minister Atal Bihari Vajpayee," *India Today*, May 15, 1998.

30. PIB, "Evolution of India's Nuclear Policy" (paper laid on the table of the Lok Sabha, May 27, 1998). Also see PIB, "Suo Motu Statement by the Prime Minister Shri Atal Bihari Vajpayee in Parliament," May 27, 1998.

31. PIB, "Evolution of India's Nuclear Policy."

32. A. K. Dhar, "India to Have Strategic N-Force: Fernandes," *Times of India*, July 4, 1998, http://web.archive.org/web/20081006192215/http://fas.org/news/india/1998/07/980704 -toi.htm.

33. "Nuclear Command to Rest with Political Leadership: Fernandes," *Rediff*, August 10, 1998, http://www.rediff.com/news/1998/aug/10geo.htm.

34. Subrahmanyam, "Nuclear Tests," 50–62.

35. PIB, "PM's Statement in Parliament on 'Bilateral Talks with United States,'" December 15, 1998.

36. Bharatiya Janata Party, "Our Foreign Policy," Election Manifesto 1998, 197, http://library.bjp.org/jspui/bitstream/123456789/241/1/BJP%20ELECTION%20MANI FESTO%201998.pdf.

37. This anomaly was explained by Vajpayee in his interview on May 15, 1998. The prime minister said, "Conducting the tests provides necessary information for this important task [strategic defence review]." See "Interview with Prime Minister."

38. PIB, "PM's Statement in Parliament."

39. J. N. Dixit, *India-Pakistan in War and Peace* (New Delhi: Books Today, 2002), 344–45.

40. MEA, "Opening Remarks by National Security Advisor Mr. Brajesh Mishra at the Release of Draft Indian Nuclear Doctrine," August 17, 1999, http://www.mea.gov.in/in-focus-article.htm?18915/Opening+Remarks+by+National+Security+Adviser+Mr+Brajesh+Mishra+at+the+Release+of+Draft+Indian+Nuclear+Doctrine.

41. Bharat Karnad (former member of NSAB), interview with the authors, December 17, 2014.

42. Interview with a former member of the NSAB, October 17, 2015.

43. Indian Pugwash Society, *Panel Discussion Report on Future of India's Nuclear Doctrine* (New Delhi: Indian Pugwash Society, 2016), http://pugwashindia.org/pdf/Report-Final-panel.pdf.

44. PIB, preamble to *India's Nuclear Doctrine* (New Delhi: GoI, 1999).

45. Rajesh Rajagopalan, "India: The Logic of Assured Retaliation," in *The Long Shadow: Nuclear Weapons and Security in the 21st Century*, ed. Muthiah Alagappa (Stanford, CA: Stanford University Press, 2008), 188–214.

46. Quoted in Lisa Schlein, "Pakistan/India Nuclear," *Voice of America*, August 19, 1999.

47. Talbott, *Engaging India*, 171–72.

48. PIB, "Statement by H.E. Ms. Savitri Kunadi, Permanent Representative of India to the United Nations in Geneva at the General Debate in the First Committee," October 15, 1999.

49. C. Raja Mohan, "Interview with Jaswant Singh, Minister of External Affairs," *The Hindu*, November 29, 1999, http://www.acronym.org.uk/old/archive/spsingh.htm.

50. Ibid.

51. Rajesh Basrur, *Nuclear Deterrence: The Wohlstetter-Blackett Debate Revisited*, RSIS Working Paper No. 271 (Singapore: S. Rajaratnam School of International Studies, 2014), http://www.rsis.edu.sg/wp-content/uploads/rsis-pubs/WP271.pdf; Rajesh Basrur, *Deterrence, Second Strike and Credibility: Revisiting India's Nuclear Strategy Debate*, IPCS Issue Brief No. 255 (New Delhi: Institute of Peace and Conflict Studies, 2014), http://www.ipcs.org/pdf_file/issue/IB255-RajeshBasrur-IndiaNuclear.pdf.

52. Basrur, *Deterrence, Second Strike*.

53. Mohan, "Interview with Jaswant Singh."

54. Ibid.

55. PIB, *India's Nuclear Doctrine*.

56. Tellis, *India's Emerging Nuclear Posture*, 325.

57. Ibid., 323.

58. Dilip Lahiri, "Formalizing Restraint: The Case for South Asia," *Strategic Analysis* 23, no. 4 (July 1999): 563–74.

59. MEA, *Annual Report 1999–2000* (New Delhi: GoI, 2000), 81.

60. Stephen Cohen, *The Indian Army: Its Contributions to the Development of a Nation* (Berkeley, CA: University of California Press, 1971); Vina Kukreja, *Civil-Military Relations in South Asia* (New Delhi: Sage, 1991); Frank O'Donnell and Harsh V. Pant, "The Evolution of India's National Security Apparatus: Persisting Structural Deficiencies," in *The*

Routledge Handbook of Indian Defence Policy, ed. Harsh V. Pant (Oxford: Routledge, 2015), 323–36.

61. Anit Mukherjee, "Correspondence: Secrecy, Civil-Military Relations and India's Nuclear Program," *International Security* 39, no. 3 (Winter 2014–15): 202–7.

62. Tellis, *India's Emerging Nuclear Posture,* 261–366.

63. Jasjit Singh, "Why Nuclear Weapons," in *Nuclear India*, ed. Jasjit Singh (New Delhi: Knowledge World, 1998), 11.

64. For an elaborate exposition of all three nuclear strategies, see Lawrence Freedman, *The Evolution of Nuclear Strategy* (London: Palgrave Macmillan, 2003); Charles L. Glaser, *Analyzing Strategic Nuclear Policy* (Princeton, NJ: Princeton University Press, 1990); McGeorge Bundy, *Danger and Survival: Choices about the Bomb in the First Fifty Years* (New York: Random House, 1988).

65. Bharat Karnad, "A Thermonuclear Deterrent," in *India's Nuclear Deterrent*, ed. Amitabh Mattoo (New Delhi: Har-Anand Publications, 1999), 120.

66. Tellis, *India's Emerging Nuclear Posture,* 338.

5

NEW CHALLENGES FOR INDIAN NUCLEAR DOCTRINE

The Doctrinal Debate, 2003–Present

This chapter will analyze India's official nuclear doctrine unveiled in 2003 and then progress to examine Indian nuclear strategic thought from the announcement of this doctrine until the present day. The doctrine and tenor of the debates that have followed the 2003 announcement demonstrate not only continued strong support for the concept of "minimum" deterrence but also growing tensions due to rising pressure within and outside government for doctrinal and force development measures that instead demonstrate "credible" deterrence. These unresolved tensions between the "minimum" and "credible" have now reached the stage at which an official strategic defense review is required to determine politically where the balance between these two imperatives is struck.

INDIA'S OFFICIAL NUCLEAR DOCTRINE OF 2003

India's official nuclear doctrine was finally promulgated in January 2003. It took approximately three years for the Indian government to review and revise the 1999 doctrine. The interlude between the 1999 and 2003 doctrines, as we saw in the previous chapter, involved a vigorous domestic debate over India's nuclear approach. New Delhi was particularly concerned that the emerging nuclear environment in the subcontinent created complications for its nuclear strategy. Emboldened by its possession of a nuclear umbrella, Pakistan's military initiated a limited land-grab exercise in the Kargil sector of Indian Kashmir.[1]

The Kargil War was fought under a nuclear shadow; India confined its military action within its border and successfully pushed out the infiltrators in a two-month military campaign, but only after incurring substantial casualties.[2] Even though it was conventionally stronger, India could not bring to bear its power on Pakistan for fear of nuclear escalation.³ Pakistan effectively used the nuclear shadow to foment subconventional war in India's troubled region of Jammu and Kashmir and also beyond to the Indian heartland.

Just over two years after the Kargil War, a major crisis erupted again when the Indian Parliament was attacked by Pakistan-sponsored terrorists in December 2001. In an act of coercive diplomacy, India amassed more than half a million of its troops alongside the international border in what was christened Operation Parakram.⁴ Frantic mobilization and grueling deployments cost India the lives of close to 800 soldiers, with approximately $2 billion spent on mobilization alone.⁵ India demobilized after nine months, with only a rhetorical assurance from Pakistan that it would not support terrorism against India.

Some have argued that India's restraint is in part due to its desire to project itself as a responsible nuclear state and thus draw a contrast with Pakistan's risk-taking attitude.⁶ A restrained approach would eventually help New Delhi to accumulate international and especially American goodwill, build a strategic relationship with Washington, ease sanctions on technology transfers, and finally be accommodated in the international nuclear order. In fact, a major driver of this Indian restraint was nuclear dynamics in the subcontinent. Pakistan's strategy of linking the nuclear and conventional domains succeeded in limiting India's conventional options. Veiled nuclear threats from Pakistan were commonplace during the Twin Peaks crisis of 2001–2, but even India's decision to demobilize in autumn 2002 was read by Pakistan as a victory of its nuclear deterrent.⁷ For President Musharraf, "South Asia's strategic balance and Pakistan's conventional and nuclear weapons . . . had deterred India. . . . India's hesitation, frustration and inability to attack Pakistan in a so called limited war were premised upon Pakistan's nuclear prowess."⁸ Although India had gone nuclear to avoid nuclear blackmail, Pakistan's subconventional warfare against India and its strategy to escape Indian conventional retribution by promising first use of nuclear weapons on the battlefield were clearly negating the advantages that India had intended to gain from its nuclear deterrent.

Notwithstanding the nuclear blackmail from Pakistan, two other developments in India's neighborhood were equally disconcerting for Indian nuclear deterrence. First, after the September 2001 terrorist attacks on the US, a global concern over the acquisition of nuclear weapons by terrorist networks such as al-Qaeda gained immediate priority in the security calculus of states worldwide.⁹ India's immediate neighborhood—Pakistan and Afghanistan—had been a safe haven for international terrorism for more than a decade. Therefore, the threat that nonstate entities could acquire nuclear assets in the future also became a security concern for the Indian government.¹⁰ Second, the United States publicly exposed the A. Q. Khan proliferation network during this period.¹¹

Although the Indian government had long been communicating its concerns about Pakistani proliferation to the US and other states, the extent of these activities was indeed alarming. All this created a perception among Indian decision makers that India might be facing an invisible nuclear threat in the future, probably backed by states that traditionally engaged in sponsoring terrorism with plausible deniability of having done so.

One last factor at the international level that influenced India's nuclear thinking in this period was the change in US nuclear strategy that came with the George W. Bush administration. On May 1, 2001, in a speech at the National Defense University, President Bush announced a "new framework for security and stability" involving new emphasis on missile defense systems to mitigate nuclear threats. Explaining the new role for missile defense in American nuclear strategy, Bush argued, "Deterrence can no longer be based solely on the threat of nuclear retaliation. . . . Defenses can strengthen deterrence by reducing the incentive for proliferation." In part, this change in policy was motivated by what Bush described as American commitments to "a credible deterrent with the lowest possible number of nuclear weapons consistent with our national security needs, including our obligations to our allies" and to quick reduction of US nuclear forces.[12] However, the shift was equally a response to the new threats emerging on the nuclear horizon: transnational terrorist networks, development of ballistic missiles by states with malevolent interests toward the United States, and the perceived risk of nuclear proliferation in Iran, North Korea, and Iraq. Some of these threats would take a new dimension with the events of September 11 and the exposure of A. Q. Khan's proliferation network.

What was promising in Bush's speech—especially for India—was the fact that this new approach was "premised on openness, mutual confidence and real opportunities for cooperation, including in the area of missile defense."[13] The threats Bush underlined comported well with India's own security perceptions, and India could take advantage of his offer of missile defense technology cooperation just as it had in the past when President Dwight Eisenhower made a similar offer through his Atoms for Peace initiative.[14] Additionally, Bush's seeming repudiation of the Cold War international nuclear order rang true for an Indian government that had long sought accommodation for its nuclear status in global nuclear policy arrangements.[15] While all these factors supported India's eventual decision to integrate missile defense into its strategic force development, this transition occurred only after the enunciation of its official nuclear doctrine.

Such was the internal, regional, and international backdrop in which India announced its official nuclear doctrine through a press statement on January 4,

2003.[16] Compared with the elaborate document that accompanied the 1999 DND, the press statement was succinct. Though the overall tenor of the doctrine remained the same, several major changes were easily visible.[17]

First, India's NFU pledge looked highly compromised. Following domestic pressure on the pledge, reportedly to the extent that the NSAB recommended its revocation in December 2002, the new doctrine introduced major conditions on NFU.[18] New Delhi now declared its right to use nuclear weapons if Indian armed forces were attacked with weapons of mass destruction (WMDs) anywhere in the world. This condition was motivated by India's experiences during the Kargil War and especially during the Twin Peaks crisis of 2001–2. It was a response to Pakistan's threat of using nuclear weapons against India on a conventional battlefield. But in responding to this threat, it also equated chemical and biological weapons with nuclear weapons; any use of such weapons could invite an Indian nuclear retaliation. Discerning the origins of the new Indian equivalence of chemical, biological, and nuclear weapons was difficult. As Rajesh Rajagopalan has argued, India by now had become a party to the Chemical Weapons Convention (CWC) and had legally forfeited chemical weapons. The Indian decision makers might have felt vulnerable to a chemical weapon attack in the absence of a similar deterrent force.[19]

The second major change in the official doctrine pertained to the quantum of punishment in Indian retaliation to nuclear first use by an adversary. As has been argued earlier, by 2000 India's nuclear doctrine was moving toward a more muscular approach in terms of quantity of punishment to be delivered in its nuclear retaliation. Following a similar trend, the new official doctrine declared, "Nuclear retaliation to a first strike will be massive and designed to inflict unacceptable punishment."[20] In deterrence literature the difference between punitive retaliation and massive retaliation is substantial; the former allows flexibility in response whereas the latter has no room for concessions. Massive retaliation necessitates that the retaliating state attack the adversary with all its nuclear might.

Last, there appeared to be a change in the order of priority between "credible" and "minimum" in the force posture of minimum credible deterrence. Whereas earlier texts and enunciations of the doctrine had always prioritized minimum over credible (at least in the sequence of these words), the 2003 document put "credible" before "minimum." In the earlier versions of the doctrine, the mere risk of a retaliatory exchange appeared to have provided India with the requisite nuclear deterrent, but the emphasis had now shifted to the credibility of India's nuclear retaliation. As Scott Sagan has argued, the emphasis on credibility pointed toward a greater increase in arsenal size than would be necessary under the "finite deterrent posture" entailed by a doctrine of minimum deterrence.[21]

2004–8: RELATIVE CALM

By the start of 2003, India's nuclear doctrine had established new caveats on its NFU policy, set its retaliatory response to the most destructive level possible, and shifted the emphasis from "minimum" to "credible" in its nuclear force posture. As mentioned previously, these revisions were largely responses to India's changing strategic context. In 2004 New Delhi saw a change in the government when the Congress-led United Progressive Alliance (UPA) took office. This new government accepted the 2003 official doctrine and attempted no change in India's professed nuclear outlook.

Although the official nuclear doctrine thus appeared frozen, changes were taking place at the level of conventional war-fighting doctrines. The Kargil War, and especially Operation Parakram in 2001–2, had illustrated that Pakistan was actively using the nuclear cover to foment subconventional or proxy war by holding India's conventional superiority hostage to its nuclear capability.[22] By 2004 Indian defense forces had started responding to this strategic imbroglio in the subcontinent by tinkering with their conventional war-fighting doctrines and looking for a way out of the impasse engendered by Pakistan's posture of nuclear first use in a conventional battle.[23] In general, the votaries of change in India's military strategy pushed for a move away from the logic of defense to one of offense.

Against this background the Indian Army in April 2004 announced its new doctrine, officially called *Indian Army Doctrine 2004*.[24] The new doctrine sought to address problems confronted by the army between 1999 and 2003.[25] First, the army intended to convert its lugubrious and unwieldy strike corps into smaller integrated battle groups (IBGs) in order to address the problem of the "mobilization differential" it had confronted in Operation Parakram. By having smaller battle groups that could mobilize quickly, India could press for surprise against both Pakistan and the international community. Second, the Indian Army had finally institutionally accepted the logic and necessity of limited rather than major war planning.[26] Last, it was turning from defense-dominated thinking to new offensive concepts.[27]

The IAF promulgated its own revised doctrine in 2007, which is not in the public domain. A few strategists who have explicated on the doctrine have suggested that the IAF was similarly responding to the new strategic situation in the subcontinent.[28] As retired vice chief of Air Staff and member of the NSAB

Vinod Patney argued in 2003, "Deterrence against large-scale conventional and nuclear war is best provided by air power." Even in deterring Pakistan from initiating a subconventional war against India, the IAF considers itself the primary instrument of punishment, providing various options to Indian decision makers. As Patney put it, the IAF "provides greater flexibility in choice of operating bases, selection of targets, target systems and geographical areas of operations," especially when the need is to "carry the conflict across the border or the Line of Control."[29] Moreover, the IAF did not suffer from a "mobilization differential" as compared to the army.[30]

Despite these developments the broader Indian nuclear doctrinal debate did not evidence major shifts from 2004 to 2008. Several reasons explain this relative calm in India's doctrinal thought. First, the 2003 doctrine provided the cover of massive retaliation if nuclear weapons or other WMDs were used against India's armed forces fighting a conventional battle against Pakistan. The Indian armed forces were actively preparing for subconventional warfare, as evident in their doctrinal and organizational revisions and in their training and exercises.[31] Second, no major incident of subconventional warfare comparable to Kargil or the attack on the Parliament occurred during this period. This suggests that the changes in India's nuclear and conventional strategies might have induced caution in Pakistan's support to terrorist networks. Moreover, India's new strategies could be tested only under such eventualities.

Third, post-2004 New Delhi's relations with both Islamabad and Beijing were on an upswing. Leaked diplomatic cables confirm that India and Pakistan came very close to solving the Kashmir issue using a "non-territorial solution."[32] President Musharraf had made promises to both Prime Minister Vajpayee in 2003 and later Prime Minister Manmohan Singh in 2005 to curb terrorist activity emanating from its soil. For a while, as mentioned previously, Pakistan appeared to be making good on its promises. After the tumult that the 1998 tests had created in Sino-Indian relations, Vajpayee undertook a historic visit to Beijing in 2003, and progress was made in stabilizing the bilateral relationship and mechanisms to resolve the boundary dispute.[33] Relations with Beijing approached their highest point of the previous two decades.

Fourth and most important, this was also the period when India was negotiating its inclusion in the international nuclear regime through a civilian nuclear agreement with the United States. One of the major arguments in support of the deal, made in both Washington and New Delhi, was that a "responsible nuclear power" such as India must be accommodated into the system. The idea of nuclear restraint was fundamental to the image of a responsible nuclear power. "Restraint" and "responsibility" had been India's mantras in explaining its nuclear behavior since the tests in May 1998. Speaking in Parliament on December 27, 1998, Prime Minister Vajpayee had said that "India is now a nuclear weapon state. . . . Our strengthened capability adds to our sense of responsibility" and that India's "nuclear policy" would be marked by "restraint and openness."[34]

The concept of responsibility would subsequently be showcased in elements of India's foreign and nuclear policy and also in its behavior.[35] Soon after the tests, India had declared a unilateral voluntary moratorium on further nuclear testing and acquiesced, at least in principle, to signing the CTBT and negotiating the FMCT.[36] It started working with the United States to implement strict export control laws in order to check nuclear proliferation.[37] Having adopted an overtly nuclear status, India also appeared to change its traditional opposition to the international nuclear nonproliferation regime by claiming that it had been a "responsible member" and "will continue to take initiatives and work with like-minded states to bring about stable, genuine and long-lasting non-proliferation."[38]

India's military restraint, in both conventional and nuclear domains, was equally visible. Even after being attacked repeatedly either by Pakistan's regular forces, as in Kargil, or by terrorist elements supported by Islamabad, as during the strike on Indian Parliament in December 2001, India's response remained limited. Although India's limited responses were in part attributable to the nuclear shadow over the subcontinent, they nevertheless generated substantial international sympathy for India's situation. When the United States finally declared its intention to negotiate a civil nuclear agreement with India in July 2005, President Bush justified this shift in long-held US policy on nuclear nonproliferation saying, "As a responsible state with advanced nuclear technology, India should acquire the same benefits and advantages as other such states." Prime Minister Manmohan Singh was equally emphatic in India's assumption of the responsibilities of a normal nuclear state: "India would reciprocally agree that it would be ready to assume the same responsibilities and practices and acquire the same benefits and advantages as other leading countries with advanced nuclear technology such as the United States."[39] Given that responsibility and restraint were the premises on which the proposed agreement was being justified to the world, and that strategic rivalries with China and Pakistan appeared then to be relatively stable, it would have made good diplomatic sense for India not to publicly revise its nuclear doctrine at that time.

POST-2008: THE DOCTRINAL DEBATE REIGNITED

The November 2008 terrorist attacks in Mumbai, in the words of Prime Minister Manmohan Singh, "shocked the nation."[40] Danger lay in a sudden deterioration of the security situation in the subcontinent. As *The Economist* explained, if "suspicions point to a Pakistani involvement . . . the slow thawing of relations between the two hostile neighbors will revert to the deep freeze."[41] The Indian government emphatically stated that the attackers had come from Pakistan; the United States concurred. As US ambassador to India David Mulford reported to the State Department, "There is war fever here. I don't know if the Prime Minister can hold out. Everyone knows that the terrorists came from Pakistan."[42]

India did not launch a war in response to the Mumbai attacks. There were two plausible reasons behind eschewing military action. First, the Indian armed forces neither had the capability to successfully execute their limited war-fighting doctrines nor could they ensure that military action would not escalate to major war and possibly a nuclear exchange.[43] Second, there was an absence of political will in New Delhi. In recollecting the deliberations of the CCS on possible responses, then-chief of Air Staff Fali Homi Major observed, "The government never made its mind to go to war."[44]

The lessons of Mumbai and India's difficult choices thereafter were apparent to Indian decision makers. As former NSA Ambassador Menon reminisced later, "Pakistan's nuclear shield permits Pakistan to undertake terrorist attacks on India without fear of retaliation. This may well have figured in the Pakistan Army's calculations behind the Mumbai attack of 26 November 2008."[45] Mumbai, therefore, reignited the doctrinal debate. The changes introduced in the 2003 nuclear doctrine and subsequent Indian enunciations of conventional limited war-fighting doctrines had evidently not improved India's strategic situation regarding Pakistan. Moreover, there appeared to be a mismatch between India's actual conventional war-fighting capabilities and those that the respective new doctrines demanded.

The domestic reaction to the Mumbai attacks also extended to questions regarding the state of nuclear force operationalization. Until 2008 the government had remained discreet regarding the process and ability of India's nuclear force to be deployed in a situation of deterrence breakdown. The fact that members of the military and strategic analysts had pointed toward lack of "political will" to respond militarily to the Mumbai attacks raised concerns regarding the credibility of Indian nuclear doctrine. Would civilian decision makers ever have the political intent to order massive nuclear retaliation against an adversary, as pledged in the 2003 doctrine?

While this question of responding to subconventional warfare continued to dominate India's conventional and nuclear strategic thinking, Pakistan's growing nuclear arsenal and miniaturization of weapons for battlefield use created a further sense of vulnerability. Reputable international sources such as the *Bulletin of the Atomic Scientists* were publishing alarming reports indicating that Pakistan had more than doubled its nuclear arsenal over the last decade.[46] The rapid vertical proliferation of the Pakistani arsenal was complemented by its diversification. Islamabad was developing plutonium-based weapons, which require less fissile material, are smaller in size, and are logistically easier to transport. These proliferation concerns were further bolstered by the news that Pakistan had successfully miniaturized nuclear warheads and developed short-range ballistic missiles for battlefield use.[47]

Since India had traditionally rejected nuclear war-fighting doctrines, it had also, at least in its official pronouncements, eschewed development of tactical nuclear capabilities. Aside from this resulting gap between Indian and Pakistani tactical nuclear capabilities, Pakistani tactical nuclear weapons also brought into question the credibility of India's retaliatory posture of "massive retaliation." Would India risk nuclear Armageddon in response to limited nuclear use by Pakistan? Pakistan's development of full spectrum deterrence, involving its intention to have ready a nuclear force package for every conceivable level of conflict with India, has raised substantial concerns in Indian nuclear strategic discourse.[48]

Although India's nuclear deterrent traditionally remained focused on Pakistan, the deterrence gap with China was a factor of growing concern in New Delhi.[49] China's assertive behavior in the Asia Pacific, as part of its increasingly aggressive post-2008 foreign and security policy approach in general, generated further anxieties. Indian strategists noted that China was modernizing its nuclear arsenal, adding new capabilities such as the DF-21 and DF-25 missiles and antisatellite weapons, which could be used to target India's command and control.[50] Beijing also reportedly diluted its NFU policy insofar as it reserves a right to use nuclear weapons in its own territory. Some strategists see a possible effect of this disclaimer to be Chinese first use in the Indian territory of Arunachal Pradesh, which is also claimed by Beijing.[51] The deterrence gap with Beijing, therefore, appeared substantial and widening.

India's own emerging capabilities also started putting pressure on its nuclear doctrine. Since the end of 2008, India has unveiled several major deterrent projects. In 2009 India's first nuclear submarine—INS *Arihant*—was launched for sea trials. In April 2012 DRDO successfully test-fired the 5,000-kilometer (3,107-mile) range Agni-V missile, bringing India closer to the select group of nations in possession of ICBMs. In 2013 DRDO also announced its plans of developing and equipping India's missiles with MIRVs, increasing the potential lethality of India's deterrent. Then–DRDO chief V. K. Saraswat remarked that the "next logical corollary as far as the long-range ballistic missile deterrents capability of this country is concerned, we will switch over to force multiplication.

Force multiplication in the case of ballistic missiles will be by way of multiple independently manoeuvrable re-entry vehicles (MIRV)."[52] During this period DRDO also claimed that India's indigenous BMD system development had been a resounding success and that these technologies would soon be deployed to shield major metropolitan areas like New Delhi and Mumbai.

Other comparatively smaller but important technological changes, such as canisterization of delivery vehicles, accompanied India's rapidly developing capability.[53] India's defense scientists gave explanations for these changes that were problematic for India's nuclear doctrine and tradition of minimum deterrence. For example, then–DRDO chief controller of strategic systems Avinash Chander linked the necessity for canisterization of missiles to the credibility of India's second-strike capability. Canisterization would, in Chander's words, "reduce the reaction time drastically," allowing "stop-to-launch" capability in a matter of minutes. This, in Chander's view, would build credibility into India's second-strike posture since "in the second strike capability, the most important thing is how fast we can react."[54] However, the Indian doctrine, as was explained by Jaswant Singh in May 2000, was one of assured retaliation, in which the response's alacrity had no relationship to the deterrent's credibility. Such doctrinal statements coming from defense scientists evidently created the perception that India was moving toward a launch-on-warning posture. In addition, as a retired Strategic Forces commander argued in 2014, "The statements by the scientists also prematurely release information on delivery systems, which later become embarrassing when time lines are overshot/delayed."[55]

All these factors—the increasing lethality and range of Pakistan's arsenal, India's inability to resolve the conventional-nuclear dilemma, China's nuclear modernization, and the growing sophistication of India's nuclear capabilities—have ignited a domestic debate in India over the need to revise the doctrine. The fear of Pakistan's increasing nuclear arsenal led Jaswant Singh, India's former external affairs and defense minister, to initiate a doctrinal debate in Parliament in March 2011.[56] Calling on the political decision makers to revisit India's nuclear doctrine, he argued that the "policy framework that the NDA [National Democratic Alliance] devised in 1998 is very greatly in need of revision because the situation that warranted the enunciation of the policy of 'no-first-use' or 'non-use against non-nuclear weapons,' 'credible deterrence with minimum force,' etc. has long been overtaken by events."[57] Rather than continuing with "yesterday's policy," India needed to "address" the problems confronting it.

Former SFC chiefs have also joined this debate. In an article written for *Force* magazine in June 2014, Lt. Gen. B. S. Nagal argued that it is time for "a dispassionate and critical evaluation of the [nuclear] doctrine." Like Jaswant

Singh, Nagal criticized some of the fundamental premises of the Indian nuclear doctrine, such as NFU and massive retaliation. Nagal claimed that while such ideas made sense in previous years, recent changes in the strategic environment necessitated a review of the doctrine.[58] Former chief of Naval Staff Arun Prakash and former national security advisor M. K. Narayanan have separately argued for "reflection at the highest level" and "robust discussion" about India's continued adherence to NFU.[59]

Civilian strategic analysts have argued similarly. As P. R. Chari, a nuclear expert and former head of the Ministry of Defence think tank, the Institute of Defence Studies and Analyses, argued, shifts in the strategic environment provided "valid ground to revisit India's nuclear doctrine."[60] These doctrinal arguments were given further impetus in April 2014, when the then principal national opposition party, the BJP, implied in its manifesto that it would revise India's nuclear doctrine. The BJP government came to power the following month and will complete its full term in May 2019. Still, no change has accompanied India's nuclear doctrine officially even though the debate on the need to review India's doctrinal precepts has not died down. In April 2016 a group of experts called for a review of some of the basic assumptions guiding India's nuclear doctrine.[61] In 2017 a major debate on nuclear doctrine followed the publication of a book by India's former foreign secretary and national security advisor, Shivshankar Menon, which many analysts considered evidence of India's shifting nuclear doctrine and force posture.[62] With the election of the Trump administration in the US and subsequent changes in America's nuclear posture review, analysts speculate that Indian nuclear doctrine may also undergo some change.[63]

The two most salient issues in today's doctrinal debate concern the continued suitability of the NFU and massive retaliation pledges in the strategic context that India presently faces.[64] These precepts were anchoring elements of Indian nuclear thought in the period immediately following the 1998 nuclear tests but are now being called into question. They will be explored in the following subsections.

The NFU Debate

That NFU has assisted India in projecting itself as a responsible and restrained nuclear power is accepted by most Indian analysts.[65] Being essentially a defensive policy, NFU has helped in "reassuring globally that India is not an aggressive power."[66] Tangible benefits have also accompanied the international community's general acceptance of India's responsible nuclear behavior, particularly the civil nuclear cooperation agreement with the US. In some sense,

India's accommodation into the global nuclear order was facilitated by nuclear restraint.

However, as critics now argue, the challenges posed by the evolving strategic situation far outweigh the soft power benefits accrued from the "passivity" of the NFU pledge.[67] First, an NFU pledge allows the adversary to carry out "large-scale destruction" even before a massive retaliation can be launched against it.[68] In the early years of the subcontinent's nuclearization, the destructive potential of Pakistani strategic assets was curtailed by the range of ballistic missiles and its limited nuclear arsenal. A "small and symbolic first strike" is easy to absorb; a "large-scale attack," on the other hand, would throw India into "chaos."[69] Today, Pakistan claims the ability to target not only the whole of continental India but also far-off islands in the Andaman Sea. Pakistan's nuclear arsenal is one of the fastest developing in the world. In the words of a former SFC commander, imperiling the populace through an NFU pledge is extremely undemocratic, especially when the "Indian public is not in sync with the government's policy and the nation is not psychologically prepared."[70]

Second, even though Pakistan has not professed a first-strike (preemptive strike) option but only declared a first-use option (defensive use of nuclear weapons in the battlefield), decision makers in New Delhi cannot guarantee that in the fog of war the distinction would remain intact.[71] As General Nagal argued, "If an adversary is to initiate a nuclear war then it must be such that it concludes on its own terms."[72] The nature of Pakistan's tactical nuclear weapon deployment adds fire to this uncertainty. Under the threat of the "use them or lose them" scenario in an Indian armored assault on the international border, Islamabad may be tempted to not only avail its battlefield nuclear forces but launch an all-out nuclear attack against India. Indeed, under the Indian nuclear doctrine, even adversary use of tactical nuclear weapons would be met with a massive Indian response leading to unacceptable damage.

Third, an NFU policy also restricts India's military options; it cannot attrite the enemy's strategic assets through selective counterstrike targeting of its nuclear forces. As Chari argues, "Pakistan is sure that India will not target its TNW's [tactical nuclear weapons] with its own nuclear missiles."[73] There is also a moral argument against NFU: to deliberately constrain India's military options is both strategically dangerous because it gives the advantage of initiative to the enemy and "morally wrong" because "the leadership has no right to place its population at peril without exhausting other options and only opting for the NFU."[74]

Preemption of Pakistan's use of tactical nuclear weapons is gaining ground among those who advocate a first-use policy. A prominent Indian think tank report justified first use in the event that Indian decision makers acquire credible information about Pakistan preparing for a nuclear attack.[75] More recently, former Indian national security advisor Shivshankar Menon argued that one "potential gray area" that would allow India to resort to preemption is when New Delhi is "certain that adversary's launch [of nuclear weapons] was imminent."[76] Some analysts have also argued that preemption may be combined with a counterforce targeting strategy that would seek to demolish Pakistan's nuclear capability to launch a retaliatory strike.[77] Preemption may not necessarily involve nuclear weapons. An ex-SFC commander has argued that India should look forward to "select conventional hardware that tracks and targets nuclear forces" because answers to the strategic situation in the subcontinent "lay not just in the promise of disproportionate retaliation but also in the credible ability to pre-empt and counter its use."[78]

Fifth, NFU has hardly helped in rebuilding the trust deficit with Pakistan. Instead, it has bolstered Pakistan's urge to support terrorism against India, as the former is sure that India will not resort to nuclear use against Islamabad's subversive activities.[79] As one expert argues, "This policy [NFU] articulation frees Pakistan of the uncertainty and angst that India might contemplate the pre-emptive use of nuclear weapons to deal with terrorist attacks or limited conventional strikes by Pakistan."[80] Although other concerns about the credibility of nuclear first use against chemical and biological weapons are also often aired in the Indian debate, the aforementioned arguments form the most common and strategically informed case for revocation of the NFU policy.[81]

What the critics have advocated is adopting a new form of ambiguity around India's nuclear use policy. Maintaining ambiguity would give India more options to choose from at its discretion, such as preemption, launch on warning, launch on launch, or NFU.[82] It would also undermine Pakistan's current comfort with India's existing NFU policy.[83] However, ambiguity would also likely bring several political and strategic costs for India. Adopting a more assertive nuclear approach toward Pakistan would only escalate its threat perceptions and would lead to commensurate conventional and nuclear developments and positioning along its borders with India. China could respond similarly.[84] Most important, as Rajesh Rajagopalan has argued, India does not have the requisite nuclear wherewithal to adopt a first-use counterforce nuclear strategy against Pakistan; it lacks not only nuclear warheads but also delivery systems.[85] A first-use counterforce strategy would demand immense material, organizational, and economic inputs.

More broadly, ending the NFU policy could significantly damage India's long-sought international image as a "responsible nuclear power." This image is the primary foundation on which India's strategic relationship with the US, its success in obtaining a waiver from NSG sanctions, and its prospective permanent membership in the UN Security Council and NSG have all been built. A retired Indian Army officer and nuclear expert comments that the present American official perception of India as a responsible nuclear power has been achieved through Indian nuclear policies such as "the doctrine, the lack of rhetoric, no threats being held out to countries like Pakistan, credible minimum deterrence, no-first-use, no move towards tactical nuclear weapons."[86] The costs of adversary misperception and a tarnished reputation have to be weighed against the benefits of nuclear flexibility to be gained from ending India's NFU policy.

Massive Retaliation

In the official 2003 nuclear doctrine, India postulated its retaliatory posture to a nuclear strike as "massive and designed to inflict unacceptable damage" to the aggressor.[87] Although India never used the Cold War terminology of "massive retaliation," its retaliation posture was construed to be so in policy analysis.[88] In any case, this was a shift away from the 1999 DND, which had depicted India's retaliatory posture as one of "punitive retaliation." Jaswant Singh later termed this a posture of "assured retaliation."[89] The shift was palpable because massive retaliation translated into certainty of an ultimate response carrying the entire weight of India's nuclear arsenal; "punitive" or "assured" retaliation, on the other hand, had some inbuilt flexibility when it came to the quantum of punishment India would direct toward an adversary for nuclear first use.

Critics now argue that the "unrealistic certitude" of massive response suffers from huge credibility problems.[90] A retired senior naval officer and nuclear expert argues that "massive retaliation was a discredited doctrine even during the Cold War."[91] The most likely use of nuclear weapons in South Asia is Pakistan's availing its tactical nuclear weapons against Indian armed forces. Such low-level nuclear use, even when deemed as first use of nuclear weapons, cannot believably invite massive retaliation from India. As analysts note, it "defies logic to threaten an adversary with nuclear annihilation to deter use of TNWs."[92]

An additional but related issue in the doctrine of massive retaliation is proportionality of use of force. To threaten extinction of the enemy, which is inherent in the policy of massive retaliation against low-yield, local use of battlefield nuclear weapons, goes against the logic of proportionality of response.[93] Beyond the credibility-proportionality dilemma, Pakistan's vast nuclear assets likely could not be fully certifiably eliminated, even after a massive strike. This could invite a similar all-out Pakistani nuclear attack on India. Thus, for India to invite unacceptable damage on itself in response to adversary use of tactical nuclear weapons smacks of irrationality.[94] It is also, as some argue, immoral to endanger a populace with counterannihilation.[95]

Most important is the issue of political will. Would Indian decision makers be ready to walk the talk if the adversary resorts to nuclear first use? The issue of political resolve is particularly problematic for a policy of "massive retaliation" because most critics believe that the Indian political class is highly risk averse. Increasingly, the strategic community is growing skeptical of whether "when it comes to the nuclear issue, the political class will have sufficient gumption to ensure assured retaliation."[96] This averseness to political risk was manifest in India's response to crisis situations in the past, whether it was the Kargil War, the Parliament attack and military mobilization crisis of 2001–2, or the more recent Mumbai attacks.[97]

Given these problems with the doctrine of massive retaliation, skeptics have argued for several other options. The common thinking behind these options, as described by one analyst, is to "settle for less than punishing Pakistan 'massively' for its temerity to use nukes first."[98] India's response to the breakdown of deterrence must not be informed by objectives of "revenge seeking" and "venting rage" as they "have no place in the decision matrix."[99] Using logic first propounded by former Indian chief of Army Staff K. Sundarji, the idea is to terminate nuclear hostilities at the lowest level possible through direct political intervention. The need is to dilute the quantum of punishment in the doctrine to the earlier posture of "punitive retaliation." This would provide the Indian decision makers the much-needed flexibility to deal with Pakistan's low-level use of battlefield nuclear weapons. If flexibility of response is the solution to various problems arising out of the "massive retaliation" doctrine, some have argued that "how India should retaliate to a nuclear first strike" must be left to the "discretion of the Prime Minister."[100] However, even critics of massive retaliation admit that adopting a more flexible retaliatory doctrine at this stage may send the "wrong signals" to Pakistan and other adversaries.[101] But most important, a flexible response posture also does not guarantee India its most important objective: to deter Pakistan's use of nuclear weapons in the first place. India is, therefore, caught between a rock and a hard place when it comes to its retaliatory posture.

The Government's Response: Staying the Course

The responses from the BJP government (2014–present) and previous UPA government (2004–2014) to these arguments have been to reinforce India's existing nuclear doctrine. Just a day after Jaswant Singh had raised the doubts on India's nuclear doctrine in Parliament, the government quickly responded to his criticisms. It issued a statement that said there was "no change" in India's nuclear doctrine, and as far as "Pakistan's increasing nuclear arsenal" was concerned, the Indian government was taking "effective steps to safeguard India's security and defense interests consistent with our doctrine of credible minimum nuclear deterrent."[102]

Ambassador Shyam Saran also gave a substantial speech on India's nuclear doctrine in April 2013.[103] Although he claimed to have spoken in an individual capacity, the speech was nevertheless widely viewed within India as explaining official views.[104] Saran was at the time the head of the NSAB, had held various prestigious appointments in the UPA government, and was considered close to the ruling elite. A noted strategic columnist observed, "Saran was placing on record India's official nuclear posture with the full concurrence of the highest levels of nuclear policy-makers in New Delhi."[105]

This impression was further validated because Saran tried to rebut many of the domestic criticisms that had enveloped India's nuclear doctrine in the previous few years, especially regarding the strategic problem posed by Pakistan's tactical nuclear weapons and doubts around the credibility of India's massive retaliation posture. Emphasizing "India's continued insistence on the central tenet of its nuclear doctrine," Saran argued that irrespective of the development of tactical nuclear weapons by Pakistan, India recognizes no such labels on nuclear weapons. All nuclear use in the subcontinent would be strategic because any nuclear use by Pakistan—tactical nuclear weapons or otherwise— would be approved at the highest level of political decision making. India's response, Saran underlined, "if it is attacked with such weapons," would be "massive and designed to inflict unacceptable damage on the adversary."[106]

The government does not appear to harbor any plans for revision of the doctrine at present. Despite the inclusion of the pledge to "revise and update" the doctrine in the BJP 2014 electoral manifesto, Prime Minister Modi, after assuming office, moved to rule out any change to the NFU policy. Modi has instead presented the NFU policy and larger Indian nuclear doctrine as a broader expression of the legacy of former Prime Minister A. B. Vajpayee and as symbolic of Indian cultural values dating back to Gandhi and Buddha.[107]

After becoming prime minister, Modi repeated his earlier pledge of continuing with India's existing nuclear doctrine. When questioned by Japanese journalists in August 2014 regarding the BJP election manifesto promise of changing the doctrine, he argued, "While every government naturally takes into account the latest assessment of strategic scenarios and makes adjustments as necessary, there is a tradition of national consensus and continuity on such issues. I can tell you that currently, we are not taking any initiative for a review of our nuclear doctrine."[108] The strength of official conservativism regarding the nuclear doctrine is further demonstrated by the BJP's ignoring calls by its influential Hindu nationalist ideological partner, the Rashtriya Swayamsevak Sangh (RSS), to revise the doctrine.[109]

The government's inaction notwithstanding, what is beyond question is the firmament enveloping Indian thinking on the nuclear doctrine at least at the level of intellectual debate and discussion among foreign policy and strategy elites. These doctrinal debates, conducted within India's nuclear strategic discourse, coincide with a greater focus on operationalization, diversification, and continued expansion of the nuclear force in the Indian government. Although the 2013 Saran speech reiterated India's traditional stance toward tactical nuclear weapons, and the incoming BJP government of 2014 reversed its manifesto pledge regarding revision of the nuclear doctrine, there is still a robust debate inside and outside the Indian government regarding the relevance of the 2003 doctrine to the nuclear forces India is developing and the security environment it faces today. The rising tension between strong support for minimum deterrence and growing pressure to demonstrate credible deterrence has reached the point that National Security Advisor Ajit Doval, speaking in October 2014, referred only to credible deterrence in describing India's future posturing intentions.[110] While it is still too soon to tell if Doval's speech signified, as one Indian analyst claimed, that "India is shifting its posture from credible minimum deterrence to credible deterrence," it at least highlighted the substantial interest in emphasizing the credible over the minimum in India's current nuclear doctrinal and force development debate.[111]

CONCLUSION

The current firmament and debate over nuclear doctrine notwithstanding, the remarkable continuity that underlines India's doctrinal journey since it tested nuclear weapons in May 1998 is indeed perplexing. More so because the doctrine has tolerated the pressure of the changing security environment, the changing organizational impulses within the military, the evolving technological sophistication of India's arsenal, growing discontent among the strategic elites on the existing doctrine, and changing governments at the center. In fact, three different prime ministers have affirmed the same doctrinal principles over a period of twenty years.[112] India's nuclear doctrine has seen some changes, with the dilution of the NFU pledge and shift from "punitive retaliation" to "massive retaliation" in 2003, but the basic philosophy underlying the doctrine has remained the same. That philosophy is, first, that nuclear weapons are political instruments to deter nuclear blackmail and nuclear use rather than war-fighting tools; second, that India's national interests are best served by a

policy of NFU of nuclear weapons; and finally, that India has a purely retaliatory nuclear strategy even though it may suffer heavily from first use of nuclear
weapons against it.

Although pinpointing the reasons behind such continuity is hard, the votaries of current nuclear doctrine argue that changes in NFU and massive retaliation may not help to answer the problems that currently confront New
Delhi. Inserting purposeful ambiguity in India's nuclear use policy might drive
India toward an arms race but would also force a more ready nuclear arsenal
entailing hair-trigger alerts and launch-on-warning postures, a scenario that
does not brook much favor among India's political class.[113] Moving away from
an assured retaliation posture to graduated use would also entail nuclear war
fighting—a futile exercise. As one retired diplomat argued, "Controlled nuclear
war between India and Pakistan is impossible."[114] The move to graduated use
would also lead to a fundamental reorientation in India's views on nuclear
weapons: from "political tools" for ensuring deterrence to "military instruments" of war fighting.[115] But there may be some other reasons for doctrinal
conservatism also.

First, as noted in chapter 4, an outline of basic nuclear doctrine was already
in place by the time India decided to test in May 1998. During the formative
years of the Cold War, Indian decision makers indeed contemplated various
patterns of nuclear deterrence and coalesced around a doctrine that emphasized the purely deterrent character of nuclear weapons vis-à-vis their war-
fighting utility. NFU was thus an integral element of India's nuclear thinking
developed during the Cold War years. The historical origins of nuclear thought
in the Indian case also point to a minimalistic orientation as far as the size of
the Indian arsenal was concerned. In fact, both NFU and minimum deterrence
were an integral part of India's institutional responses to questions of nuclear
deterrence, as was demonstrated by the conclusions of various committees
formed between 1985 and 1998 to address the nuclear question. Continuity in
doctrinal thinking, therefore, can be located in India's institutional memory on
nuclear deterrence.

Second, Indian strategic decision making suffers from a lack of strategic
planning. Decisions are not made until they are absolutely necessary. Strategic planning is always at a premium in a polity where immediate, pressing
concerns require the time and attention of the political class much more
than vague requirements of strategy do. The post-1998 nuclear doctrine was
a necessity born out of the nuclear tests, and India, as explained in chapter
4, pronounced a draft doctrine only grudgingly. It took India approximately
five years to enunciate its nuclear doctrine officially. A strategic defense review

never accompanied the official nuclear doctrine even though it was supposedly prioritized above doctrine by the BJP-led NDA government. This trend of inaction is also visible in issues concerning national security. Even after several high-level committees on national security—the Kargil Review Committee (1999), the Group of Ministers Report (2001), the Satish Chandra Committee (2011)—had submitted their findings to the government, changes were hard to come by and, if made, were only cosmetic.[116]

Third, India has a perennial problem in the unique structure of its civil-military relations. The civilian bureaucracy dominated by the Indian Administrative Service has continuously acted as the only gatekeeper when it comes to interaction between the political class and the military.[117] The military's concerns are always filtered through the bureaucratic lens; some have argued that rather than civilian control, India's military suffers from excessive "bureaucratic control." Thus, the military's viewpoints on strategy are always at a premium. The fact that many military officers who suffered in the SFC are currently critiquing India's nuclear doctrine points to their sense of frustration with nuclear decision-making structures when they were in office.[118]

Fourth, doctrinal evolution is also conditioned by India's external environment. Isomorphic pressures from major nuclear powers, especially the US, have indeed induced change in India's doctrinal policy.[119] For a start, post-1998 US pressure was critical in India's enunciating a doctrine in the first place. Strobe Talbott's criticisms of the 1999 DND and Singh's course correction in his November 1999 interview indicate that the process of formulating the nuclear doctrine was influenced by an important foreign policy goal: to stabilize Indo-US relations after the tests. And as we will see in the next chapter, during this period India also veered toward signing the CTBT. However, changes in US nonproliferation policy with the Bush administration allowed New Delhi to tweak its nuclear doctrine accordingly. Some have argued that India's permitting nuclear weapon use in response to chemical and biological weapon attacks in 2003 was influenced by a 2002 US nuclear posture review.[120] India's changing missile defense policy, however, is the most concrete evidence in this regard. As Ashley Tellis has shown, India's missile defense policy in 2002–3 was a complete mirror image of its traditional missile defense policy. Although this reversal was not reflected in the 2003 doctrine, New Delhi later in the year formally announced to the US its intentions to incorporate missile defense in its nuclear posture and, by implication, in its nuclear doctrine.

Fifth, one of the most important yet undermentioned factors in India's doctrinal evolution is that many in India continue to view its nuclear doctrine as a statement of its unique nuclear philosophy, which underlines "responsibility" and "restraint" as the basic guiding principles not only of its nuclear behavior but also its historical worldview.[121] India's responsibility and restraint have helped the country to make inroads into the global nuclear regime. India has a unique status "as a responsible state with advanced nuclear technology"—as close to a recognized nuclear weapon state under the NPT as a non-NPT member can get—and it has achieved this status through the Indo-US nuclear deal.[122] The doctrine, therefore, is not just a military statement; it is also a pitch for Indian foreign policy: nuclear weapons "impose immense responsibility and demand prudence and sobriety in how we conduct ourselves in the community of nations."[123]

To ensure that this tradition of restraint remains entrenched in Indian nuclear thought, however, an official defense review is required. More so because doctrines are evolutionary concepts; they depend on threat perceptions and security objectives and, therefore, if the need arises, should be subject to change. These policy decisions require meticulous weighing of various options. With developments in Pakistani and Chinese nuclear strategies and India's increasing technical capabilities, Indian nuclear planners are approaching a decision point, with a response required to the following question: How does India intend to strike a balance between the continued substantial support for minimum deterrence (including the international diplomatic advantages accrued by a "responsible" minimum deterrence doctrine) and the pressures, generated by India's worsening strategic environment and the growing sophistication of its technical nuclear capabilities, to elevate the role of nuclear weapons in Indian defense? This question can be settled only through an official strategic defense review.

As is becoming increasingly clear, proceeding on the current trajectory without conducting a review risks even greater doctrinal and posturing incohesion. As we have seen, the 2003 nuclear doctrine, statements of defense scientists, actual force capabilities being planned and fielded, and remarks by the national security advisor already contradict each other at times. A review would provide a public assessment of the threats facing India; suggestions for how India can best use and develop conventional and nuclear forces to deter these threats; and a clear understanding that nuclear forces attain relevance only in situations where national survival is at risk. In this way, an official defense review would provide a better articulation of India's nuclear doctrine and posture, and the relationship of India's nuclear forces to its broader defense projection in 2018, than is available at present.

India's nonproliferation policy approaches are also of relevance to its profile as a regional and global nuclear actor in the twenty-first century. We will now explore these in detail.

NOTES

1. V. P. Malik, *Kargil: From Surprise to Victor* (New Delhi: HarperCollins, 2009), 293; Kartik Bommakanti, "Coercion and Control: Explaining India's Victory in Kargil War," *India Review* 10, no. 3 (2011): 283–328.

2. John H. Gill, "Military Operations in Kargil Conflict," in *Asymmetric Warfare in South Asia: The Causes and Consequences of Kargil War*, ed. Peter R. Lavoy (Cambridge: Cambridge University Press, 2009), 92–129.

3. Timothy D. Hoyt, "Kargil: The Nuclear Dimension," in Lavoy, *Asymmetric Warfare in South Asia*, 144–70.

4. On Operation Parakram, see V. K. Sood and Praveen Sawhney, *Operation Parakram: The War Unfinished* (New Delhi: Vision Books, 2003); S. Kalyan Raman, "Operation Parakram: An Indian Exercise in Coercive Diplomacy," *Strategic Analysis* 26, no. 4 (2002): 478–92.

5. Gurmeet Kanwal, "Lost Opportunities in Operation Parakram," *Indian Defence Review*, December 13, 2011, http://www.indiandefencereview.com/spotlights/lost-opportunities-in-operation-parakram; "Indian Army Lost 798 Soldiers," *Times of India*, July 31, 2003, https://timesofindia.indiatimes.com/india/Op-Parakram-claimed-798-soldiers/articleshow/104948.cms.

6. Karthika Sasikumar, "India's Emergence as a Responsible Nuclear Power," *International Journal* 62, no. 4 (Autumn 2007): 825–44; Ashley J. Tellis, C. Christine Fair, and Jamison J. Moby, *Limited Conflicts under the Nuclear Umbrella: Indian and Pakistani Lessons from the Kargil War* (Santa Monica, CA: RAND, 2001), 3.

7. Polly Nayak and Michael Krepon, *US Crisis Management in South Asia's Twin Peaks Crisis*, Report 57 (Washington, DC: Stimson Center, September 2006), https://www.stimson.org/sites/default/files/file-attachments/Twin_Peaks_Crisis.pdf.

8. Quoted in Praful Bidwai, "India-Pakistan: Back from the Brink, but Confrontation Persists," *Inter-Press Service*, June 25, 2002, http://www.ipsnews.net/2002/06/india-pakistan-back-from-the-brink-but-confrontation-persists/.

9. On how 9/11 shaped fears of nuclear terrorism, see Graham Allison, *Nuclear Terrorism: The Ultimate Preventable Catastrophe* (New York: Owl Books, 2007), 123.

10. Reshmi Kazi, *Nuclear Terrorism: The New Terror of the 21st Century*, IDSA Monograph No. 27 (New Delhi: Institute for Defence Studies and Analyses, December 2013), 26, https://idsa.in/system/files/Monograph27.pdf.

11. Michael Lauffer, "The A.Q. Khan Nuclear Chronology," Carnegie Endowment for International Peace, September 7, 2005, http://carnegieendowment.org/2005/09/07/a.-q.-khan-nuclear-chronology.

12. White House, "Speech by the President George W. Bush at the National Defense University, Washington D.C.," May 1, 2001, http://fas.org/nuke/control/abmt/news/010501bush.html.

13. Ibid.

14. Ashley Tellis, "The Evolution of US-India Ties: Missile Defense in an Emerging Strategic Relationship," *International Security* 30, no. 4 (Spring 2006): 128. See also Jaswant Singh, *Call to Honour: In Service of Emergent India* (New Delhi: Rupa, 2006), 330.

15. C. Raja Mohan, "In Praise of Diplomatic Exuberance," *The Hindu*, May 6, 2001, http://www.thehindu.com/2001/05/07/stories/05071348.htm.

16. PIB, "Operationalizing India's Nuclear Doctrine."

17. Although Scott Sagan mentions five major changes in the 2003 document, in strict doctrinal terms they can be summarized to essentially three, as outlined in the text. See Scott Sagan, "The Evolution of Pakistani and Indian Nuclear Doctrine," in Sagan, *Inside Nuclear South Asia*, 245–51.

18. Rajesh Rajagopalan, "India's Doctrinal Options," in Kanwal and Chansoria, *Pakistan's Tactical Nuclear Weapons*, 197; "Abandon No-First Use Policy, Security Board Tells Govt," *Rediff*, January 9, 2003, http://www.rediff.com/news/special/ia/20030109.htm.

19. Rajagopalan, "India," 197.

20. PIB, "Operationalizing India's Nuclear Doctrine."

21. Sagan, "Indian and Pakistani Nuclear Doctrine," 246.

22. Ali Ahmed, *India's Doctrine Puzzle: Limiting War in South Asia* (New Delhi: Routledge, 2014), 53–55; G. D. Bakshi, *The Rise of Indian Military Power: Evolution of an Indian Strategic Culture* (New Delhi: Knowledge World, 2010), 224.

23. Bakshi, *Rise of Indian Military Power*, 224.

24. Army Training Command (ATC), *Indian Army Doctrine 2004*, October 2004, https://www.files.ethz.ch/isn/157030/India%202004.pdf; Ladwig, "Cold Start," 158–90.

25. The three strike corps based in India's hinterland were to be converted into eight division-sized IBGs. The IBGs would be a combination of mechanized infantry, armor, and artillery with emphasis on integrated firepower and swift maneuver. They also sought close air support from both the air force and the navy for firepower mobilization. Rather than fighting a full-scale conventional war, IBGs would make shallow territorial ingress into Pakistan. The limited nature of these offensives would allow India not to cross the nuclear threshold while simultaneously punishing Pakistan for its proxy wars. If the doctrine intended to change the structure of the army's offensive force, it also suggested infusing elements of offense in its defensive formations called the pivot corps. One of the major changes in the defense formations was making them firepower intensive rather than troop intensive; additional armor and artillery were sought for these formations to relieve troops for offensive operations. This doctrine later came to be known as the Cold Start. See Ladwig, "Cold Start," 158–90; Joshi and Pant, "India and the Changing Nature of War," 74–93.

26. V. P. Malik, "National Seminar on the Challenge of Limited War: Parameters and Options—Closing Address," Institute of Defence Studies and Analyses, January 5, 2000, http://www.idsa-india.org/chief6-2000.html.

27. Ahmed, *India's Doctrine Puzzle*, 3.

28. A. Subramaniam, "The Strategic Role of Air Power: An Indian Perspective on How We Need to Think, Train and Fight in the Coming Year," *Air Power Journal* 22, no. 3 (Fall 2008): 56–66.

29. Vinod Patney, "Air Power and Joint Operations: Doctrine and Organizational Challenges," *United Service Institution Journal* 133, no. 553 (July–September 2003): 366–87.

30. Bakshi, *Rise of Indian Military Power*, 239.

31. Ladwig, "Cold Start," 158–90.

32. Sachin Parashar, "Manmohan Singh, Musharraf Came Close to Striking Kashmir Deal: Wikileaks," *Times of India*, September 3, 2011, https://timesofindia.indiatimes.com/india/Manmohan-Singh-Musharraf-came-close-to-striking-Kashmir-deal-WikiLeaks/articleshow/9841701.cms.

33. Joseph Kahn, "Indian Premier's Talks in Beijing Signal Better Relations," *New York Times*, June 24, 2003.

34. PIB, "Suo Motu Statement by Vajpayee."
35. Sasikumar, "India's Emergence," 825–44.
36. PIB, "Evolution of India's Nuclear Policy."
37. PIB, "PM's Statement in Parliament."
38. PIB, "Suo Motu Statement by Shri Jaswant Singh, Minister of External Affairs on the Nuclear Non-Proliferation Treaty Review Conference," May 9, 2000, http://www .acronym.org.uk/old/archive/46india.htm.
39. DAE, "Joint Statement on U.S.-India Civil Nuclear Co-operation," July 18, 2005, http://www.dae.nic.in/?q=node/61.
40. Reuters, "Text: Prime Minister's Statement on Mumbai Attack," November 27, 2008, https://in.reuters.com/article/idININdia-36741320081127.
41. "The Mumbai Attacks: Terror in India," *The Economist*, November 27, 2008, http:// www.economist.com/node/12701072.
42. Condoleezza Rice, *No Higher Honor: A Memoir of My Years in Washington* (New York: Simon & Schuster, 2011), 719.
43. Sandeep Unnithan, "Why India Didn't Strike Pakistan after 26/11," *India Today*, October 14, 2015, http://indiatoday.intoday.in/story/why-india-didnt-strike-pakistan-after -26-11/1/498952.html.
44. "Govt Never Made Up Its Mind to Go to War with Pak after 26/11: Former Air Chief Homi Major on 26/11," *Rediff*, November 16, 2009, http://www.rediff.com /news/slide-show/slide-show-1-govt-never-made-up-its-mind-to-go-to-war-with -pak-after-26-11/20091116.htm.
45. Menon, *Choices*, 172.
46. Hans M. Kristensen and Robert S. Norris, "Pakistani Nuclear Forces, 2009," *Bulletin of Atomic Scientists* 65, no. 5 (September–October 2009): 82–89.
47. Ashish Kumar Sen, "Pakistan Making Small Nukes to Target India," *Tribune*, December 2, 2010, http://www.tribuneindia.com/2010/20101202/main1.htm; Vipin Narang, "Posturing for Peace: Pakistan's Nuclear Posture and South Asian Stability," *International Security* 34, no. 3 (Winter 2009–10): 38–78.
48. Shyam Saran, "Dealing with Pakistan's Brinksmanship," *The Hindu*, December 7, 2012, http://www.thehindu.com/opinion/lead/Dealing-with-Pakistan%E2%80%99s -brinkmanship/article14641185.ece.
49. Gaurav Kampani, "India: The Challenge of Nuclear Operationalization and Strategic Stability," in *Strategic Asia 2013–14: Asia in the Second Nuclear Age*, ed. Ashley Tellis, Abraham M. Denmark, and Travis Turner (Washington, DC: National Bureau of Asian Research, 2014): 115–17.
50. W. P. S. Sidhu, "Updating India's Nuclear Doctrine," *Livemint*, April 27, 2014, http:// www.livemint.com/Opinion/rkEybO3sf1wA2vWbxXr0GM/Updating-Indias-nu clear-doctrine.html.
51. Anupam Srivastava and Seema Gahlot, "The Influence of Bureaucratic Politics on India's Nuclear Strategy," in Yoshihara and Holmes, *Strategy in the Second Nuclear Age*, 146; Bartendu Kumar Singh, "Fearing a Chinese Nuclear Attack in Arunachal Pradesh," Institute for Peace and Conflict Studies, July 25, 2001, http://www.ipcs .org/article/china/fearing-a-chinese-nuclear-attack-in-arunachal-pradesh-530 .html.
52. NDTV, "India's Nuclear Deterrent Capability Is in Place, the Country Can Sleep Well: Defence Research Chief," May 4, 2013, https://www.ndtv.com/india-news

/indias-nuclear-deterrence-capacity-is-in-place-the-country-can-sleep-well-defence
-research-chief-521179.

53. Narang, "Five Myths," 148–49.

54. NDTV, "India's Nuclear Deterrent Capability."

55. B. S. Nagal, "Checks and Balances," *Force*, June 2014, 12–16.

56. Lok Sabha Secretariat, Fifteenth Series, Vol. 16, "Discussion on the Demand for Grant No. 31 under the Control of the Ministry of External Affairs," Seventh Session, 2011/1932, March 15, 2011, 149.

57. Ibid., 148.

58. Nagal, "Checks and Balances."

59. Arun Prakash, "India's Nuclear Deterrent: The More Things Change . . . ," S. Rajaratnam School of International Studies, March 2014, 4, https://www.rsis.edu.sg/wp-content/uploads/2014/07/PR140301_India_Nuclear_Deterrent.pdf; M. K. Narayanan, "Lurking Dangers," *Seminar* 665 (January 2015), http://india-seminar.com/2015/665/665_m_k_narayanan.htm.

60. P. R. Chari, "India's Nuclear Doctrine: Stirrings of Change," Carnegie Endowment for International Peace, June 4, 2014, http://carnegieendowment.org/2014/06/04/india-s-nuclear-doctrine-stirrings-of-change.

61. Iftikhar Gilani, "Time to Review and Articulate India's Nuclear Doctrine, Experts Tell PM," *Daily News and Analysis*, April 30, 2016, http://www.dnaindia.com/india/report-time-to-review-and-articulate-india-s-nuclear-doctrine-experts-tell-pm-2207513.

62. See Menon, *Choices*, 105–23. For analysts who saw in Menon's writing a change in Indian doctrine and posture, see Vipin Narang, "Beyond the Nuclear Threshold: Causes and Consequences of First Use" (prepared remarks delivered to Carnegie International Nuclear Policy Conference, Washington, DC, March 20, 2017), 2, https://southasianvoices.org/sav-dc-nukefest2017-potential-indian-nuclear-first-use/#vnr; Shashank Joshi, "India's Nuclear Doctrine Should No Longer Be Taken for Granted," *Lowy Interpeter*, March 22, 2017, https://www.lowyinstitute.org/the-interpreter/indias-nuclear-doctrine-should-no-longer-be-taken-granted. Many argued against such an interpretation of Menon's writings. See Harsh V. Pant and Yogesh Joshi, "Why a Rethink on India's Nuclear Doctrine May Be Necessary," *The Quint*, March 27, 2017, https://www.thequint.com/opinion/2017/03/27/why-a-rethink-of-india-no-first-use-nuclear-doctrine-may-be-necessary; Abhijnan Rej, "India Is Not Changing Its Policy on No First Use of Nuclear Weapons," *War on the Rocks*, March 29, 2017, https://warontherocks.com/2017/03/india-is-not-changing-its-policy-on-no-first-use-of-nuclear-weapons/. For a summary of these debates, see Sameer Lalwani and Hannah Haegeland, "The Debate over India's Nuclear Strategy Is Heating Up," *War on the Rocks*, April 5, 2017, https://warontherocks.com/2017/04/the-debate-over-indian-nuclear-strategy-is-heating-up.

63. Manoj Joshi, "Donald Trump's Review Could Help India Nuance Its Nuclear Doctrine," *Hindustan Times*, February 25, 2018, https://www.hindustantimes.com/analysis/donald-trump-s-review-could-help-india-nuance-its-nuclear-doctrine/story-JV5esVtIZ7wKpT0qbp2M9L.html; Debak Das, "Nuclear Posture Review 2018: Implications for India," *ORF*, February 21, 2018, http://www.orfonline.org/expert-speaks/nuclear-posture-review-2018-its-implications-for-india/.

64. Bharatiya Janata Party, *Ek Bharat, Sreshta Bharat, Sabka Saath Sabka Vikas: Election*

Manifesto 2014 (New Delhi: BJP, 2014), 39, http://www.bjp.org/images/pdf_2014/full_manifesto_english_07.04.2014.pdf.

65. Gurmeet Kanwal, "India's Nuclear Doctrine: Need for a Review," CSIS, December 5, 2014, http://csis.org/publication/indias-nuclear-doctrine-need-review; Chari, "Stirrings of Change."

66. Nagal, "Checks and Balances," 13.

67. Anil A. Athale, "Why India Needs Nuclear Weapons," *Rediff*, September 25, 2009, http://news.rediff.com/column/2009/sep/25/why-india-needs-nuclear-weapons.htm.

68. Nagal, "Checks and Balances," 14. See also General Nagal's comments in Indian Pugwash Society, "Panel Discussion Report on Future of India's Nuclear Doctrine," April 25, 2016, 3, http://pugwashindia.org/pdf/Report-Final-panel.pdf.

69. Kampani, "India's Evolving Civil-Military Institutions."

70. Nagal, "Checks and Balances," 14.

71. Gilani, "Time to Review and Articulate."

72. Nagal, "Checks and Balances," 14.

73. Chari, "Stirrings of Change."

74. Nagal, "Checks and Balances," 14.

75. Institute of Peace and Conflict Studies, *India's Nuclear Doctrine: An Alternative Blueprint* (New Delhi: Institute of Peace and Conflict Studies, 2012), http://www.ipcs.org/Indias-Nuclear-Doctrine.pdf.

76. Menon, *Choices*, 164.

77. Narang, "Beyond the Nuclear Threshold," 2; Joshi, "India's Nuclear Doctrine."

78. Vijay Shankar, "Strategic Non-Nuclear Weapons: An Essential Consort to a Doctrine of NFU," Institute of Peace and Conflict Studies, January 13, 2014, http://www.ipcs.org/article/indo-pak/the-strategist-strategic-non-nuclear-weapons-an-essential-consort-to-4256.html.

79. D. Suba Chandran, "Should India Give Up Its NFU Doctrine?" Institute of Peace and Conflict Studies, June 24, 2010, http://www.ipcs.org/article/india/should-india-give-up-its-nfu-doctrine-3169.html.

80. Chari, "Stirrings of Change."

81. P. R. Chari, "India and NFU: The Doctrinal Conundrum," Institute of Peace and Conflict Studies, http://www.ipcs.org/article/india-and-the-new-nuclear-order/india-and-no-first-use-the-doctrinal-conundrum-4392.html.

82. Nagal, "Checks and Balances," 14.

83. Pant and Joshi, "Why a Rethink."

84. Narang, "Beyond the Nuclear Threshold," 2; Joshi, "India's Nuclear Doctrine."

85. Rajesh Rajagopalan, "India's Nuclear Strategy: A Shift to Counterforce?" *ORF*, March 30, 2017, http://www.orfonline.org/expert-speaks/india-nuclear-strategy-shift-counterforce.

86. Gurmeet Kanwal (Visiting Fellow, Vivekananda International Foundation), interview by the authors, February 16, 2015.

87. PIB, "Operationalizing India's Nuclear Doctrine."

88. Rajesh Rajagopalan, "India's Nuclear Doctrine Debate," Carnegie Endowment for International Peace, June 30, 2016, http://carnegieendowment.org/2016/06/30/india-s-nuclear-doctrine-debate-pub-63950.

89. Mohan, "Interview with Jaswant Singh."

90. Chari, "Stirrings of Change."

91. Raja Menon (Distinguished Fellow, Institute of Peace and Conflict Studies), interview by the authors, February 18, 2015.

92. Ali Ahmed, "India's Nuclear Doctrine: Don't Leave It to the Hawks," *Foreign Policy Journal*, July 11, 2014, https://www.foreignpolicyjournal.com/2014/07/11/indias -nuclear-doctrine-review-dont-leave-it-to-the-hawks/.

93. Manoj Joshi (Distinguished Fellow, Observer Research Foundation), interview by the authors, February 17, 2015.

94. Ali Ahmed, "An Indian Nuclear Doctrine Review: A Third Model," Institute of Peace and Conflict Studies, April 30, 2014, http://www.ipcs.org/article/india/an-indian -nuclear-doctrine-review-a-third-model-4410.html; Ali Ahmed, "Reviewing India's Nuclear Doctrine (Policy Brief)," Institute of Defence Studies and Analyses, April 24, 2009, http://www.idsa.in/policybrief/reviewingindiasnucleardoctrine_aahmed_240409.

95. Nagal, "Checks and Balances."

96. In August 2014 the Observer Research Foundation New Delhi think tank organized a one-day conference on India's nuclear doctrine during which the issue of political resolve was discussed at length. See Pushan Das, "Re-examining India's Nuclear Doctrine," Issue Brief No. 97, Observer Research Foundation, July 2015, 4, http://www .orfonline.org/research/re-examining-indias-nuclear-doctrine/.

97. For example, the then-chief of Air Staff later accused the government of lacking the political will to issue a robust response to Pakistan following the 2008 Mumbai terrorist attacks. "Govt Never Made Up Its Mind to Go to War with Pak after 26/11," *Rediff*, November 16, 2009, http://www.rediff.com/news/slide-show/slide-show-1-govt -never-made-up-its-mind-to-go-to-war-with-pak-after-26-11/20091116.htm.

98. Ahmed, "Don't Leave It to the Hawks."

99. Koithara, *Managing India's Nuclear Forces*, 245.

100. Chari, "Stirrings of Change."

101. Nagal, "Checks and Balances."

102. Lok Sabha Secretariat, Fifteenth Series, Vol. 16, Seventh Session, "Discussion on the Demand for Grant No. 31 under the Control of the Ministry of External Affairs," 2011/1932, March 16, 2011, 98.

103. Saran, "Is India's Nuclear Deterrent Credible?"

104. Seema Sirohi, "A Battle of Nuclear Narratives," *Gateway House*, Mumbai, May 23, 2013, http://www.gatewayhouse.in/a-battle-of-nuclear-narratives/.

105. Indrani Bagchi, "Strike by Even a Midget Nuke Will Invite Massive Response, India Warns Pak," *Times of India*, April 30, 2013, https://timesofindia.indiatimes.com /india/Strike-by-even-a-midget-nuke-will-invite-massive-response-India-warns-Pak /articleshow/19793847.cms. See also Sirohi, "Nuclear Narratives."

106. Saran, "Is India's Nuclear Doctrine Credible?" 16.

107. Excerpts from the interview can be found on Modi's personal website. "I Want to Run a Professional Government: Narendra Modi (Excerpts of the Interview with ANI)," April 16, 2014, http://www.narendramodi.in/i-want-to-run-the-government -professionally-narendra-modi-3173.

108. Indrani Bagchi, "India Not Revisiting Its Nuclear Doctrine, India Assures Japan," *Times of India*, August 30, 2014, https://timesofindia.indiatimes.com/india/India-not-revis iting-its-nuclear-doctrine-Modi-assures-Japan/articleshow/41231521.cms.

109. Ajmer Singh, "RSS Body Wants Narendra Modi Government to Revisit India's Nuclear Doctrine," *Economic Times*, December 3, 2014, https://economictimes.indiatimes.com/news/politics-and-nation/rss-body-wants-narendra-modi-government-to-revisit-nuclear-doctrine/articleshow/45354727.cms.

110. "Will Address Problems with Pakistan, China, through Talks; Deterrence Key to Good Relations: Ajit Doval," *Indian Express*, October 22, 2014, http://indianexpress.com/article/india/india-others/nsa-on-pakistan-china-talks-key-but-also-deterrence/.

111. Abhijit Iyer-Mitra, "Era of Effective Deterrence," *Pioneer*, October 31, 2014, http://www.dailypioneer.com/columnists/oped/era-of-effective-deterrence.html.

112. Menon, *Choices*, 157.

113. Sheel Kant Sharma, "Reviewing India's Nuclear Doctrine," *South Asia Monitor*, May 22, 2014, http://southasiamonitor.org/detail.php?type=n&nid=8084. See also Rakesh Sood, "Policy Brief No. 18—Should India Revise Its Nuclear Doctrine?" AJRC Working Papers, Centre for Nuclear Non-Proliferation and Disarmament, December 2014, 9, https://cnnd.crawford.anu.edu.au/publication/cnnd/5078/policy-brief-no-18-should-india-revise-its-nuclear-doctrine.

114. Jayant Prasad, "For a Clear Nuclear Doctrine," *The Hindu*, May 6, 2014, http://www.thehindu.com/opinion/lead/for-a-clear-nuclear-doctrine/article5979229.ece.

115. Ibid.; Shyam Saran, "The Dangers of Nuclear Revisionism," *Business Standard*, April 22, 2014, http://www.business-standard.com/article/opinion/shyam-saran-the-dangers-of-nuclear-revisionism-114042201335_1.html.

116. See Arun Prakash, "National Security Reforms: Ten Years after the Kargil Committee Report," *United Service Institution Journal* 141, no. 590 (October–December 2012): 504–22; Anit Mukherjee, *Failing to Deliver: Post-Crisis Defence Reforms in India, 1998–2010*, IDSA Occasional Paper No. 18 (New Delhi: Institute for Defence Studies and Analyses, 2011), http://www.idsa.in/system/files/OP_defencereform.pdf.

117. Mukherjee, "Secrecy, Civil-Military Relations," 202–7; Koithara, *Managing India's Nuclear Forces*, 10–11.

118. Shashank Joshi, "India's Nuclear Anxieties: The Debate over Doctrine," *Arms Control Today*, May 6, 2015, https://www.armscontrol.org/ACT/2015_05/Features/India-Nuclear-Anxieties-The-Debate-Over-Doctrine.

119. Joshi, "Evolving Indian Nuclear Doctrine?" 69–94.

120. Sagan, "Indian and Pakistani Nuclear Doctrine," 245–51.

121. There appears to be a division of opinion between the foreign policy establishment and the military on precisely this point. Most of the commentators who argue that India should continue with the current nuclear doctrine hail from the Indian Foreign Service. It is the retired military officers and some civilian strategists who have casted doubts on the effectiveness of the current doctrine. For arguments by diplomats, see Saran, "Is India's Nuclear Deterrent Credible?"; Sood, "Should India Revise Its Nuclear Doctrine?"; Prasad, "For a Clear Nuclear Doctrine"; Sharma, "Reviewing India's Nuclear Doctrine." For arguments from the military and civilian strategists, see Nagal, "Checks and Balances"; Koithara, *Managing India's Nuclear Forces*; Chari, "Stirrings of Change."

122. White House, "Joint Statement by President George W. Bush and Prime Minister Manmohan Singh," July 18, 2005, http://2001-2009.state.gov/p/sca/rls/pr/2005/49763.htm.

123. Saran, "Dangers of Nuclear Revisionism."

6

INDIAN NONPROLIFERATION POLICY

Approaches and Challenges in the
Twenty-First Century

If India's nuclear force structure and its ideological position on nuclear deterrence constitute the first and second pillars of its nuclear policy, its approach to questions of nuclear nonproliferation and arms control forms the third. This chapter provides analysis of India's evolving behavior on issues of nuclear nonproliferation and arms control since its nuclear tests in May 1998. It is divided into three sections: the first deals with issues of nonproliferation and India's policies on mechanisms such as the NPT and the NSG; the second focuses on India's policies on arms control measures such as the CTBT and the FMCT; and the third covers India's reactions to state-specific nuclear challenges posed by countries such as Iran and North Korea.

India has demonstrated a substantial commitment to curtailing global proliferation. However, its method of developing and implementing nonproliferation policies has often been willingly conducted independently of principal structures for global nonproliferation policymaking, such as the NPT, CTBT, NSG, and FMCT processes. India's overall approach has tended to involve extensive actions to address external proliferation so long as these do not threaten important national interests. This approach will likely continue to characterize Indian nonproliferation policymaking and helps explain many of the idiosyncrasies of India's engagement with international regimes and execution of its policies to limit proliferation.

INDIA, THE NUCLEAR NONPROLIFERATION TREATY, AND THE NUCLEAR SUPPLIERS GROUP

Until the 1998 nuclear tests, India remained a perennial outlier to the international nuclear nonproliferation regime. It had actively engaged in the negotiations leading to the NPT in the Eighteen-Nation Committee on Disarmament during the mid-1960s. However, as the treaty took shape, India declined to be part of this global mechanism to combat nuclear proliferation. India's reservations obtained from two features of the treaty. First, it legitimized the nuclear weapons of the existing nuclear powers. All states that had exploded nuclear devices before January 1, 1968, according to the treaty, were deemed nuclear weapon states and could continue with their nuclear weapon programs. This included China too. For India, this amounted to nuclear apartheid since New Delhi had the requisite expertise to go nuclear but had conscientiously decided to remain nonnuclear. Second, the NPT had failed to provide any explicit security guarantees against the nuclear threat from China. Hedging against the Chinese threat, therefore, required India to keep its nuclear option open to ensure national security in the future.[1]

New Delhi's refusal to be a signatory to the NPT in the late 1960s initiated India's long but difficult relationship with the nonproliferation regime.[2] In fact, India went from being an initial architect of the nonproliferation regime to one of its principal targets. After India had conducted its PNE in 1974, a cartel of major technologically developed states combined their efforts to deny India the requisite technology for its civilian nuclear program, lest such assistance could be diverted to a weapon program.[3] This resulted in the formation of the NSG.[4] Under NSG guidelines India's civilian nuclear program came under heavy sanctions. The denial of technology—most visibly the American refusal to supply India with enriched uranium fuel for its Tarapur nuclear plant in the late 1970s and early 1980s—crippled India's civilian nuclear program.[5]

Sanctions, however, were not limited to India's nuclear program. As India slowly trudged down the path of developing a weapon capability including ballistic missiles in the late 1980s, its entire strategic program was targeted. For New Delhi, the MTCR, established in 1988, was yet again a manifestation of the nonproliferation regime's continuous targeting of India's capabilities and strategic autonomy.[6]

With the end of the Cold War, nuclear nonproliferation acquired significant momentum. The global balance of power shifted to the United States, which perceived nuclear nonproliferation as one of the most important issues in post–Cold War global politics. This period immediately after the Cold War, in the words of William Walker, was one of "nuclear enlightenment." Many states, such as South Africa, Ukraine, Kazakhstan, and Belarus, gave up their nuclear weapons; the NPT was indefinitely extended in 1995; and serious negotiations began on the CTBT.[7] These developments translated into increasing international pressure on India to formally join international nonproliferation policy structures and to give up its military nuclear option.

Within India, however, these developments forced policymakers toward a defiant posture.[8] The 1998 Indian nuclear weapon tests released some of the pressure that had gradually accumulated on India owing to its ambiguous nuclear policy and its difficult relationship with the nonproliferation regime.[9] However, as C. Raja Mohan has observed, within a decade of the 1998 nuclear tests, India obtained de facto recognition as a nuclear weapon state with the successful conclusion of the Indo-US civilian nuclear agreement in 2008.[10] India was recognized as a "state with advanced nuclear technology," and the technological barriers resulting from India's difficult relationship with the nonproliferation regime were removed.[11] The NSG, originally conceived to target India's nuclear program, unanimously granted an exemption to New Delhi to trade in sensitive nuclear technologies and materials.

This turnaround in India's fortunes was a result of two important strategic developments between 1998 and 2008.[12] First, the economic reforms promulgated in the early 1990s led to high economic growth rates by the early 2000s. India's economic rise therefore provided a geo-economic heft hitherto enjoyed by Indian diplomacy. Accommodation of this rising power fit well with historical trends in international politics. Second, for the US, despite its position as the chief architect and enforcer of the nonproliferation regime, India was a natural partner in checking the strategic rise of China, the United States' most probable future challenger.

These strategic reasons for accommodation of India in the international nuclear regime were complemented by India's nonproliferation policy approaches from 1998 to 2008. Although India was a perennial outlier to the nonproliferation regime, two facets of its nonproliferation policy were well entrenched by the time it conducted its nuclear tests in 1998. First, even though India argued against the NPT, it maintained its support for the general principle of nonproliferation. India's major argument was not against horizontal proliferation; rather, its complaints pertained to the lack of attention and focus on vertical proliferation within the NPT. Simply put, the goal of nonproliferation was not fundamentally against India's interest; its selective application was. The difference between India's support for the principle of nonproliferation and its resistance to the NPT is well documented in its 1995 Annual Defence Report: "India makes a distinction between the NPT and non-proliferation. While maintaining reservations on the former, India is fully committed to the goal of curbing nuclear proliferation."[13]

Second, as far as New Delhi was concerned, India had followed an export control policy of refusing nuclear technology commerce when there could be a potential proliferation hazard. In the aftermath of the 1974 PNE, New Delhi had promised the United States that it would not export Indian nuclear technology to states of proliferation concern.[14] India maintained this export control policy through the turmoil-filled years of its relationship with the nonproliferation regime. Even as India argued against technology denial regimes imposed by the developed countries, it strived to align its own export control policies with global standards.[15] Prime Minister Vajpayee declared to the world in the aftermath of the nuclear tests, "Our strengthened capability [of nuclear weapons] adds to our sense of responsibility and obligation of power." This responsibility translated into a modest nuclear arsenal, a highly limited nuclear doctrine, and several arms control measures, such as the unilateral moratorium on nuclear testing and a willingness to negotiate an FMCT and CTBT. The Indian government also suggested that even though India was not a party to the NPT or a member of the NSG, it was "committed to non-proliferation and maintaining of stringent export controls" to ensure that indigenous knowhow and technology was not clandestinely leaked.[16]

Immediately after the 1998 nuclear tests, the UN Security Council called on India and Pakistan to join the NPT through Resolution 1172. Although New Delhi rejected this demand, it still moderated its position on the NPT in the post-1998 period.[17] In the midst of the 2000 NPT Review Conference (RevCon), India's external affairs minister, Jaswant Singh, issued a *suo motu* statement in Parliament: "Though not a party, India's policies have been consistent with key provisions of NPT that apply to nuclear weapon states." This was indeed an interesting formulation because the obligations India claimed to be adhering to under the NPT were those of "nuclear weapon states." These obligations largely translated to articles 1 and 3 of the treaty, which restricted nuclear weapon states from supplying nuclear technology and material to nonnuclear-weapon states for purposes other than peaceful uses of atomic energy. As Singh stated in Parliament, "One of the basic obligations of nuclear weapons states under the NPT was to prevent further proliferation."[18] On one level, this statement could be read as a political convenience; having gone nuclear, India was now much more comfortable espousing the rationale behind the NPT. However, it was also consistent with India's approach of supporting nonproliferation principles while boycotting the inherent divisions created by the NPT.[19]

Supporting the nonproliferation principle was also a strategy to help India's accommodation in the nonproliferation regime. Immediately after the 1998 tests, the Indian government initiated a nuclear dialogue with the US. The dialogue was aimed at revoking the economic sanctions the US imposed because of the nuclear tests but also at finding a modus vivendi to reconcile India's nuclear weapon program with the larger nonproliferation regime. One of the first concessions that India offered the American interlocutors during this dialogue had to do with export controls. India promised to enact strict export control laws commensurate with international standards. By early 1999 a group on strategic export controls had been set up to "review the implementation of the existing system and make recommendations to increase effectiveness." By 2000 India's director general of foreign trade had enacted a list of special chemicals, organisms, materials, equipment, and technologies (SCOMET), further tightening India's export control policy.[20]

The real breakthrough, however, occurred with the enactment of the Weapons of Mass Destruction and Their Delivery Systems (Prevention of Unlawful Activities) Act, also known as the WMD Act, by the Indian Parliament in June 2005. This legislation was part of India's commitment to UN Security Council Resolution 1540. Adopted in April 2004, this resolution mandated that all states "take and enforce effective measures to establish domestic controls to prevent the proliferation of nuclear, chemical, or biological weapons and their means of delivery."[21] India had actively participated in the negotiations leading up to the adoption of Resolution 1540. Since the resolution's adoption, India has also used the 1540 committee guidelines to submit its national reports on export controls to the UN Security Council.[22]

These shifts in India's nonproliferation policy did indeed help its quest for accommodation in the international nuclear order. When the US president declared in June 2005 that "as a responsible state with advanced nuclear technology, India should acquire the same benefits and advantages as other states," India's track record on nuclear nonproliferation was held to be one of the benchmarks of its responsible nature.[23] As US undersecretary of state R. Nicholas Burns argued in June 2005,

> India has a record of nonproliferation, which is exceptional; very strong commitment to protection of fissile material, other nuclear materials and nuclear technology; and there's a transparency about the Indian Government's program, which has been very welcomed. India has safeguarded reactors. In Tarapur, for instance, the reactors built long ago by the United States, American firms, and what was significant about yesterday's agreement is that India committed itself in public, very specifically, to a series of actions to which it had not previously committed itself. Actions, which will, in effect, in a de facto sense, have India agreeing to the same measures that most of the NPT states have agreed to.[24]

For three long years beginning in 2005, India and the US negotiated India's accommodation in the nuclear nonproliferation regime.[25] India agreed to structurally separate its nuclear weapon program from its civilian nuclear energy program, sign an IAEA Additional Protocol, and give guarantees to continue its nuclear test moratorium and to negotiate an FMCT. The US, for its part, changed its domestic nuclear laws to restart nuclear technology trade with India and promised to secure an Indian exemption from the NSG on nuclear technology export restrictions. In September 2008 the NSG unanimously agreed to permit India to engage in nuclear trade. In October the civilian nuclear deal was finally approved by President Bush.

The NSG waiver was a historic landmark in India's relations with the nonproliferation regime. As Prime Minister Manmohan Singh argued, "[The waiver] marks the end of India's decades-long isolation from the nuclear mainstream and of the technology denial regime." However, the civilian nuclear agreement with the US constitutes only a partial accommodation. Under the NPT system, India is still considered a nuclear outlier; it is also not a member of any of the major technology denial regimes, such as the NSG, even though it has recently become a member of the MTCR, the Australia Group, and the Wassenaar Arrangement. Post-2008 the debate within India has veered toward gaining full accommodation in the international nuclear order. Two issues have garnered maximum attention: India's joining the NPT as a nuclear weapon state and India's membership in the NSG.

The debate over India's permanent membership in the NPT as a nuclear weapon state reached its crescendo just before the NPT RevCon in 2010. In an interview given to Fareed Zakaria on CNN, Prime Minister Singh argued that India was a "nuclear weapons state, but we are a responsible nuclear power." This was widely interpreted as a call for formal Indian inclusion in the NPT as a nuclear weapon state. As Sumit Ganguly and David P. Fidler argued at the time, "Singh's statement represents the first public announcement by a high-ranking official that India wants to be an NWS [nuclear weapon state] within the NPT. Indian press reports indicate that Singh is serious about this proposal, despite opposition within India."[26] The arguments presented in favor of India's candidacy ranged from its being a responsible nuclear power to the idea that India's inclusion in the treaty would ultimately help in strengthening the nonproliferation regime.[27] Some even argued that reforming the NPT to create a third category of states—advanced states with nuclear technological capability—could be the best way to include India in the treaty.[28]

This debate died down following the recommendations made by the 2010 NPT RevCon. For the first time in its history, the NPT RevCon explicitly called on the non-NPT states (India, Israel, and Pakistan) to join the NPT as non-nuclear-weapon states.[29] The RevCon declaration also reaffirmed that a majority of the states did not accept India as a nuclear weapon power, notwithstanding the Indo-US nuclear deal. What this debate in the strategic community highlighted was a long-held aspiration among the Indian elites: the prestige and legitimacy of being a nuclear weapon state within the NPT.[30] Even though this aspiration remains subdued owing to adverse reactions among the non-nuclear-weapon states in the NPT, it is an ideal that New Delhi would very much like to obtain. However, for the time being, the best possible option for India is to maintain the status quo.[31]

Since securing the NSG exemption in September 2008, India has sought admission to all four technology-control regimes—the NSG, MTCR, the Australia Group, and the Wassenaar Arrangement—which regulate the export of missile, chemical/biological, and sensitive conventional technologies. India's diplomatic crusade for accommodation in these technology control regimes has met with a fair amount of success. It is now a member of all technology control regimes except the NSG. For India's strategic community, however, NSG membership is crucial; winning admission to the NSG will strengthen its claims as a "responsible" nuclear weapon state. Joining that most exclusive state grouping, the permanent membership of the UN Security Council, would also be a boon for India.[32]

India regularly engages leading states of the NSG to argue its case for admission.[33] President Barack Obama endorsed India's candidacy for NSG membership when he visited India in 2010. In 2011 the US introduced a "food for thought" paper to NSG deliberations regarding potential Indian membership, suggesting that the group could waive the normal NPT membership criterion for India. Britain issued a similar paper in 2013.[34] In addition to US support, India has won the support of Australia, France, Germany, Russia, South Korea, and the United Kingdom. Still, India's NSG challenges remain substantial.[35]

NSG membership is agreed on by group consensus, and India's diplomacy has not yet been able to overcome continuing opposition by several members, including Ireland, Japan, the Netherlands, and Switzerland. India is unwilling to yield to demands for stronger nonproliferation commitments, which could include adopting a permanent test ban or ending fissile material production.[36] Given that the Indian package of nonproliferation commitments is substantially the same as it was for securing an NSG sanctions waiver in 2008, the situation is at an impasse today.[37] The impasse on nonproliferation commitments notwithstanding, the biggest obstacle to India's NSG membership is China.[38]

Unlike other major powers, China has not been particularly enthusiastic about accepting India as a nuclear weapon state. China viewed the Indo-US nuclear deal with hostility—as a US attempt to prop up India as a challenger to China's hegemony in Asia. Also, by granting de facto nuclear status to India, the nuclear deal placed the two Asian rivals on the same pedestal. It is not without reason, therefore, that Beijing left no stone unturned to block the consensus in the NSG when in 2008 the issue of an India-specific waiver came up for discussion.[39] China's strategy to effectively sabotage India's NSG membership is by advocating a quid pro quo for Pakistan. Given Islamabad's past problems with proliferation—that is, the A. Q. Khan network—China's proposal has hardly any takers in the NSG. Its strategic merit, however, lies somewhere else. Linking India's membership with Pakistan not only invokes the fear that the nuclear regime is crumbling under the weight of the exceptions being granted to India, as many committed nonproliferationists argue, but also takes care of China's all-weather friendship with Pakistan. China's resistance to India's membership in the NSG is further symptomatic of the rivalry among these rising powers in other global institutions, such as the UN Security Council.

Some positive movement on India's membership bid has followed Narendra Modi's appointment as prime minister. The new government was able to garner support from South Korea when Modi visited Seoul in 2015.[40] Given that the US remains the preeminent global power, its support is critical for India's candidacy. However, seven years into the Indo-US nuclear deal, India has not been able to make a breakthrough. This has led to some palpable frustration in New Delhi; as an Indian expert observes, "The fact that this has lingered on for so many years doesn't speak well of either side in terms of fulfilling their commitments and obligations."[41] Washington has in principle accepted that India's membership in the NSG and other export control regimes would "strengthen global nonproliferation and export control regimes," as was evident in the text of the joint declaration issued when President Obama visited India in January 2015. The joint statement also indicated that the US agrees that "India meets MTCR requirements and is ready for NSG membership" and "that it supports India's early application and eventual membership in all four regimes."[42] Concerted efforts on both sides allowed India to gain membership of the MTCR in June 2016.[43] The fact that China is not a member of the MTCR definitely helped India's cause. However, for India's NSG quest, the two countries will have to push much harder.

As illustrated in this section, India is willing to implement nonproliferation policies independent of the formal NPT and NSG structures and seeks alignment with their export control standards insofar as these do not compel sacrifice of core perceived Indian interests, including, most visibly, India's right to a nuclear weapon capability. The outcomes of this Indian approach will be further examined in the next section, which explores Indian perceptions of the CTBT and FMCT.

INDIA'S APPROACH TOWARD THE CTBT AND THE FMCT

The two major issues in arms control that have huge consequences for India's nuclear policy are its attitude to the CTBT and the FMCT. Just like its relationship with the nonproliferation regime, India's relationship with these arms control measures has a highly checkered history. In August 1993 India played a constructive role in the decision to initiate negotiations of the Ad Hoc Committee on Nuclear Test Ban at the CD in Geneva.[44] India was one of the firm supporters of a test ban treaty in the early 1990s. Similarly, India played a pivotal role in leading the negotiations of the FMCT. In December 1993 New Delhi cosponsored with the US a Canadian resolution in the UN General Assembly calling on the CD to initiate negotiations on a treaty banning further production of fissile material for weapon purposes.[45] This initial leadership, however, did not translate into India's final sponsorship of arms control measures. In 1996 India declined to sign the CTBT on the pretext that the treaty did not sufficiently address its national security interests.[46] Since the CD adopted the Shannon Mandate in 1995, FMCT progress has remained logjammed owing to the reservations of the G-21 states (including India) about including existing stocks of fissile material in the treaty's purview. India had supported this interpretation between 1995 and 1998.[47]

The nuclear weapon tests of 1998, however, paved the way for a qualitative shift in India's posture on both arms control measures. Soon after the tests, India declared a unilateral moratorium on further nuclear testing. During the initial phase of the Indo-US nuclear dialogue, New Delhi also showed interest in signing the CTBT. In September 1998 Prime Minister Vajpayee declared in the UN that India was now looking forward to signing the CTBT: "[India] having harmonised its national imperatives and security obligations and desirous of continuing to cooperate with the international community is now engaged in discussions with key interlocutors on a range of issues including the CTBT. We are prepared to bring these discussions to a successful conclusion, so that the entry into force of the CTBT is not delayed beyond September 1999."[48]

This was indeed a significant statement highlighting the change in India's national position and the Indian government's more positive disposition toward the treaty after the 1998 tests. Several reasons explained India's volte-face. First, India had achieved its primary security interests by exploding a series of nuclear devices. Weaponization of India's nuclear deterrent could, therefore, proceed satisfactorily. Second, a positive approach toward the CTBT could also help New Delhi end its diplomatic isolation in the international community. Last, the US had preconditioned normalization of relations and revocation of economic sanctions on India's adherence to the CTBT. All these factors contributed to the change in policy. However, before negotiations could achieve any desired results, the US Senate rejected the CTBT in October 1999. The effect of the Senate's verdict on India's behavior was palpable. As External Affairs

Minister Jaswant Singh argued later, the "Senate vote was like a pressure valve for India, too suddenly, the sting from US efforts [to force India's signing of the CTBT] was gone."[49]

Prime Minister Vajpayee was indeed facing a lot of domestic pressure not to sign the CTBT. The political opposition was united against what it construed as compromises to Indian security and the government's willingness to prostrate before the US, and the Indian military establishment was also not convinced of the strategic logic of the test ban. In early 1999 the Chiefs of Staff Committee recommended that the government not sign the CTBT. Interviews with one member of the Chiefs of Staff Committee during this time reflect uneasiness in the military about the technical success of the 1998 nuclear weapon tests, especially the hydrogen bomb test.[50] The military, it appears, was skeptical of the yields produced by the hydrogen device tested in 1998. There was some controversy regarding the yields of the tests, and in fact, many foreign scientists challenged the claims made by the Indian nuclear establishment.[51] The government, however, had sided steadfastly with the estimates of the scientific enclave.

Both Indian domestic opposition to the treaty and the American rejection had contributed to India's decision not to sign the CTBT. India continued with its voluntary moratorium on nuclear testing. In September 2000, during the fifty-fifth session of the UN General Assembly, Prime Minister Vajpayee indefinitely extended India's voluntary moratorium.[52] The Indo-US nuclear deal further formalized India's unilateral moratorium. Under the treaty additional nuclear tests by New Delhi may lead to revocation of the agreement.

Many commentators have argued that by acquiescing to an indefinite testing moratorium as a quid pro quo in the nuclear deal, India has given up its autonomy to conduct nuclear tests. The most significant criticism of India's voluntary moratorium emanates from the controversy regarding the yield of the 1998 test. Doubts around the 1998 nuclear tests have been rekindled by testimonies of some senior nuclear scientists. In August 2009 K. Santhanam, project director of the 1998 tests, publicly declared that the thermonuclear device was a "fizzle," or that it had unexpectedly underperformed compared to its planned yield.[53] This sparked a fierce public debate fueled by Santhanam's claim that he had broken his silence only because the Obama administration had pressed New Delhi to sign the CTBT.[54] As a response, the Manmohan Singh government formed a special committee of the Atomic Energy Commission (AEC) to look into the matter. According to one member of the committee, the DAE was able to convince the committee that the fusion warhead was reliable.[55] Despite the public assurances provided by Prime Minister Singh and senior Indian scientists, concerns about weapon reliability make it difficult for New Delhi to accept the CTBT in the near future.[56]

The controversy continues to inform the debate on India's nuclear posture and its deterrence capability in several ways. First, if in the future India decides to set limits on its nuclear program, warhead yields would be a major determinant. The controversy around the 1998 thermonuclear test persists, and there is still substantial domestic opposition to the CTBT. Second, new delivery systems such as SLBMs will require further miniaturization of nuclear warheads.[57] In the face of this technological challenge and the reported failure of the thermonuclear device tested in 1998, India may not find it attractive to surrender its option to test. Last, the military's confidence in India's warhead capabilities will be equally consequential. As a retired admiral has argued, "There is a unanimous agreement outside the AEC-DRDO circles that India will not be able to build safe and reliable two-stage fusion weapons on the basis of a single 1998 test, since the fusion stage of the test was only a partial success."[58] As the end user of India's nuclear capability, the military must have confidence in warhead yields, and this important issue has not received enough attention in the discourse over India's attitude to the CTBT.

As was mentioned earlier, in the period immediately after the 1998 tests, the armed forces argued against signing the CTBT. If a political decision is made to sign the CTBT, India would have to rely mostly on boosted fission weapons. This may compel India to address the question of what it would technically consider "massive" retaliation, as mandated by its nuclear doctrine.[59] These questions have no easy answers, but their existence points to an important debate that must be resolved before India can decide on signing the CTBT.

As with the CTBT, India's position on the FMCT, in the post-1998 period, has seen a positive change. After the 1998 nuclear tests, the Vajpayee government indicated its willingness to negotiate an early conclusion of the FMCT.[60] Similar assurances were provided to the US during the Indo-US dialogue.[61] Consequently, when in August 1998 the CD finally agreed to establish an ad hoc committee to negotiate the FMCT, India dropped both of the conditions on which it had earlier opposed the treaty, bringing its position in harmony with other nuclear weapon states.[62] In September 1998 the Vajpayee government declared in the CD that "such a treaty will not eliminate existing arsenals." The reference to a time-bound framework for disarmament was dropped.[63] In 1999 India also dropped its reservation on effective, multilateral, and intrusive verification mechanisms under the FMCT, which it had earlier insisted on.[64] Therefore, by the end of 2000, India's position on the FMCT was aligned with that of the US.

These changes were also evident during the negotiations of the Indo-US civilian nuclear agreement. As a quid pro quo to the easing of US restrictions on nuclear trade, India committed itself to "working with the United States for the conclusion of a multilateral Fissile Material Cut-off Treaty."[65] However, unlike other P-5 countries, with the exception of China, India had declined to observe a unilateral moratorium on further production of fissile material.[66] The change in India's orientation toward the FMCT has hardly borne any positive results in the CD. In June 2009 the CD unanimously agreed to pursue the FMCT after sixteen years of dillydallying. Since then Pakistan has consistently blocked all resolutions on the treaty. Pakistan's principal opposition is on the issue of stocks of fissile material, which the treaty in its present form does not address. According to Islamabad, a treaty that does not lead to verifiable elimination of fissile material stocks and is only concerned with stopping future production of nuclear material is inherently discriminatory, does not serve the purpose of global nuclear disarmament, and most important, from Pakistan's perspective, renders the strategic balance in South Asia in favor of its archrival, India.[67] For one, India possesses huge stocks of RgPu.[68] Plus, the Indo-US nuclear deal has allowed India to further enhance its fissile material stocks by diverting its indigenous production of natural uranium to its weapon program.[69]

Like the CTBT, the FMCT is intricately linked with India's deterrence posture.[70] India's future policy on the FMCT will be defined by its deterrence requirements: How much fissile material would be needed to ensure a credible deterrent posture? There are no easy answers to this question. While some minimalists in India's strategic community have argued that a total of around one hundred nuclear warheads would provide India with sufficient capability, some maximalists have argued for a force strength of over four hundred weapons.[71]

The policy of credible minimum deterrence is also undergoing a shift. Sophisticated weapon systems and an increase in delivery vehicles will automatically generate pressure to increase the number of warheads.[72] For example, a fleet of six ballistic missile submarines with a capacity of sixteen SLBMs each would themselves require around a hundred warheads. India is also experimenting with MIRV technology. This technological determinism will automatically increase the pressure for more fissile material. However, a crucial determinant is also future changes in India's nuclear doctrine. If India gives up its NFU policy and adopts a retaliatory posture of flexible response rather than massive retaliation, its nuclear arsenal will likely increase. All these factors will determine the trajectory of India's policies on the FMCT.

As this section has shown, India's perceived national interests—principally including the need to build and maintain a nuclear force of sufficient size and reliability to provide an adequate deterrent—play an important role in Indian willingness to fully join the CTBT structure and FMCT processes. While India still has nonproliferation policies aligned with the intentions of these regimes—that is, a unilateral testing moratorium and regular formal participation in FMCT dialogues at the CD—the degree to which its nonproliferation policy is determined by prior broader strategic interests is becoming increasingly clear. Having examined Indian approaches to regime-specific nonproliferation structures, we will now explore Indian responses to state-specific nonproliferation challenges.

STATE-SPECIFIC NONPROLIFERATION CHALLENGES

India's policies regarding state-specific nuclear nonproliferation issues—in recent years, those involving Iran, North Korea, and Syria—follow the same conceptual approach as its policies regarding structures of the nonproliferation regime. Through its policies India demonstrates a genuine concern and interest in preventing nuclear proliferation. However, this interest is conditioned and limited by overarching Indian imperatives, including India's multifaceted relationship with the state in question, in which the nuclear issue is but one of the many interactions between the state and India; India's shared membership with each of these states in the Non-Aligned Movement (NAM), which has further moderated India's stance toward them; and underpinning this, deep-rooted preferences in Indian policymaking for dialogue over force to solve diplomatic issues.

Although India has worked with other states to pressure each of the states in question to resolve the nuclear issue, the manner in which it does so reflects its tendency to prioritize its own strategic interests. This behavior has remained relatively constant since 1998, with few of the transitions to new approaches seen elsewhere in this study. India is likely to continue its present policy of advocating peaceful diplomatic solutions to nuclear disputes while maintaining overall effective relationships with the states in question.

Iran

The Iranian nuclear problem—the most complex of the proliferation dilemmas that the world has recently faced—has posed the thorniest challenge for India. Iran's relations with the West are still today almost entirely determined by its nuclear activities. The West has little interest in Iran outside the nuclear issue, and diplomatic relations between the two still largely reflect this reality.

India is in a dramatically different position from the West. For India, Iran is a necessary hydrocarbon source, a crucial and like-minded partner in stabilizing Afghanistan, and in the words of an Indian minister of external affairs, a "gateway to Central Asia" and India's energy and security interests in that region. Looming in the background of these interests is the specter of China. New Delhi is convinced that limiting its interactions with Iran for the sake of global nonproliferation objectives will only create room for China to fill this space.[73]

Although India is concerned with Iran's nuclear activities and their possible consequences for global security, this concern is only one of several elements of India's relationship with Iran. New Delhi has "de-linked" or "carved out" the nuclear issue from other aspects of its relationship with Iran; that is, the health of other projects with Iran is largely not determined by the status of the nuclear issue. This approach is not unconventional. Washington had attempted to separate its concerns with India's nuclear program from other interactions with New Delhi in the late 1990s, before it opted to implicitly accept India's nuclear force a few years later.[74] India has genuine concerns about Iran's nuclear activities and communicates these in its diplomacy. However, its other interests in the bilateral relationship and its perception that China is waiting in the wings to swallow any opportunity India forsakes on behalf of the global nonproliferation cause limit its nuclear pressures on Iran.

India has a good relationship with Iran that long predates the emergence of Iran's nuclear program as a global concern in 2003 and the subsequent restructuring of Western relations with Iran around the status of this issue. As a fellow member of the NAM, India enjoyed cordial relations with Iran to the extent that its Iran policy has not been a notable topic of concern in the Indian Parliament.[75] Bilateral initiatives of the last six years have expanded the ambit of cooperation to include antiterrorism dialogue and trade and transport projects.[76] A particularly prominent statement of intent in the Indo-Iran relationship was the New Delhi Declaration of January 2003, issued just before the Iranian nuclear issue began attracting global attention. This statement cleared barriers to bilateral investment and prioritized energy cooperation, bluntly stating, "Iran with its abundant energy resources and India with its growing energy needs as a rapidly developing economy are natural partners."[77]

Iranian dissidents' revelation of the concealed Natanz uranium enrichment and Arak heavy water reactor facilities in August 2002 and subsequent demands by the leading Western states and the IAEA that Iran address concerns about its nuclear intentions brought a new challenge to Indo-Iran relations. While New Delhi and Tehran still sought progress on the objectives outlined previously, the political and economic costs to the Indian government of advancing these

projects dramatically escalated as Tehran stonewalled international verification of its nuclear program. As resolving the Iranian nuclear file rose up the
hierarchy of American policy priorities, Washington increasingly paid attention to the degree that other states were pressuring Iran in its evaluations of
the health of US bilateral relationships with those states.

This approach extended to American diplomacy toward India. The US-
India Next Steps in Strategic Partnership dialogue, expanding to the 2005 joint
statement and following negotiations concerning a civil nuclear agreement,
necessarily entailed greater Indian exposure to American pressure that it curtail
its relations with Iran in response to its nuclear intransigence. This emerging
strategic partnership with the United States was in itself a controversial topic
in India, especially among Leftist parties, which formed part of India's coalition
government at the time. Convinced that closer Indian relations with the US involved sacrificing Indian strategic autonomy to the wishes of a new imperialist
superior, the Left opposed the prospective nuclear agreement. It furthermore
spotlighted India's Iran policy as a litmus test of New Delhi's ability to act
independently of Washington.[78] At the same time, Washington set a litmus
test for the Indian government's ability to act as a worthy strategic partner and
align with it against Iran in its global diplomacy.[79] In this way, the India-Iran
relationship and its various components came under unprecedented pressure.

New Delhi sought a diplomatic line that would satisfy these various pressures. This middle approach would be conditioned by the fact that New Delhi
could hardly berate Tehran for its disputes in a treaty regime that India had
never belonged to and had publicly condemned as hypocritical and unfair. As
a further complication, Tehran was beginning to appropriate the Indian diplomatic language of "nuclear apartheid" to delegitimize the nonproliferation
regime.[80] This language highlighted India's status as an outlier and even potential wrecker of the NPT system just when long-desired accommodation in this
system was nearly in India's grasp. Reflecting these conditions, the line India
adopted was legalistic: Iran should fully meet the obligations it had committed
to as a member of the NPT, and negotiations on this issue should be resolved
through dialogue rather than the use of force. India has adhered to this line
since 2003.[81]

However, this has not stopped the US from setting Iran-related litmus tests
for its continued relationship with India. The most public and visible test was
the February 2006 IAEA vote on whether to refer Iran's continuing obfusca-
tions to the UN Security Council. Several members of the US Congress, responsible for authorizing the prospective civil nuclear agreement, stressed that they
would be watching India's ongoing relationship with Iran closely as a marker
of its respect for US policy priorities. The US ambassador to India publicly

remarked on the dim prospects for the future of the civil nuclear agreement should India not vote with the United States to refer the Iran nuclear file to the Security Council.[82]

Under weight of this tremendous pressure, Indian diplomats sought face-saving ways to prevent India's alignment with the United States from looking like capitulation. Voting "with the United States" and "against Iran," as the decision was almost universally portrayed in the Indian media, New Delhi argued that it had toned down the resolution's language and successfully fought to grant Iran an additional six weeks before the next IAEA board meeting to recover dialogue with its EU 3+3 interlocutors.[83] Nevertheless, the Indian government was excoriated by significant elements of its polity and media for this vote.[84] This episode evidently signified India's reaching the outer limits of its possible hawkish activism on the Iranian nuclear issue.

A subsequent Indian vote to censure Iran at the IAEA was merely an effort to maintain a consistent voting stance given the absence of change in Iranian behavior. Indeed, Indian remarks after the 2009 IAEA vote featured largely the same diplomatic language, emphasizing that "the coming weeks should be used by all concerned to expand the diplomatic space to satisfactorily address all outstanding issues. India firmly supports keeping the door open for dialogue and avoidance of confrontation."[85]

India's other activities directed against Iran's nuclear intransigence include responses to the tremendous economic pressures brought on New Delhi by unilateral Iran-focused US sanctions. Under these sanctions a failure to significantly reduce oil imports from Iran can lead to Indian banks' being denied access to the US financial system.[86] This grave threat led to various Indian efforts to prevent this blockage from materializing. India reduced its imports of crude oil from 21 million metric tons in 2009–10 to 11 million metric tons in 2014–15. India cut its Iranian oil imports by nearly a third following a May 2012 visit to New Delhi by then–US secretary of state Hillary Clinton, during which she concentrated talks on urging such a measure.[87] India's central bank canceled participation in the Asian Clearing Union system of payment settlements with Iran. Several Indian firms ceased transport of Iranian hydrocarbons and other forms of trade with Iran because of their fear of losing access to the US financial system and also EU sanctions threatening their ability to insure their businesses.[88]

However, New Delhi has specified its support for only the UN sanctions in its diplomacy and has considered ways around the more aggressive unilateral US sanctions in the past. Ideas included creating official front companies for trade with Iran designed to have no exposure to the US or EU financial systems; encouraging Indian firms to partner with Chinese, Russian, or Kuwaiti peers to render the joint venture more difficult for Western investigators to individually sanction; and doing more business in the Iranian rial currency.[89]

Unlike the West, which views Iran solely through the prism of the nuclear issue, India has other important interests in its relationship with Iran. This explains New Delhi's relative moderation toward Tehran compared to Western capitals' stringency. India's other interests include its mutual opposition with Iran to a Pakistan-sponsored rehabilitation of the Taliban in Afghanistan's government; the Chabahar Port project, which will improve its trade links with Iran, Afghanistan, and Central Asia; its economic and power-projection ambitions in Central Asia; and a pervading sentiment that Indian withdrawal from economic projects with Iran will merely be gifting these to China.

Iran has historic trade links with and an interest in stabilizing its border areas in western Afghanistan. It has long cultivated links with Afghan politicians and certain anti-Taliban militant groups in order to oppose the efforts of the Taliban and other Sunni militant groups to gain a foothold in Afghanistan. Although nominally independent movements, these latter groups also represent significant arms of Pakistani influence in Afghanistan. India has a mutual interest with Iran in minimizing Pakistan's influence in Afghanistan. India has devoted over $2 billion since 2001 to reconstruction projects in Afghanistan and has focused its attention on building infrastructure and training civilian officials.[90] This project is intended to build an Afghan state strong enough to withstand efforts by the Taliban and other Pakistani-sponsored groups to render Afghanistan a weak client state of Islamabad. India cannot afford to let its relationships with like-minded regional states deteriorate.

A related element of the Afghanistan imperative is the Chabahar Port. Sitting at the far edge of the Indian Ocean and close to the Pakistani border in Iran, the port permits India a trade route with Iran and Central Asia without the need to transit through Pakistan. The first delivery of goods from the completed port took place in September 2013.[91] While Indian investment in such infrastructure projects is frowned on in Washington, they are crucial for India to build its regional trade relationships. Following the announcement of the Lausanne Accord in April 2015, two Indian state firms—Jawaharlal Nehru Port Trust and Kandla Port Trust—agreed to devote $85 million to developing container and general cargo berths at the port.[92]

India has several other potentially lucrative economic projects with Iran. An Indian state company, Oil and Natural Gas Corporation Videsh (OVL), discovered the Farzad-B gas field in the Farsi block in Iranian waters in 2008. The field is estimated today to contain 759 billion cubic meters of gas reserves. OVL operated the field's development but had to relinquish its development rights owing to growing international pressure on India to cease economic investments in Iran, plus problems with obtaining adequate development technology due to multilateral nuclear-related sanctions on Iran. Iran established an auction for the Farzad-B development rights in 2014. With a less restrictive Western economic approach toward Iran following the conclusion of the Lausanne Accord and Joint Comprehensive Plan of Action in 2015, Western firms are likely to compete with OVL for the development contract.[93]

The Chabahar Port project, while already substantial, forms one part of a larger Indian initiative to expand its economic connections and influence in Central Asia. The Chabahar Port is planned to be an important node in the International North-South Transport Corridor (INSTC) connecting Moscow to Mumbai with an integration of rail, road, and sea links. The INSTC group was established in 2000 and includes India, Iran, Russia, and several Central Asian states.[94] This corridor is estimated to reduce transport time by up to 40 percent and costs by up to 30 percent as compared to the current route through the Mediterranean and Suez Canal.[95] INSTC will improve India's access to the considerable hydrocarbon resources of Central Asia. The region is estimated to hold 11 percent of global gas reserves, along with significant oil and coal resources.[96] As the world's fourth-largest energy consumer, India needs to secure access to hydrocarbon opportunities like this in Iran and Central Asia for its development.

In opening new ground trade routes to Central Asia that avoid Pakistan and Chinese territory, the corridor through Iran also has important geostrategic incentives for India. New Delhi has hitherto faced an effective veto from Beijing and Islamabad on developing land connections to Central Asia owing to the unavailability of a route that circumvents their territory.[97] For these reasons, India's minister of external affairs in 2012 described Iran as "a gateway for India to Central Asia."[98]

Thus, India's relationship with Iran involved several major elements, of which the nuclear issue is but one. India's nonproliferation policy toward Iran communicates its opposition to continued Iranian opacity over its nuclear intentions through condemnatory votes at the IAEA, implementation of UN sanctions, and less enthusiastically, implementation of unilateral US sanctions. However, India also seeks to balance this nuclear stance in light of the other important objectives India has for its economic and security development, such as stabilizing Afghanistan, diversifying trade links, extending influence in Central Asia, and preventing Chinese domination of its neighborhood. Balancing these interests differentiates India's relationship with Iran from Western approaches toward Iran that often solely focus on the nuclear file. Balance and a preference for a holistic view also characterize India's stances toward the North Korean and Syrian nuclear disputes.

North Korea and Syria

India has a much more distant relationship with North Korea than it has with Iran, and Pyongyang has far less to offer New Delhi in economic and strategic opportunities than Tehran does. India robustly opposes North Korea's efforts to develop nuclear weapons and to use these weapons to blackmail states for economic and technological concessions. However, it also seeks to develop its relationship with Pyongyang in order to potentially moderate North Korean nuclear behavior and help North Korea diversify its trade sources and thus reduce its economic dependence on China. The overall aim of India's North Korea policy evinces the same principles that guide its Iran nonproliferation policy: joining with other states in opposing questionable nuclear activities, but not to the extent that nuclear issues threaten other mutually beneficial aspects of the relationship.

India implements UN Security Council sanctions against technology trade with North Korea and communicates its opposition to North Korean nuclear activities through diplomacy. New Delhi is also aware of Pyongyang's historic links with the A. Q. Khan proliferation network and regularly emphasizes its concern with "clandestine proliferation networks" in comments on North Korea. India's minister of external affairs, meeting his North Korean counterpart at an Association of Southeast Asian Nations (ASEAN) meeting in July 2013, demanded a halt to any continuing nuclear cooperation between Pakistan and North Korea.[99] India's activism against North Korean nuclear developments extends to several instances of North Korean ships' being detained by Indian officials and their cargo investigated for any nuclear-sensitive material. A 2009 case involved the Indian Coast Guard firing live ammunition to force a North Korean ship to yield to the investigation.[100] As some remnants of the A. Q. Khan proliferation network undoubtedly survive, India has strong incentives to prevent Pyongyang from reconstituting these remnants for its benefit and for the benefit of states such as Pakistan or Iran.

However, aside from these efforts to contain North Korea's nuclear activities, New Delhi is also engaged in building other aspects of its relationship with Pyongyang. Indian exports to North Korea primarily include metals, pharmaceuticals, and textiles, and North Korea exports mostly iron and steel to India in turn. Indian trade with North Korea amounted to $208 million in 2014–15, and India was the third-largest trading partner with North Korea in 2013, behind only China and Russia.[101]

India has also sought other approaches to brighten its image in Pyongyang. It received a North Korean diplomatic mission seeking food aid in 2011 and subsequently donated $1 million in food aid through the World Food

Programme.[102] North Korea's foreign minister visited New Delhi in April 2015, meeting with the minister for external affairs and vice president. It was likely that a North Korean request for additional aid featured in the discussion.[103] An Indian analyst explains Indian outreach to North Korea as New Delhi's seeking a status as a counterweight to the influence of Beijing and Islamabad in Pyongyang.[104] Creating economic and aid instruments of leverage in North Korea could indeed strengthen the influence of India's aforementioned nuclear diplomacy. While New Delhi continues to oppose North Korea's nuclear activities, it simultaneously attempts to cultivate political and economic links with Pyongyang and broaden their bilateral relationship. As in its policy toward Iran, the nuclear issue has been de-linked from other beneficial aspects of India's relationship with North Korea.

This de-linked approach also characterizes India's previous position on the nuclear developments of Syria. Syria is a fellow member of the NAM, and an Indian commentator has observed, "Damascus has always been helpful within the Organization of Islamic Cooperation, Arab League, Non-Aligned Movement and such other forums in regard of Indian interests."[105] An IAEA vote came due in 2011 regarding whether to refer Syria to the UN Security Council for continued obstruction of IAEA efforts to resolve questions regarding its nuclear activities, questions that stemmed from the destruction of a secret Syrian nuclear reactor, built with North Korean assistance, in an Israeli air strike in 2007.[106] In considering its vote, India faced a dilemma similar to the one it faced in the 2006 vote on Iran. If India acceded to US pressure to vote to censure Syria, it could have faced a backlash in its domestic politics and among NAM peers for doing Washington's bidding. However, voting against censure would have been hypocritical given India's well-expressed opposition to nuclear proliferation elsewhere. Remaining on the fence, India abstained from the vote. Indian diplomats explained the vote claiming that the evidence for a covert Syrian reactor was not fully persuasive.[107] This position permitted India to continue good relations with Syria. It also demonstrated again that nuclear policy concerns are but one element of India's overall relationship with a state and that these concerns are never allowed to threaten the other planks of a relationship.

In each of these cases, India demonstrated a genuine concern with halting nuclear proliferation. In its multilateral diplomacy at the IAEA and UN, it frequently joins coalitions pressuring for greater clarity from the state in question regarding its activities. In its bilateral diplomacy with the states in question, it urges that the state fully cooperates with the IAEA and UN. However, these stances are moderated by India's traditional holistic view of the nuclear issue as merely one of several different elements in its relationship with a state. Its activism in seeking a resolution to the nuclear issue does not become the prime characteristic of its relationship with a state. Even with North Korea, a state with little foreign policy activities that are not related to its nuclear behavior, India seeks to build additional elements into their bilateral relationship through economic trade and food aid. This holistic perspective toward nonproliferation issues looks set to continue.

CONCLUSION

This chapter has shown that India has a long-standing and deeply held commitment to restricting global proliferation. However, it does not seek to develop the existing structures through which many global nonproliferation policies are coordinated—such as the NPT, CTBT, NSG, and FMCT negotiation process—as an end in itself. India has tended to support these institutions insofar as they themselves recognize India's strong nuclear export control record and communicate a willingness to consider India's institutional inclusion without demanding disarmament as the price of entry. Indeed, the degree to which India has pursued nonproliferation objectives independent of these institutional settings has been highlighted in this chapter and is especially visible in India's adoption of a unilateral testing moratorium and its implementation of new nuclear export control regulations. Unlike many Western states, India can and does consider nonproliferation policy deliverable without specific linkage to or within the above institutions.

India's overarching attitude toward nonproliferation policy, as we have seen, is indeed to advance efforts to limit external proliferation that do not involve the sacrifice of important national interests. This may appear an obvious point but explains the continuing Indian refusal to countenance both its unilateral nuclear disarmament and its virtual termination of relations with Iran and North Korea in the service of global nonproliferation objectives. The current dilemmas for New Delhi in considering prospective CTBT and FMCT membership reflect unresolved questions regarding the requirements of Indian nuclear deterrence. The influence of these questions outweighs any desires in India to advance these treaties in order to strengthen their influence as core elements of the present global nonproliferation policy structure as an end in itself.

This overall approach—a careful conditioning of Indian nonproliferation policy commitments by its broader strategic interests—has lasted decades and looks likely to continue. However, as this chapter has shown, this stance has not prohibited extensive Indian actions in support of global nonproliferation objectives nor excluded its present energetic advocacy for NSG membership and a larger role in global nonproliferation policymaking.

This chapter has highlighted these elements of India's nonproliferation policy approach as part of this book's analysis of its nuclear policies and perceptions. However, the chapter has also supported a recurring theme of the book: the need for an Indian strategic defense review, as particularly highlighted by the substantial influence of unresolved questions regarding Indian nuclear force sizing and reliability on domestic CTBT and FMCT debates. A strategic defense review would help deliver assessments and decisions on these issues, with obvious resultant significance for the broader Indian nonproliferation policy stances examined in this chapter.

NOTES

1. Kennedy, "India's Nuclear Odyssey," 120–53.
2. Jayita Sarkar, "The Making of a Non-Aligned Nuclear Power: India's Proliferation Drift," *International History Review* 37, no. 5 (2015): 933–50.
3. William Burr, "A Scheme of 'Control': The United States and the Origins of the Nuclear Suppliers' Group, 1974–76," *International History Review* 36, no. 2 (2014): 252–76.
4. Richard Braneau, "Engaging a Nuclear India: Punishment, Reward and Politics of Non-Proliferation," *Journal of International and Public Affairs* 17, no. 1 (2006): 33.
5. N. Ram, "India's Nuclear Policy: A Case Study in the Flaws and Futility of Non-Proliferation" (paper presented at the 34th Annual Meeting of the Association of Asian Studies, Chicago, April 1–2, 1982), 70–71.
6. Savita Pandey, "Missile Technology Control Regime: Impact Assessment," *Strategic Analysis* 22, no. 6 (September 1999): 923–45.
7. William Walker, "Nuclear Enlightenment and Counter-enlightenment," *International Affairs* 83, no. 3 (2007): 431–53.
8. Jyotika Saxena, "Regime Design Matters: The CTBT and India's Nuclear Dilemma," *Comparative Strategy* 25, no. 3 (2006): 209–29; Dinshaw Mistry, "The Unrealized Promise of International Institutions: The Test Ban Treaty and India's Nuclear Breakout," *Security Studies* 12, no. 4 (2003): 116–51.
9. Jaswant Singh, "Against Nuclear Apartheid," *Foreign Affairs* 77, no. 5 (September–October 1998): 41–52.
10. C. Raja Mohan, "India's Nuclear Exceptionalism," in *Nuclear Proliferation and International Security*, ed. Morten Bremer Mærli and Sverre Lodgaard (London: Routledge, 2007), 152.
11. MEA, "US Joint Statement," Embassy of India, Washington, DC, July 18, 2005, https://www.indianembassy.org/archives_details.php?nid=568.
12. See C. Raja Mohan, *Impossible Allies: Nuclear India, United States and the Global Nuclear Order* (New Delhi: India Research Press, 2006).
13. MoD, *Annual Report 1994–95* (New Delhi: GoI, 1995), 2.
14. "Joint Communiqué between India and the US," File No. WII/121/14/74 Vol. II, October 29, 1974, Ministry of External Affairs Files, NAI.
15. MEA, "India's System of Controls over Export of Strategic Goods and Technologies," August 1, 2004, http://mea.gov.in/in-focus article.htm?18843/Indias+System+of+Controls+over+Exports+of+Strategic+Goods+and+Technology.

16. PIB, "Suo Motu Statement by Vajpayee."

17. A. Vinod Kumar, *India and the Nuclear Nonproliferation Regime: The Perennial Outlier* (Cambridge: Cambridge University Press, 2014), 76.

18. PIB, "Suo Motu Statement Made in the Parliament by the Minister of External Affairs on the NPT Review Conference," May 9, 2000, http://mea.gov.in/in-focus-article .htm?19220/Suo+Motu+Statement+in+Parliament+by+the+EAM+on+the+NPT +Review+Conference.

19. Kate Sullivan, "Is India a Responsible Nuclear Power?" S. Rajaratnam School of International Studies, March 2014, 3, https://www.rsis.edu.sg/wp-content/uploads /2014/07/PR140301_Is_India_a_Responsible_Nuclear_Power.pdf.

20. Rajiv Nayan and Ian J. Stewart, "Export Controls and India," CSSS Occasional Paper, Centre for Science and Security Studies, King's College London, London, August 2013,9,https://www.kcl.ac.uk/sspp/departments/warstudies/research/groups/csss /pubs/India-export-control.pdf; MEA, "India's System of Controls over Export of Strategic Goods and Technologies," August 1, 2004, http://mea.gov.in/in-focus-ar ticle.htm?18843/Indias+System+of+Controls+over+Exports+of+Strategic+Goods +and+Technology.

21. UN Security Council, "Resolution 1540 (2004)," April 28, 2004, http://www.un.org /ga/search/view_doc.asp?symbol=S/RES/1540(2004).

22. Rajiv Nayan, "UNSCR 1540: A Decade of Existence," Institute for Defence Studies and Analyses, April 28, 2014, http://www.idsa.in/idsacomments/UNSCR1540 _rnayan_280414.

23. Sasikumar, "India's Emergence," 825–44; Jayshree Bajoria and Esthar Pan, "The US-India Nuclear Deal," Council on Foreign Relations, November 5, 2010, http://www .cfr.org/india/us-india-nuclear-deal/p9663#p3.

24. Department of State, "Briefing on the Signing of Global Partnership Agreement between the United States and India," June 19, 2005, http://2001-2009.state.gov/p/us /rm/2005/49831.htm.

25. For a comprehensive account of the Indo-US nuclear deal, see Harsh V. Pant, *The US–India Nuclear Pact: Policy, Process and Great Power Politics* (New Delhi: Oxford University Press, 2011).

26. David P. Fidler and Sumit Ganguly, "India Wants to Join the Non-Proliferation Treaty as a Nuclear Weapon State," *Yale Global*, January 27, 2010, http://yaleglobal.yale.edu /content/india-wants-join-non-proliferation-treaty?page=1.

27. Rajiv Nayan, "NPT and India: Accommodating the Exception," *Strategic Analysis* 34, no. 2 (2010): 309–21; Fidler and Ganguly, "India Wants to Join."

28. A. Vinod Kumar, "Reforming the NPT to Include India," *Bulletin of the Atomic Scientists*, May 1, 2010, https://thebulletin.org/reforming-npt-include-india.

29. 2010 Review Conference of the Parties to the Treaty on the Non-proliferation of Nuclear Weapons, "Draft Final Document," May 27, 2010, https://web.archive.org /web/20111012175829/http://www.reachingcriticalwill.org/legal/npt/revcon 2010/DraftFinalDocument.pdf.

30. Yogesh Joshi, "2010 RevCon and India as a Nuclear Weapon State," *Indian Pugwash Society*, accessed December 19, 2017, http://www.pugwashindia.org/Issue_Brief_De tails.aspx?Nid=290.

31. Yogesh Joshi, "India and the NPT: What Next?" *Open Democracy*, July 21, 2010, https:// www.opendemocracy.net/yogesh-joshi/india-and-npt-what-next.

32. Menon, interview.
33. Ji Yeonjung, "A Path to NSG: India's Rise in the Global Nuclear Order," *Rising Powers Quarterly* 2, no. 3 (2017): 19–37; Saira Bano, "India and Nuclear Suppliers Group (NSG) Membership," *Global Change, Peace and Security* 27, no. 2 (2015): 136.
34. Bano, "India and Nuclear Suppliers Group," 134.
35. White House, "U.S.-India Joint Statement: Shared Effort; Progress for All," January 25, 2015, https://www.whitehouse.gov/the-press-office/2015/01/25/us-india-joint -statement-shared-effort-progress-all.
36. Bano, "India and Nuclear Suppliers Group," 135–36.
37. Happymon Jacob (Associate Professor of Disarmament Studies, Jawaharlal Nehru University), interview by the authors, February 26, 2015.
38. Yogesh Joshi, "China Rivalry Keeping India out of Nuclear Suppliers Group," *World Politics Review*, June 14, 2013, http://www.worldpoliticsreview.com/articles/13020 /china-rivalry-keeping-india-out-of-nuclear-suppliers-group.
39. Saibal Dasgupta, "China Red-Flags India's Entry into the NSG, May Push for Pakistan," *Times of India*, January 27, 2015, https://timesofindia.indiatimes.com/india/China -red-flags-Indias-entry-into-NSG-may-push-for-Pakistan/articleshow/46024533.cms.
40. PTI, "PM Modi's 3-Nation Tour: South Korea Backs India's NSG Membership," *Economic Times*, May 18, 2015, https://economictimes.indiatimes.com/news/politics-and -nation/pm-modis-3-nation-tour-south-korea-backs-indias-nsg-membership-bid/ar ticleshow/47330124.cms.
41. Kanwal, interview.
42. White House, "U.S.-India Joint Statement."
43. MEA, "India Joins Missile Technology Control Regime," June 27, 2016, http://mea.gov .in/press-releases.htm?dtl/26953/India_joins_Missile_Technology_Control_Regime.
44. MEA, *Annual Report 1992–93* (New Delhi: GoI, 1993), 88.
45. MEA, *Annual Report 1993–94* (New Delhi: GoI, 1994), 84.
46. "Statement Made by Arundhati Ghose in Conference on Disarmament on June 20, 1996 on CTBT," in *Documents on India's Nuclear Disarmament Policy*, vol. I–III, ed. Gopal Singh and S. K. Sharma (New Delhi: Anamika Publishers and Distributors, 2000), 1386–87.
47. Shannon Kile, "Nuclear Arms Control and Non-proliferation," in *SIPRI Yearbook 1999* (Stockholm: Stockholm International Peace Research Institute, 1999), 519–35.
48. PIB, "Address of the Prime Minister of India to 53rd UN General Assembly," September 24, 1998, http://www.satp.org/satporgtp/countries/india/document/papers /pm_address_2_un_millenium_summit.htm.
49. Singh, *Call to Honour*, 317.
50. Interview with Indian senior military official, March 21, 2016.
51. For Indian assessments, see B. Manohar, B. S. Tomar, S. S. Rattan, V. K. Shukla, V. V. Kulkarni, and Anil Kakodkar, "Post Shot Radioactivity Measurement on Samples Extracted from Thermonuclear Test Site," *BARC News Letter*, no. 186 (July 1999), http:// www.fas.org/nuke/guide/india/nuke/990700-barc.htm. For international assessments, see William R. Walters, Arthur J. Rodgers, Kevin Mayeda, Stephen C. Myers, Michael Pasyamos, and Marvin Denny, "Preliminary Regional Seismic Analysis of Nuclear Explosions and Earthquakes in Southwest Asia," Lawrence Livermore National Laboratory, Livermore, CA, 1998, https://e-reports-ext.llnl.gov/pdf/903991 .pdf.

52. Shannon N. Kile, "Nuclear Arms Control and Ballistic Missile Defence," in *SIPRI Yearbook 2001* (Stockholm: Stockholm International Peace Research Institute, 2001), 423–56.

53. K. Santhanam and Ashok Parthasarathi, "Pokhran-II Thermonuclear Test, a Failure," *The Hindu*, July 9, 2011, http://www.thehindu.com/opinion/op-ed/Pokhran-II-ther monuclear-test-a-failure/article13736892.ece; Sachin Parashar, "Pokhran II Not Fully Successful: Scientist," *Times of India*, August 27, 2009, https://timesofindia.in diatimes.com/india/Pokhran-II-not-fully-successful-Scientist/articleshow/4938610 .cms; "AEC Ex-chief Backs Santhanam on Pokhran-II," *The Hindu*, September 25, 2009, http://www.thehindu.com/sci-tech/science/AEC-ex-chief-backs-Santhanam -on-Pokhran-II/article16883345.ece.

54. Rajya Sabha Secretariat, "Success of Pokhran Tests," Unstarred Question No. 1524, December 3, 2009, http://rsdebate.nic.in/; Rajya Sabha Secretariat, "Revelation Regarding Pokhran Tests," Unstarred Question No. 748, November 26, 2009, http:// rsdebate.nic.in/; "Why K Santhanam Said Pokharan II Was Not a Success," *Rediff*, August 28, 2009, http://news.rediff.com/inter/2009/aug/28/why-santhanam-said -pokharan-ii-was-not-a-success.htm.

55. Telephone interview with a member of the Atomic Energy Commission, May 15, 2017.

56. Sunny Sebastian, "Pokhran-II Was Successful, Says Manmohan," *The Hindu*, August 29, 2009, http://www.thehindu.com/news/national/Pokhran-II-was-successful-says -Manmohan/article16877789.ece; PTI, "Pokhran II Successful, Insists Kalam," *Times of India*, August 27, 2009, https://timesofindia.indiatimes.com/india/Pokhran-II -successful-insists-Kalam/articleshow/4941553.cms.

57. Prakash, "India's K-15 Launch."

58. Koithara, *Managing India's Nuclear Forces*, 124.

59. Ibid., 125.

60. PIB, "Suo Motu Statement by Vajpayee."

61. Talbott, *Engaging India*, 126–27; Singh, *Call to Honour*, 296–97.

62. Shannon Kile, "Nonproliferation, Arms Control and Disarmament," in *SIPRI Yearbook 2000* (Stockholm: Stockholm International Peace Research Institute, 2000), 443–77. See also Kumar, *India and the Nuclear Nonproliferation Regime*, 101.

63. Arundhati Ghose, "India and Fissile Material Cut-Off Treaty," in *India in a Changing Global Nuclear Order*, ed. Arvind Gupta (New Delhi: IDSA-Pugwash, 2009).

64. Kile, "Nonproliferation, Arms Control and Disarmament," 530.

65. MEA, "Indo-U.S. Joint Statement," July 18, 2005.

66. R. Rajaraman, "India," in *Banning the Production of Fissile Materials for Nuclear Weapons: Country Perspectives on Challenges to a Fissile Material (Cut-off) Treaty* (Princeton, NJ: International Panel on Fissile Materials, 2008), 22, http://fissilematerials.org/library /gfmr08cv.pdf.

67. Yogesh Joshi, "Logic May Help: Pakistan and FMCT (Pacnet#14)," Pacific Forum, Center for Strategic and International Studies, March 3, 2011, http://csis.org/files /publication/pac1114.pdf.

68. Zia Mian, A. H. Nayyar, R. Rajaraman, and M. V. Ramana, *Fissile Materials in South Asia: Implications of the Indo-US Nuclear Deal* (Princeton, NJ: International Panel on Fissile Materials, 2006), 12–13.

69. Zia Mian and A. H. Nayyar, "Pakistan," in *Banning the Production of Fissile Materials: Country Perspectives on Challenges to a Fissile Material (Cut-off) Treaty* (Princeton, NJ: International Panel on Fissile Materials, 2008), 40–41.

70. Indian Pugwash Society, "Panel Discussion Report on Future of India's Nuclear Doctrine," May 5, 2016. See also Koithara, *Managing India's Nuclear Forces*, 128.

71. For some minimalist interpretations, see Jasjit Singh, "Planning Military Power for the Future," *Air Power Journal* 2, no. 4 (Winter 2005): 63; Rajaraman, "India," 25. For a maximalist viewpoint, see Bharat Karnad, *Nuclear Weapons and Indian Security: The Realist Foundations of Strategy* (New Delhi: Macmillan India, 2005), 620.

72. Yogesh Joshi, "Nuclear Stability in South Asia and the Challenge of Strategic Technologies," in *Perspectives on Nuclear Strategy of India and Pakistan*, ed. Mohammed Badrul Alam (New Delhi: Kalpaz, 2012).

73. Harsh V. Pant, "Iran Sanctions: Is India between a Rock and Hard Place? (Policy Q&A)," National Bureau of Asian Research, March 2012, http://nbr.org/downloads/pdfs/outreach/NBR_IndiaCaucus_March2012.pdf; Bharat Karnad, "U.S. Wrong on India's Iran Policy," *The Diplomat*, March 19, 2012, https://thediplomat.com/2012/03/u-s-wrong-on-indias-iran-policy/.

74. Ashley J. Tellis, "What Should We Expect from India as a Strategic Partner?" in *Gauging U.S.-Indian Strategic Cooperation*, ed. Henry D. Sokolski (Carlisle, PA: US Army War College, 2007), 235.

75. Atul Mishra, "Necessary Oppositions: Domestic Debates on Iran," *Strategic Analysis* 36, no. 6 (November–December 2012): 882–98.

76. MEA, "Transcript of the Joint Media Interaction of External Affairs Minister of India and Foreign Minister of Iran," May 31, 2012, http://www.mea.gov.in/bilateral-documents.htm?dtl/19673/Transcript+of+the+Joint+Media+Interaction+of+External+Affairs+Minister+of+India+and+Foreign+Minister+of+Iran.

77. GoI and Islamic Republic of Iran, "The New Delhi Declaration," January 25, 2003, http://www.satp.org/satporgtp/countries/india/document/papers/iran_delhidecl.htm.

78. S. Samuel C. Rajiv, "India and Iran's Nuclear Issue: Three Policy Determinants," *Strategic Analysis* 35, no. 5 (2011): 823–25.

79. Rama Lakshmi, "India's Long-Established Ties with Iran Straining Alliance with U.S.," *Washington Post*, September 20, 2007, http://www.washingtonpost.com/wp-dyn/content/article/2007/09/19/AR2007091902202.html.

80. "Iranian President Won't Accept 'Nuclear Apartheid,'" *Radio Free Europe*, May 11, 2014, http://www.rferl.org/content/iran-nuclear-rohani-apartheid/25380607.html; "Iran Calls Fuel Bank 'Nuclear Apartheid,'" CNN, December 5, 2010, http://edition.cnn.com/2010/WORLD/meast/12/04/iran.nuclear/; Christiane Amanpour, "Iranian President: No 'Nuclear Apartheid,'" CNN, September 17, 2005, http://edition.cnn.com/2005/WORLD/meast/09/17/ahmadinejad/.

81. MEA, "Official Spokesperson's Response to a Question on the Iranian Nuclear Deal," July 14, 2015, http://www.mea.gov.in/media-briefings.htm?dtl/25480/Official_Spokespersons_response_to_a_question_on_the_Iranian_nuclear_deal; Siddharth Varadarajan, "The IAEA Votes to Refer Iran," February 5, 2006, https://svaradarajan.com/2006/02/05/the-iaea-votes-to-refer-iran/.

82. Harsh V. Pant, "India's Relations with Iran: Much Ado about Nothing," *Washington*

Quarterly 34, no. 1 (Winter 2011): 62; M. Mahtab Alam Rizvi, "Interpreting India's Vision in West Asia: A Study of India-Iran Relations," *South Asian Survey* 18, no. 1 (2011): 88–89.

83. Varadarajan, "IAEA Votes to Refer Iran."
84. Rizvi, "Intepreting India's Vision," 88–89.
85. PTI, "Why India Voted against Iran in IAEA," *Rediff*, November 27, 2009, http://www.rediff.com/news/report/why-india-voted-against-iran-in-iaea/20091127.htm.
86. Amitav Ranjan, "To Engage Iran, India Looks to Beat US, UN Sanctions by Being 'Creative,'" *Indian Express*, August 3, 2010, http://indianexpress.com/article/news-archive/web/to-engage-iran-india-looks-to-beat-us-un-sanctions-by-being-creative/.
87. Chaitanya Mallapur, "How Iran's Nuclear Deal Could Benefit India," *Economic Times*, August 14, 2015, http://capsindia.org/files/documents/CAPS_NSNL_15Aug2015.pdf; Hillary Clinton, *Hard Choices* (London: Simon & Schuster, 2014), 440.
88. Nidhi Verma, "India Plans to Bring Iran Back into Banking Clearing Union," Reuters, March 2, 2016, http://in.reuters.com/article/india-iran-idINKCN0W41NU; Uttara Choudhury, "India's Plan to Buy More Iran Oil Will Irk US, but It's Good Economics," *Firstpost*, August 13, 2013, http://www.firstpost.com/business/economy/indias-plan-to-buy-more-iran-oil-will-irk-us-but-its-good-economics-1028973.html.
89. Ranjan, "To Engage Iran."
90. Robert M. Shelala II, Nori Kasting, and Anthony H. Cordesman, *U.S. and Iranian Strategic Competition: The Impact of Afghanistan, Pakistan, India and Central Asia* (Washington, DC: CSIS, 2013), 5, 22.
91. Shubhajit Roy, "India Uses Iran Port to Import Afghan Dry Fruits," *Indian Express*, September 17, 2013, http://indianexpress.com/article/news-archive/web/india-uses-iran-port-to-import-afghan-dry-fruits/.
92. Natalie Obiko Pearson, "With Iran's Help, India Eludes China in Race for Gas Riches," Bloomberg, August 6, 2015, http://www.bloomberg.com/news/articles/2015-08-06/india-opens-gateway-to-central-asian-gas-riches-after-iran-deal; Mallapur, "How Iran's Nuclear Deal."
93. Michael Tanchum, "India Seeks 'Auspicious Re-Birth' in Iran's Energy Sector," *The Diplomat*, August 21, 2015, http://thediplomat.com/2015/08/india-seeks-auspicious-re-birth-in-irans-energy-sector/; Mallapur, "How Iran's Nuclear Deal."
94. International North-South Transport Corridor, accessed December 19, 2017, http://www.instc-org.ir/Pages/Home_Page.aspx.
95. Archis Mohan, "India Nudges Iran on Route," *Telegraph* (Kolkata), March 1, 2012, https://www.telegraphindia.com/1120301/jsp/frontpage/story_15198569.jsp.
96. Pearson, "India Eludes China."
97. Ibid.
98. MEA, "Transcript of the Joint Media Interaction of External Affairs Minister of India and Foreign Minister of Iran," May 31, 2012, http://www.mea.gov.in/bilateral-docu ments.htm?dtl/19673/Transcript+of+the+Joint+Media+Interaction+of+External +Affairs+Minister+of+India+and+Foreign+Minister+of+Iran.
99. Elizabeth Roche, "India Raises Nuclear Proliferation Issue with North Korea," *Livemint*, July 1, 2013, http://www.livemint.com/Politics/LODdydiXBZ0K64pBqL27xJ/India-to-hold-nuclear-talks-with-North-Korea.html.
100. Arun Ram, "Suspicious North Korean Ship Detained off Andamans," *Times of*

India, August 8, 2009, https://timesofindia.indiatimes.com/india/Suspicious-North -Korean-ship-detained-off-Andamans/articleshow/4869270.cms.

101. Department of Commerce (DoC), "Export Import Data Bank," May 16, 2016, http:// commerce.nic.in/eidb/iecnt.asp; Sojin Shin, "Political Risks in India-North Korea Ties," ISAS Brief No. 382, Institute of South Asian Studies, National University of Singapore, July 31, 2015, 4, https://www.isas.nus.edu.sg/ISAS%20Reports/ISAS%2 0Brief%20No.%20382%20-%20Political%20Risks%20in%20India-North%20 Korea%20Ties.pdf.

102. Palah Ghosh, "Why Does India Have Relations with North Korea?" *International Business Times*, December 30, 2011, http://www.ibtimes.com/why-does-india-have-rela tions -north-korea-213592.

103. Ankit Panda, "North Korea's Foreign Minister Makes Rare Visit to India," *The Diplomat*, April 14, 2015, http://thediplomat.com/2015/04/north-koreas-foreign-minis ter-makes-rare -visit-to-india/?allpages=yes&print=yes.

104. Ghosh, "Why Does India Have Relations?"

105. M. K. Bhadrakumar, "Did India Vote 'Yes' or 'No' at the IAEA?" *Indian Punchline* (blog), June 10, 2011, http://blogs.rediff.com/mkbhadrakumar/2011/06/10/did -india-vote-yes-or-no-at-the-iaea/.

106. International Atomic Energy Agency (IAEA), "Implementation of the NPT Safe-guards Agreement in the Syrian Aran Republic: Report by the Director General (GOV/2012/42)," August 30, 2012, https://www.iaea.org/sites/default/files/gov 2012-42.pdf.

107. Peter Crail, "IAEA Sends Syria Nuclear Case to UN," *Arms Control Today*, July/August 2011, https://www.armscontrol.org/act/2011_%2007-08/%20IAEA_Sends_Syria _Nuclear_Case_to_UN.

CONCLUSION

A s we have seen, Indian nuclear policy faces many challenges in the coming years. These challenges have been comprehensively explored in each chapter of this volume.

Our survey of Indian nuclear force transitions in chapter 1 revealed the emergence of a new, sophisticated generation of delivery vehicles. New Delhi appears to have few political boundaries regarding the technical parameters of nuclear force development, which brings into question India's adherence to a posturing concept of credible minimum deterrence. The Agni-V will bring Chinese east coast targets into range for the first time, but DRDO remains engaged in a prospective program to develop an Agni-VI missile of even greater range. Indian interest in multiple-warhead technologies, including potentially MIRVs, arguably further undermines "credible minimum deterrence" as a descriptive term for directions in India's nuclear posture development.

These dynamics are further amplified by emerging intermediate- and short-range missiles, including the Prahaar, Brahmos, Nirbhay, and Shourya. While the Nirbhay and Shourya appear most likely to be assigned nuclear missions, these new platforms all contribute to ambiguity about the constitution of India's nuclear force and increase the potential for adversary misinterpretation of missile deployment and use in a crisis. Even if the Prahaar and Brahmos models are not used for nuclear purposes, they remain especially suited for conventional counterforce strike operations. Again, their preparation, stationing, and launch could be viewed as evidence of an Indian counterforce attack on Pakistan or China, threatening escalatory implications.

These potential concerns are also arising in the air and naval domains. The Sukhoi Su-30MKI fighter has been assigned both nuclear and conventional missions as India continues to develop its network of airfields in border areas. The arming of the Sukhoi with Nirbhay or Brahmos missiles could further elevate the potential for adversary misinterpretation of Indian air operations, including concluding that a conventional counterforce strike is being planned or launched. In the sea environment, the *Arihant*-class SSBN fleet enters operational service in a naval context characterized by contested boundaries and aggressive brinkmanship initiatives. Chapter 1 also studied the progress of India's ballistic missile defense program, which could potentially incentivize Pakistan and China to dedicate additional nuclear force assets to overcoming its interception capabilities.

While India's nuclear command and control mechanisms are becoming gradually more integrated, further efforts are needed to ensure the operational credibility of India's existing nuclear forces through this system. Given the multiple nuclear posturing options these force developments provide to India's nuclear planners, this chapter concluded that a public official defense review should be conducted to clarify growing ambiguities regarding India's future nuclear direction and to ensure that its emerging nuclear force can be characterized by the core posturing concepts of assured retaliation and credible minimum deterrence, as opposed to movements toward a flexible response doctrine and posture.

Chapters 2 and 3 investigated the contemporary nuclear and conventional threats posed to India by shifts in doctrinal thought and strategic planning in Pakistan and China. Pakistan's previous nuclear operative concept of credible minimum deterrence has been replaced with a new framework of full spectrum deterrence, which intends to generate a tailored nuclear threat for virtually every level of militarized crisis with India. The Nasr tactical nuclear missile, as the symbol of this new concept, generates significant nuclear escalatory complications for an Indian conventional strike against Pakistani forces or targets in the land domain. At the upper missile range levels, Rawalpindi is constructing the Shaheen-III, intended to extend its nuclear reach to the Andaman and Nicobar Islands, and the multiple-warhead Ababeel, which will further ensure the technical certainty of a nuclear strike in an Indian environment that potentially features BMD systems.

Pakistan's efforts to introduce seaborne nuclear deterrence are also slowly taking shape and will further complicate India's strategic context. The dual-use nature of the submarines that Pakistan is most likely to use for its naval nuclear arm threatens escalation dangers for Indian antisubmarine operations. Indeed, there is a distinct risk that Pakistan will extend its full spectrum deterrence efforts in the land domain into the naval arena, lowering the bilateral nuclear threshold and threatening seaborne nuclear responses to perceived Indian maritime incursions.

Indian reactions to these developments illuminate the blurring of perceived thresholds in the subcontinental nuclear competition. The Indian military is persisting with "proactive strike" planning to seize Pakistani territory in a conventional conflict. This planning includes exercises that involve fighting through a nuclear attack. The increasing divergence between New Delhi and Islamabad regarding the location of their nuclear thresholds on the escalation spectrum joins a history of misperception in their previous crises.

As chapter 2 highlighted, these developments further indicate the necessity of an official Indian defense review to detangle the evolving threats that Pakistan poses to India and to ensure that nuclear forces remain a last-resort option in addressing these threats. In addition, the different perspectives on regional nuclear thresholds in each country's strategic discourse and evidence that these discrete perspectives are becoming entrenched in strategic planning merit beginning a trilateral strategic dialogue among India, Pakistan, and China. This dialogue would clarify nuclear doctrinal and posturing intentions and reduce the growing risk of these misinterpretations informing crisis responses.

Chinese military posturing and doctrinal debates are introducing additional complexity into India's strategic environment, as detailed in chapter 3. China's naval projection already challenges India's traditional presence in the Indian Ocean, and the emergence of *Jin*-class SSBN fleet operational patrols could add a nuclear edge to already tense naval interactions between the two countries. Recent wide-ranging Chinese defense reforms involve the creation of a new unified Western Theater Command facing India, which will host military forces with rapid mobilization capabilities and a more aggressive posture. Chinese security managers are developing new generations of conventional and nuclear missiles that will likely be assigned Indian targeting missions. These new models feature greater mobility and multiple-warhead potential. Recent missile training programs simulate environments highly similar to Tibet, and doctrinal writings emphasize use of missiles to counteract India's early air and ground force superiority in border regions. To bolster India's military presence against China, Indian planners are establishing new army corps and airfields in border areas, including stationing Brahmos units to pose a credible deep-strike threat.

These mutual developments create new opportunities for misperception and can inform ongoing doctrinal debates in Beijing and New Delhi. Strategic planners are assigning greater importance to potentially nuclear-capable missiles, as security discourses in both states begin to revisit the relationship of conventional conflict to nuclear NFU pledges. In India, a former SFC chief has proposed that New Delhi could retract its NFU commitment in a conventional war with China; in China, military analysts have suggested that a conventional attack on nuclear forces could be treated as nuclear first use and permit a nuclear response.

In addition, Indian nuclear force advancements and the implications of its deepening defense partnership with the United States could soon begin to more directly affect Chinese nuclear debates, threat perceptions, and posturing. In particular, these advancements and the US partnership could strengthen the Chinese school of thought that prefers a flexible response doctrine and a larger and more technically diverse nuclear force. As chapter 3 found, a closer degree of interactivity between Indian and Chinese nuclear force modernizations, in a context of virtually no dialogue between the countries on this topic, could begin to introduce arms race dynamics.

Chapters 4 and 5 described the history and core organizing concepts of Indian nuclear thought and explored how the evolving strategic context is being perceived and debated in Indian strategic circles. Indian nuclear thinking has long been characterized by minimum deterrence, including a strong consensus around the consonance of an NFU pledge with Indian perspectives on nuclear deterrence. The posture of minimum deterrence and the NFU pledge have been visible in official and nongovernmental nuclear debates and planning reviews since the 1960s and were more recently expressed in the 1999 and 2003 nuclear doctrines.

As chapter 5 highlights, however, the two core tenets of the 2003 doctrine—NFU and massive retaliation—are being subjected to increasing debate given the immensely complex strategic environment that India presently inhabits. The NFU pledge is still widely supported, but significant sections of the Indian strategic elite are beginning to question its viability. Several retired senior officials, including national security advisors and heads of the Chiefs of Staff Committee and SFC, have called for the NFU policy to be abandoned, subjected to critical review, or reinterpreted.

A case of reinterpretation is a new suggested nuclear doctrine, issued by a panel of highly respected former officials and nuclear experts, that would reframe India's NFU policy as extending to prohibit "initiation of a nuclear strike." "Initiation" would involve activities such as mating warheads to delivery vehicles. This more expansive definition implies that adversary efforts to ready strategic forces could now be viewed by India as equivalent to first use and thereby permit an Indian nuclear attack.[1] This line of thought would indeed seem to dovetail with the remarks of former national security advisor Shivshankar Menon, who has appeared to claim that the NFU pledge, as he understood it, allowed preemptive counterforce strikes if an adversary were judged to be planning a nuclear strike.

While very few signs indicate that India's NFU pledge will be revoked in the near future, these debates still highlight that the changing security scenario in South Asia is forcing India to rethink some of its doctrinal requirements.

Indeed, as Menon seems to suggest, the pledge may be quietly reinterpreted (or may already have been) to permit a wider range of preemptive strike options. Revoking the NFU pledge, and even merely suggesting that it has been revoked, would elevate Pakistan's nuclear threat perceptions and further escalate its nuclear force production to ensure survivability. For China, expectations of Indian first use could encourage early Chinese counterforce strikes in strategic planning and further pressure Chinese nuclear decision makers to adopt a similar preemption-friendly interpretation of NFU or to revoke the pledge entirely to develop flexible response concepts and forces.

The second commitment—of massive retaliation—enjoys less of an Indian consensus around its continuation compared to NFU. Considering Pakistan's threat to conduct a highly limited, localized Nasr attack against Indian conventional forces, India's promise to visit widespread nuclear devastation in response is becoming more difficult to uphold as a credible pledge. However, resuming the punitive retaliation commitment outlined in the original 1999 doctrine could entail developing nuclear war-fighting capabilities and would still not address the ongoing challenge of deterring first use by Pakistan. These nuclear debates, as well as the increasing pressure they place on the tenets of India's 2003 nuclear doctrine, again highlight the need for an official Indian defense review to situate the country's emerging nuclear capabilities in the changed strategic context of 2018.

Chapter 6 analyzed how India is managing its rise in the global nuclear order as an important aspect of its overarching nuclear policy. The chapter found that, in its approach to both state-specific nonproliferation challenges and the broader regimes that constitute the nuclear order, India is deeply committed to limiting proliferation as long as these efforts do not require New Delhi to sacrifice its other important national interests in the service of this objective. India has supported the NPT, CTBT, and NSG insofar as they themselves recognize India's strong nuclear export control record and communicate a willingness to consider India's institutional inclusion without demanding disarmament as the price of entry. To address recent proliferation challenges, such as Iran and North Korea, India has taken substantive measures to enforce sanctions intended to curtail their nuclear activities.

However, taking a view of its broader strategic interests toward these states, India has continued economic and energy engagements with Iran to counteract Pakistan's regional presence and support India's internal economic development. Indian diplomats continue to interact with North Korea and engage in food aid and limited trade initiatives to potentially reduce Beijing's economic leverage over Pyongyang and to amplify India's voice in efforts to moderate North Korea's nuclear adventurism. India will remain committed to reducing nuclear proliferation, but efforts by the United States and other actors to pressure New Delhi to take actions that more directly threaten its broader national interests—such as the survival of its nuclear force, its pressing energy and economic developmental needs, and the necessity for a rising power to maintain positive relations with core states in its regional calculus—are unlikely to succeed.

This book has argued that all these developments represent conditions particularly conducive to accidental and inadvertent escalation. Risk of inadvertent escalation—in which a decision is made at the military operational level that has unplanned escalatory consequences—is visible in multiple areas of the current regional security context. The first principal factor conducive to inadvertent escalation risk is the looming extension of South Asia's nuclear competition into the naval domain. China, India, and Pakistan have little operational experience of managing naval nuclear deterrent forces or of ensuring safe patrols in contested naval environments. There has been little discussion about, for example, how to limit the escalatory implications of one state targeting the nuclear-armed submarines of its adversary with an antisubmarine operation. These dangers are worsened by all three states' intentions to expand their naval spheres of influence. India intends to increase patrols into the South and East China Seas, and recent Chinese forays have approached the Indian Andaman and Nicobar Islands. As Pakistan invests in a new generation of naval forces, including eight Chinese submarines, it is likely to want to expand its own patrol areas.

Even if the nuclear-armed vessels of each state do not regularly stray close to other national littorals, these developments still create increased risk of nuclear vessels' coming into contact with adversary conventional forces. Indeed, Pakistan may be particularly incentivized to falsely claim that far-reaching patrols are nuclear-armed in order to deter any Indian responses and thus bolster new naval territorial claims. Such a nuclear threat would be an application of Pakistan's full spectrum deterrence to the naval domain, just as the nuclear-armed Nasr is used to deter significant Indian conventional actions in the land domain. The increased risk of intermingling conventional and nuclear naval competition should be addressed by naval services in their training programs and by policymakers through enhanced strategic dialogue.

The second area of inadvertent escalation risk identified in this book is the rising prominence of dual-use platforms as potential nuclear delivery vehicles. In the realm of seaborne deterrence, the Type-041 Chinese submarine model is a likely candidate to serve as part of Pakistan's emerging nuclear force, as it simultaneously constitutes the core of the next generation of Rawalpindi's conventional naval projection. The Babur cruise missile and the C-802 antiship missile could also receive dual conventional and nuclear assignments. In India, Sukhoi Su-30MKI fighters have been allocated nuclear missions by the SFC, and they are an essential component of the IAF's deep strike planning. Furthermore, the Brahmos, Nirbhay, and Prahaar missiles could all be designated with nuclear roles or could be perceived as having nuclear roles by adversaries. This trend is also highlighted in Chinese strategic planning. Conventionally armed variants of DF-21 missiles, for example, likely have Indian nuclear targeting missions. These developments increase ambiguities among adversaries regarding the true constitution of regional nuclear forces and create risk of misperception of the nuclear significance of an adversary missile movement or launch.

These transitions link with the third area of growing inadvertent escalation risk: the rising interest of China, India, and Pakistan in early consequential missile strikes on enemy territory to seize the operational initiative. This thinking assigns increased importance to dual-use missile platforms in conventional orders of battle and to efforts to quickly locate and destroy adversary missile units to avoid their use. In China, military analysis of potential conflict scenarios with India has focused on using conventional missile strikes to counteract Indian air and ground force advantages in border areas. More broadly, Chinese strategic thought has emphasized the heavy early use of conventional missile attacks on enemy command hubs, population centers, and significant force concentrations to ensure conflict termination on its terms. These targets could include Indian bases or forces that have nuclear roles, such as the IAF Ambala base. Such tactics could also force a significant degradation of Indian conventional forces in the initial stages of conflict, placing intracrisis pressure on its nuclear threshold. In India, the Prahaar and Brahmos are attaining increasing significance in Indian Army and IAF forward strike planning and are well-suited to targeting enemy missile units. Retired Indian military officials have indicated that destruction of adversary missile capabilities is indeed an early priority in conflict scenario planning and that they do not differentiate between the conventional and potential nuclear missions of these targets in attaining this aim. Pakistan is assessed to be likely to integrate conventionally armed Babur cruise missiles into its strike planning against India.

These shifts create a danger of inadvertent counterforce strikes and additional room for crisis misperception in adversaries' determination of the mission of missile deployments or launches. Moreover, the high-intensity, low-duration conflict promised by such emphases on early missile strikes threatens to pressure the nuclear thresholds of all three states if they judge that their conventional defenses have been substantively and unexpectedly eroded at only the early stages of the exchange.

These three inadvertent escalation risks are joined, and amplified, by two accidental escalation concerns. Accidental escalation, as defined in this book, emphasizes the implications of misperceptions by political leaders and security communities, rather than by military operational commanders, for unplanned escalation dynamics. The first area of inadvertent escalation concern is aggressive trends in the doctrinal debates of China, India, and Pakistan. In China a school of nuclear thought that urges abandonment of the NFU policy and building of a larger and more diversified nuclear force to ensure China's general deterrence has emerged. This school draws some of its argumentative power from an assessment that China's surrounding strategic environment, including the credibility of Indian nuclear forces, is becoming more threatening. Should such thinking gain ground in Chinese doctrinal planning, it would be far more difficult for Indian security managers to discern which operations and targets could approach China's nuclear threshold. As covered in chapters 4 and 5, there exist similar growing pressures in Indian strategic discourse to adopt a flexible response doctrine and nuclear war-fighting capabilities. These pressures coincide with the recent claims by some scholars that Indian decision makers may have reinterpreted their understanding of NFU to enable preemptive counterforce strikes and with development of new dual-use platforms, such as the Shourya, Prahaar, Brahmos, and Nirbhay missiles. Watching these developments, security planners in Pakistan and China may conclude that Indian nuclear force capabilities no longer correspond with a credible minimum deterrence posture and NFU pledge and may further expand their forces to prepare for nuclear war fighting. Doctrinal transitions in Pakistan are more undeniable. The new full spectrum deterrence concept, in threatening nuclear escalation in most Indian conventional attack scenarios, significantly elevates escalation dangers in the subcontinent. These dangers are not alleviated by Indian efforts to develop proactive strike concepts that fight through first nuclear use by Pakistan, signifying core differences between New Delhi and Rawalpindi regarding strategic stability.

These nuclear debates and doctrinal transitions are exacerbated by the second area of accidental escalation risk: the near-absence of regional strategic dialogue, denying policymakers opportunities to reduce the dangers arising from each of the inadvertent and accidental escalation concerns. Instituting a dialogue would help all three capitals better determine adversary nuclear and conventional intentions and perceptions; potentially lead to the development of CBMs and crisis resolution mechanisms; and reduce the risk of unplanned escalation based on misperceptions taking root in a conflict.

Early topics for discussion, based on the developments outlined in this book, could include the meaning of the doctrinal concepts of NFU, full spectrum

deterrence, minimum deterrence, and credible minimum deterrence as decision makers apply them in strategic planning. This could lead to interactions
regarding how each state would view significant conventional strikes, including those on nuclear or nuclear-capable bases and units, in relationship to their
nuclear thresholds. As this dialogue advanced, more sensitive topics could include listing the precise delivery vehicle types that constitute national nuclear
forces so as to reduce the risk of inadvertent targeting of nuclear units and
the misperception of conventional force movements or attacks in the early
stages of a nuclear strike. Procedures to enable the safe operation of seaborne
nuclear forces, including demarcating the likely patrol areas and units consti-
tuting these forces, could also be discussed. During the dialogue, India, China,
and Pakistan could develop protocols to deconflict patrol routes and manage
scenarios in which a nuclear-armed vessel comes into contact with adversary
conventional forces.

As mutual strategic trust developed through regular iterations of this dialogue and progress on these concerns, further initiatives could be adopted to
address the growing risks of nuclear misperception highlighted in this book.
Negotiating a regional flight-test pre-notification agreement, incorporating
both ballistic and cruise missile tests, would reduce the potential for missile
test launches to be read as initial nuclear strikes. Dialogues on BMD intentions,
including potential limits on the systems fielded and areas protected, could
curtail a potential source of demand for larger nuclear arsenals with multiple-
warhead capabilities. The three states could also agree to structurally disag-
gregate their conventional and nuclear forces, with platforms assigned to the
two separate missions located at different bases and operating with different
preparation and movement signatures as far as is practicable.

Although decision makers in all three capitals may be tempted to increase
the ambiguity that new dual-use platforms promise at land or sea—for example, to bolster conventional brinkmanship by suggesting to the adversary that a
platform involved is nuclear-armed—this risks activating one or several of the
unplanned escalatory dynamics. As Catherine Kelleher argued regarding the
North Atlantic Treaty Organization–Soviet context, clearly dividing nuclear
and conventional forces permits a state to better signal the precise escalatory
rung of a conflict to an adversary and thus avoid unplanned escalation and aid
crisis resolution efforts.[2] Following the same logic, deliberate conventional targeting of nuclear forces should also be avoided by all three states.

As well as arguing that India attempt to initiate a trilateral dialogue, this
book has argued that Indian security would be furthermore well served by conducting a public official defense review. India's nuclear doctrine has not been
updated since 2003, and its general defense policy and force development have

never been subjected to a review process. Pressures to assign a more expansive role to nuclear weapons in India's nuclear doctrinal debate emanate from a concern that Indian conventional force modernization is not keeping up with the evolving threats posed by Pakistan and China. A public official defense review would include new assessments of the specific strategic challenges posed by China and Pakistan, both conventional and nuclear, and of which threats are best met by conventional and nuclear defenses, respectively. This public dis-aggregation of threats, in line with the structural detangling of conventional from nuclear forces suggested previously, should ultimately reiterate the historical Indian perspective of nuclear weapons' serving only a last-resort role, with an assured retaliation rather than war-fighting posture. This review could further lead to political limits on force size and destructive capacity in train with this rejection of a nuclear war-fighting concept.

India's future nuclear policy will necessarily be a significant part of its growing influence in international politics in the twenty-first century. Renewed effort to conduct an official public defense review and to establish trilateral strategic dialogue is required. A review and dialogue will help reduce the risk of India's rise being complicated by the challenges of its strategic environment and accidental or inadvertent escalation arising from misinterpretation of these challenges. As India's nuclear context obtains increasing significance in its global ascent, New Delhi will need to pay close attention to addressing these concerns in the coming years.

NOTES

1. Institute of Peace and Conflict Studies, *India's Nuclear Doctrine*.
2. Catherine McArdle Kelleher, "Thresholds and Theologies: The Need for Critical Reassessment," *Survival* 26, no. 4 (1984): 159–60.

SELECTED BIBLIOGRAPHY

PRIMARY SOURCES

Archives

Central Intelligence Agency, Freedom of Information Act Collection.
Haksar, P. N. Papers. Nehru Memorial Museum and Library, New Delhi.
Kaul, T. N. Papers. Nehru Memorial Museum and Library, New Delhi.
Ministry of External Affairs Files. National Archives of India, New Delhi.
Mitra, Asok. Papers. Nehru Memorial Museum and Library, New Delhi.
Nehru, B. K. Papers. Nehru Memorial Museum and Library, New Delhi.
Nuclear Proliferation International History Project. Woodrow Wilson Center, Washington, DC.
Prime Minister Secretariat Files. National Archives of India, New Delhi.

Government Publications: China

Ministry of Foreign Affairs. "Foreign Ministry Spokesperson Hua Chunying's Regular Press Conference." December 27, 2016.
State Council Information Office. *China's Military Strategy*. Beijing: Government of the People's Republic of China, 2015.

Government Publications: India

Cabinet Secretariat. "Composition of Cabinet Committees." September 11, 2017.
Defence Research and Development Organisation (DRDO). *IGMDP: Integrated Guided Missile Development Program*. New Delhi: DRDO, 2008.
Department of Atomic Energy. "Joint Statement on U.S.-India Civil Nuclear Co-operation." July 18, 2005.
Department of Commerce. "Export Import Data Bank." May 16, 2016.
Government of India and Islamic Republic of Iran. "The New Delhi Declaration." January 25, 2003.
Indian Army Training Command. *Indian Army Doctrine 2004*. October 2004.
Indian Navy. *Ensuring Secure Seas: Indian Maritime Security Strategy*. New Delhi: Government of India, 2015.
———. *Freedom to Use the Seas: India's Maritime Military Strategy*. New Delhi: Government of India, 2007.
———. *Indian Maritime Doctrine*. INBR 8. New Delhi: Government of India, 2004.

Kargil Review Committee. *Kargil Review Committee Report*. New Delhi: Government of India, 1999.

Lok Sabha Secretariat, Fifteenth Series, XVI, Seventh Session, 2011/1932, March 15 and 16, 2011.

Malik, V. P. "National Seminar on the Challenge of Limited War: Parameters and Options—Closing Address." New Delhi: Institute of Defence Studies and Analyses, January 5, 2000.

Manohar, B., B. S. Tomar, S. S. Rattan, V. K. Shukla, V. V. Kulkarni, and Anil Kakodkar. "Post Shot Radioactivity Measurement on Samples Extracted from Thermonuclear Test Site." *BARC News Letter*, no. 186 (July 1999).

Ministry of Defence. *Annual Report 1994–95*. New Delhi: Government of India, 1995.

———. *Annual Report 2013–14*. New Delhi: Government of India, 2014.

———. *Annual Report 2014–15*. New Delhi: Government of India, 2015.

Ministry of External Affairs. *Annual Report 1992–93*. New Delhi: Government of India, 1993.

———. *Annual Report 1993–94*. New Delhi: Government of India, 1994.

———. *Annual Report 1999–2000*. New Delhi: Government of India, 2000.

———. "India Joins Missile Technology Control Regime." June 27, 2016.

———. "India's System of Controls over Export of Strategic Goods and Technologies." August 1, 2004.

———. "Indo-US Joint Statement." July 18, 2005.

———. "Official Spokesperson's Response to a Question on the Iranian Nuclear Deal." July 14, 2015.

———. "Opening Remarks by National Security Advisor Mr. Brajesh Mishra at the Release of Draft Indian Nuclear Doctrine." August 17, 1999.

———. "Statement by H.E. Ms. Savitri Kunadi, Permanent Representative of India to the United Nations in Geneva at the General Debate in the First Committee." October 15, 1999.

———. "Transcript of the Joint Media Interaction of External Affairs Minister of India and Foreign Minister of Iran." May 31, 2012.

National Security Advisory Board. "Draft Report of National Security Advisory Board on Indian Nuclear Doctrine." August 17, 1999.

Press Information Bureau. "Address of the Prime Minister of India to 53rd UN General Assembly." September 24, 1998.

———. "Cabinet Committee on Security Reviews Progress in Operationalizing India's Nuclear Doctrine." January 4, 2003.

———. "Evolution of India's Nuclear Policy: Paper Laid on the Table of the Lok Sabha." May 27, 1998.

———. "PM's Statement in Parliament on 'Bilateral Talks with United States.'" December 15, 1998.

———. "Road Building along China Borders." May 12, 2015.

———. "Suo Motu Statement by Shri Jaswant Singh, Minister of External Affairs on the Nuclear Non-Proliferation Treaty Review Conference." May 9, 2000.

———. "Suo Motu Statement by the Prime Minister Shri Atal Bihari Vajpayee in Parliament." May 27, 1998.

Rajya Sabha. "Revelation regarding Pokhran Tests." Unstarred Question No. 748. November 26, 2009.

———. "Success of Pokhran Tests." Unstarred Question No. 1524. December 3, 2009.

"Statement Made by Arundhati Ghose in Conference on Disarmament on June 20, 1996, on CTBT." In *Documents on India's Nuclear Disarmament Policy*, vol. I–III, edited by Gopal Singh and S. K. Sharma, 1386–87. New Delhi: Anamika Publishers and Distributors, 2000.

Swamy, Subramaniam. "India's Nuclear Strategy in the Nineteen Seventies." In *Nuclear Weapons: A Compilation Prepared by the Department of Atomic Energy*, edited by Department of Atomic Energy, 201–19. Bombay: Government of India, November 1970.

Government Publications: Pakistan

Inter Services Public Relations. "Meeting of the National Command Authority," news release. September 9, 2015.

———. "Naval Chief Inaugurates Naval Strategic Force Headquarters." May 19, 2012.

———. Press Release No. PR-10/2017-ISPR. January 9, 2017.

———. Press Release No. PR-34/2017-ISPR. January 24, 2017.

———. "Shaheen 3 Missile Test." March 9, 2015.

———. "22nd Meeting of the National Command Authority." News release. February 24, 2016.

Khan, Muhammad. "From Cold Start to Cold Storage!" Inter Services Public Relations, November 2013.

Ministry of Planning, Development and Reform. "CPEC Is a National Project: Ahsan Iqbal." January 5, 2016.

Government Publications: United States

Defense Security Cooperation Agency. "Pakistan—Refurbishment of Oliver Hazard Perry Class Frigate." February 19, 2010.

Department of State. "Briefing on the Signing of Global Partnership Agreement between the United States and India." June 19, 2005.

Grimmett, Richard F. *U.S. Arms Sales to Pakistan*, RS22757. Washington, DC: Congressional Research Service, 2009.

———. *U.S. Defense Articles and Services Supplied to Foreign Recipients: Restrictions on Their Use*, RL30982. Washington, DC: Congressional Research Service, 2005.

National Air and Space Intelligence Center. *Ballistic and Cruise Missile Threat 2009*. Wright-Patterson Air Force Base, OH: National Air and Space Intelligence Center, 2009.

Office of Naval Intelligence. *The PLA Navy: New Capabilities and Missions for the 21st Century*. Washington, DC: US Government Printing Office, 2015.

Office of the Secretary of Defense. *Military and Security Developments Involving the People's Republic of China 2015*. Washington, DC: US Government Printing Office, 2015.

Rinehart, Ian E. *The Chinese Military: Overview and Issues for Congress*, R44196. Washington, DC: Congressional Research Service, 2016.

US-China Economic and Security Review Commission. *2015 Report to Congress*. Washington, DC: US-China Economic and Security Review Commission, 2015.

Walters, William R., Arthur J. Rodgers, Kevin Mayeda, Stephen C. Myers, Michael Pasyamos, and Marvin Denny. "Preliminary Regional Seismic Analysis of Nuclear Explosions and Earthquakes in Southwest Asia." Livermore, CA: Lawrence Livermore National Laboratory, 1998.

White House. "Joint Statement by President George W. Bush and Prime Minister Manmohan Singh." July 18, 2005.

———. "Speech by the President George W. Bush at the National Defense University, Washington D.C." May 1, 2001.

———. "U.S.-India Joint Statement: Shared Effort; Progress for All." January 25, 2015.

Selected Bibliography

International Organizations

2010 Review Conference of the Parties to the Treaty on the Non-proliferation of Nuclear Weapons. "Draft Final Document." May 27, 2010.

International Atomic Energy Agency. "Implementation of the NPT Safeguards Agreement in the Syrian Arab Republic: Report by the Director General (GOV/2012/42)." August 30, 2012.

UN Security Council. "Resolution 1540 (2004)." April 28, 2004.

INTERVIEWS

Interview by telephone with a member of the Atomic Energy Commission, New Delhi, April 23, 2017.

Interview with former member of the NSAB, New Delhi, October 17, 2015.

Interview with Indian senior military official, Mumbai, March 21, 2016.

Interview with member of the Sundarji Committee, New Delhi, October 17, 2015.

Interview with senior nuclear scientist, Mumbai, April 9, 2017.

Jacob, Happymon (Associate Professor of Disarmament Studies, Jawaharlal Nehru University), interview by the authors, New Delhi, February 26, 2015.

Joshi, Manoj (Distinguished Fellow, Observer Research Foundation), interview by the authors, New Delhi, February 17, 2015.

Kanwal, Gurmeet (Visiting Fellow, Vivekananda International Foundation), interview by the authors, New Delhi, February 16, 2015.

Karnad, Bharat (Research Professor in National Security Studies, Centre for Policy Research, and former member, NSAB), interview by the authors, New Delhi, November 22, 2014.

Menon, Raja (Distinguished Fellow, Institute of Peace and Conflict Studies), interview by the authors, February 18, 2015.

SECONDARY SOURCES

Ahmed, Ali. *India's Doctrine Puzzle: Limiting War in South Asia*. New Delhi: Routledge, 2014.

Allison, Graham. *Nuclear Terrorism: The Ultimate Preventable Catastrophe*. New York: Owl Books, 2007.

Bakshi, G. D. *The Rise of Indian Military Power: Evolution of an Indian Strategic Culture*. New Delhi: Knowledge World, 2010.

Bano, Saira. "India and Nuclear Suppliers Group (NSG) Membership." *Global Change, Peace and Security* 27, no. 2 (2015): 123–37.

Basrur, Rajesh. *Minimum Deterrence and India's National Security*. Stanford, CA: Stanford University Press, 2006.

Berger, Andrea. *The P-5 Nuclear Dialogue: Five Years On*. London: Royal United Services Institute, 2014.

Bhalla, Puneet. "India Chooses Rafale." *Scholar Warrior*, Spring 2012, 139–44.

Bommakanti, Kartik. "Coercion and Control: Explaining India's Victory in Kargil War." *India Review* 10, no. 3 (2011): 283–328.

Bracken, Paul. *The Second Nuclear Age: Strategy, Danger, and the New Power Politics*. New York: Times Books, 2012.

Braneau, Richard. "Engaging a Nuclear India: Punishment, Reward and Politics of Non-Proliferation." *Journal of International and Public Affairs* 17, no. 1 (2006): 27–46.

Bundy, McGeorge. *Danger and Survival: Choices about the Bomb in the First Fifty Years*. New York: Random House, 1988.

Burr, William. "A Scheme of 'Control': The United States and the Origins of the Nuclear Suppliers' Group, 1974–76." *International History Review* 36, no. 2 (2014): 252–76.

Cai Penghong. "China's Evolving Overseas Interests and Peaceful Competition." In *Beyond the Wall: Chinese Far Seas Operations*, edited by Peter A. Dutton and Ryan D. Martinson, 63–72. Newport, RI: US Naval War College, 2015.

Chakma, Bhumitra. "Escalation Control, Deterrence Diplomacy and America's Role in South Asia's Nuclear Crises." *Contemporary Security Policy* 33, no. 3 (2012): 554–76.

Chase, Michael S., Jeffrey Engstrom, Tai Ming Cheung, Kristen A. Gunness, Scott Warren Harold, Susan Puska, and Samuel K. Berkowitz. *China's Incomplete Military Transformation: Assessing the Weaknesses of the People's Liberation Army (PLA)*. Santa Monica, CA: RAND, 2015.

Chhatwal, Ravinder. "Analysis of PLAAF Potential against India." *Air Power Journal* 8, no. 4 (Winter 2013): 61–89.

Clary, Christopher. "The Future of Pakistan's Nuclear Weapons Program." In *Strategic Asia 2013–14: Asia in the Second Nuclear Age*, edited by Ashley J. Tellis, Abraham M. Denmark, and Travis Tanner, 131–62. Washington, DC: National Bureau of Asian Research, 2014.

Clinton, Hillary. *Hard Choices*. London: Simon & Schuster, 2014.

Cohen, Stephen P. *The Indian Army: Its Contributions to the Development of a Nation*. Berkeley: University of California Press, 1971.

Cohen, Stephen P., and Sunil Dasgupta. *Arming without Aiming: India's Military Modernization*. Washington, DC: Brookings Institution Press, 2014.

Cordesman, Anthony H. *Strategic Threats and National Missile Defenses: Defending the U.S. Homeland*. Westport, CT: Praeger, 2002.

Dalton, Toby, and Michael Krepon. *A Normal Nuclear Pakistan*. Washington, DC: Stimson Center and Carnegie Endowment for International Peace, 2015.

Dixit, J. N. *Anatomy of a Flawed Inheritance: Indo-Pak Relations, 1970–94*. New Delhi: Konark, 1995.

———. *India-Pakistan in War and Peace*. New Delhi: Books Today, 2002.

Erickson, Andrew S., Abraham M. Denmark, and Gabriel Collins. "Beijing's 'Starter Carrier' and Future Steps: Alternatives and Implications." *Naval War College Review* 65, no. 1 (Winter 2012): 15–55.

Erickson, Andrew S., and Lyle J. Goldstein. "China's Future Nuclear Submarine Force: Insights from Chinese Writings." *Naval War College Review* 60, no. 1 (Winter 2007): 54–79.

Fravel, M. Taylor, and Evan S. Medeiros. "China's Search for Assured Retaliation: The Evolution of Chinese Nuclear Strategy and Force Structure." *International Security* 35, no. 2 (Fall 2010): 48–87.

Freedman, Lawrence. *The Evolution of Nuclear Strategy*. London: Palgrave Macmillan, 2003.

Ganguly, Sumit, and Devin T. Hagerty. *Fearful Symmetry: India-Pakistan Crises in the Shadow of Nuclear Weapons*. Seattle: University of Washington Press, 2006.

Gates, Robert M. *Duty: Memoirs of a Secretary at War*. London: WH Allen, 2014.

Ghose, Arundhati. "India and Fissile Material Cut-Off Treaty." In *India in a Changing Global Nuclear Order*, edited by Arvind Gupta, 159–68. New Delhi: IDSA-Pugwash, 2009.

Gill, John H. "Military Operations in the Kargil Conflict." In *Asymmetric Warfare in South Asia: The Causes and Consequences of the Kargil Conflict*, edited by Peter R. Lavoy, 92–129. Cambridge: Cambridge University Press, 2009.

Glaser, Alexander, and M. V. Ramana. "Weapon-Grade Plutonium Production Potential in the Indian Prototype Fast Breeder Reactor." *Science and Global Security* 15, no. 2 (November 2007): 85–105.

Glaser, Charles L. *Analyzing Strategic Nuclear Policy*. Princeton, NJ: Princeton University Press, 1990.

Gopalaswamy, Bharath, and Ting Wang. "The Science and Politics of an Indian ASAT Capability." *Space Policy* 26, no. 4 (November 2010): 229–35.

Gupta, Amit. "Communication: Building a Nuclear Triad; India's Draft Nuclear Doctrine." *Pacifica Review: Peace, Security and Global Change* 12, no. 2 (June 2000): 189–95.

———. "India's Third-Tier Nuclear Dilemma: N Plus 20?" *Asian Survey* 41, no. 6 (November–December 2001): 1044–63.

Heginbotham, Eric, et al. *China's Evolving Nuclear Deterrent: Major Drivers and Issues for the United States*. Santa Monica, CA: RAND, 2017.

Hoyt, Timothy D. "Kargil: The Nuclear Dimension." In *Asymmetric Warfare in South Asia: The Causes and Consequences of the Kargil Conflict*, edited by Peter R. Lavoy, 144–70. Cambridge: Cambridge University Press, 2009.

International Institute for Strategic Studies. *The Military Balance 2015*. London: International Institute for Strategic Studies, 2015.

———. *The Military Balance 2016*. London: International Institute for Strategic Studies, 2016.

Jaspal, Zafar Nawaz. "Ballistic Missile Defense: Implications for India-Pakistan Strategic Environment." *National Defence University Journal 2011*, 1–26.

Ji Yeonjung. "A Path to NSG: India's Rise in the Global Nuclear Order." *Rising Powers Quarterly* 2, no. 3 (2017): 19–37.

Joshi, Shashank. "An Evolving Indian Nuclear Doctrine?" In *Deterrence Instability and Nuclear Weapons in South Asia*, edited by Michael Krepon, Joshua T. White, Julia Thompson, and Shane Mason, 69–94. Washington, DC: Stimson Center, 2015.

———. "Pakistan's Tactical Nuclear Nightmare: Déjà Vu?" *Washington Quarterly* 36, no. 3 (Summer 2013): 159–72.

Joshi, Yogesh. "Between Principles and Pragmatism: India and the Nuclear Nonproliferation Regime in the Post-PNE Era, 1974–1980." *International History Review*, January 2, 2018.

———. "Nuclear Stability in South Asia and the Challenge of Strategic Technologies." In *Perspectives on Nuclear Strategy of India and Pakistan*, edited by Mohammed Badrul Alam, 158–73. New Delhi: Kalpaz, 2012.

———. "Waiting for the Bomb: PN Haksar and India's Nuclear Policy in 1960s." Working Paper No. 10, Nuclear Proliferation International History Project, Woodrow Wilson Center for Scholars, September 2017.

Joshi, Yogesh, Frank O'Donnell, and Harsh V. Pant. *India's Evolving Nuclear Force and Implications for US Strategy in the Asia-Pacific*. Carlisle, PA: US Army War College, 2016.

Joshi, Yogesh, and Harsh V. Pant. "India and the Changing Nature of War: Gradual Incrementalism?" In *Handbook of Indian Defence Policy*, edited by Harsh V. Pant, 79–98. Routledge: London, 2015.

Joshi, Yogesh, and Alankrita Sinha. "India and Ballistic Missile Interception: From Theory to Practice." *Nuclear Notes* 2, no. 1 (June 2012): 25–31.

Kak, Kapil. "Rationale and Implications." In *Pakistan's Tactical Nuclear Weapons: Conflict Redux*, edited by Gurmeet Kanwal and Monika Chansoria, 63–84. New Delhi: KW Publishers, 2014.

Kampani, Gaurav. "India: The Challenge of Nuclear Operationalization and Strategic Stability." In *Strategic Asia 2013–14: Asia in the Second Nuclear Age*, edited by Ashley J. Tellis,

Abraham M. Denmark, and Travis Tanner, 99–130. Washington, DC: National Bureau of Asian Research, 2014.

———. "Is the Indian Nuclear Tiger Changing Its Stripes?" *Nonproliferation Review* 21, no. 3/4 (2014): 383–98.

———. "Stakeholders in the Indian Strategic Missile Program." *Nonproliferation Review* 10, no. 3 (Fall–Winter 2003): 48–70.

Kamphausen, Roy. "China's Land Forces: New Priorities and Capabilities." In *Strategic Asia 2012–13: China's Military Challenge,* edited by Ashley J. Tellis and Travis Tanner, 27–60. Seattle: National Bureau of Asian Research, 2012.

Karnad, Bharat. *India's Nuclear Policy.* Westport, CT: Praeger, 2008.

———. *Nuclear Weapons and Indian Security: The Realist Foundations of Strategy.* New Delhi: Macmillan India, 2005.

———. "A Thermonuclear Deterrent." In *India's Nuclear Deterrent,* edited by Amitabh Mattoo, 108–49. New Delhi: Har-Anand, 1999.

Kelleher, Catherine McArdle. "Thresholds and Theologies: The Need for Critical Reassessment." *Survival* 26, no. 4 (1984): 156–63.

Kemburi, Kalyan. "Recalibrating Deterrence Theory and Practice: The View from India." In *The China-India Nuclear Crossroads,* edited by Lora Saalman, 82–93. Washington, DC: Carnegie Endowment for International Peace, 2012.

Kennedy, Andrew B. "India's Nuclear Odyssey: Implicit Umbrellas, Diplomatic Disappointments, and the Bomb." *International Security* 36, no. 2 (Fall 2011): 120–53.

Khan, Feroz Hassan. *Eating Grass: The Making of the Pakistani Bomb.* Stanford, CA: Stanford University Press, 2012.

———. "Reducing the Risk of Nuclear War in South Asia." In *Pakistan's Nuclear Future: Reining in the Risk,* edited by Henry D. Sokolski, 63–102. Carlisle, PA: US Army War College Strategic Studies Institute, 2009.

Khan, Muhammad Azam. "S-2: Options for the Pakistan Navy." *Naval War College Review* 63, no. 3 (Summer 2010): 85–104.

Khan, Zafar. "Emerging Shifts in India's Nuclear Policy: Implications for Minimum Deterrence in South Asia." *Strategic Studies* 34, no. 1 (Spring 2014): 94–112.

———. "Pakistan's Nuclear First Use Doctrine: Obsessions and Obstacles." *Contemporary Security Policy* 36, no. 1 (2015): 149–70.

Kile, Shannon N. "Nonproliferation, Arms Control and Disarmament." In *SIPRI Yearbook 2000,* 443–76. Stockholm: Stockholm International Peace Research Institute, 2000.

———. "Nuclear Arms Control and Ballistic Missile Defence." In *SIPRI Yearbook 2001,* 423–56. Stockholm: Stockholm International Peace Research Institute, 2001.

———. "Nuclear Arms Control and Non-proliferation." In *SIPRI Yearbook 1999,* 519–45. Stockholm: Stockholm International Peace Research Institute, 1999.

Kile, Shannon N., Phillip Schell, and Hans M. Kristensen. "Indian Nuclear Forces." In *SIPRI Yearbook 2012: Armaments, Disarmament and International Security,* 332–36. Oxford: Oxford University Press, 2012.

Koithara, Verghese. *Managing India's Nuclear Forces.* New Delhi: Routledge, 2012.

Kondapalli, Srikanth. "The Chinese Military Eyes South Asia." In *Shaping China's Security Environment: The Role of the People's Liberation Army,* edited by Andrew Scobell and Larry M. Wortzel, 197–282. Carlisle, PA: US Army War College Strategic Studies Institute, 2006.

Kostecka, Daniel J. "Places and Bases: The Chinese Navy's Emerging Support Network in the Indian Ocean." *Naval War College Review* 64, no. 1 (Winter 2011): 59–78.

Kristensen, Hans M., and Robert S. Norris. "Chinese Nuclear Forces, 2015." *Bulletin of the Atomic Scientists* 71, no. 4 (July–August 2015): 77–84.

———. "Chinese Nuclear Forces, 2016." *Bulletin of the Atomic Scientists* 72, no. 4 (October 2016): 205–11.

———. "Indian Nuclear Forces, 2012." *Bulletin of the Atomic Scientists* 68, no. 4 (July–August 2012): 96–101.

———. "Indian Nuclear Forces, 2015." *Bulletin of the Atomic Scientists* 71, no. 5 (September 2015): 77–83.

———. "Pakistani Nuclear Forces, 2009." *Bulletin of Atomic Scientists* 65, no. 5 (September–October 2009): 82–89.

———. "Pakistani Nuclear Forces, 2015." *Bulletin of the Atomic Scientists* 71, no. 6 (November–December 2015): 59–66.

———. "Pakistani Nuclear Forces, 2016." *Bulletin of the Atomic Scientists* 72, no. 6 (October 2016): 368–76.

———. "Worldwide Deployments of Nuclear Weapons, 2014." *Bulletin of the Atomic Scientists* 70, no. 5 (September–October 2014): 96–108.

Kukreja, Vina. *Civil-Military Relations in South Asia.* New Delhi: Sage, 1991.

Kumar, A. Vinod. *India and the Nuclear Nonproliferation Regime: The Perennial Outlier.* Cambridge: Cambridge University Press, 2014.

Ladwig, Walter C., III. "A Cold Start for Hot Wars? The Indian Army's New Limited War Doctrine." *International Security* 32, no. 3 (Winter 2007–8): 158–90.

———. "Indian Military Modernization and Conventional Deterrence in South Asia." *Journal of Strategic Studies* 38, no. 5 (2015): 729–72.

Lahiri, Dilip. "Formalizing Restraint: The Case for South Asia." *Strategic Analysis* 23, no. 4 (July 1999): 563–74.

Lavoy, Peter R. "Islamabad's Nuclear Posture: Its Premises and Implementation." In *Pakistan's Nuclear Future: Worries Beyond War,* edited by Henry D. Sokolski, 129–66. Carlisle, PA: US Army War College Strategic Studies Institute, 2008.

Lewis, Jeffrey. *Paper Tigers: China's Nuclear Posture,* Adelphi Paper 446. London: International Institute for Strategic Studies, 2014.

Lin, Herbert. "Escalation Dynamics and Conflict Termination in Cyberspace." *Strategic Studies Quarterly* 6, no. 3 (Fall 2012): 46–70.

Malik, V. P. *Kargil: From Surprise to Victor.* New Delhi: HarperCollins, 2009.

Markey, Daniel S. *No Exit from Pakistan: America's Tortured Relationship with Islamabad.* Cambridge: Cambridge University Press, 2013.

Menon, Raja. *A Nuclear Strategy for India.* New Delhi: Routledge, 2000.

———. "Parallel Stories: Soldiers, Scientists and Nuclear Logic." *India International Centre Quarterly* 25, no. 2/3 (Summer/Monsoon 1998): 71–80.

Menon, Shivshankar. *Choices: Inside the Making of India's Foreign Policy.* Washington, DC: Brookings Institution Press, 2016.

Mian, Zia. "Pakistan." In *Assuring Destruction Forever,* 2015 ed., edited by Ray Acheson, 54–63. Geneva: Reaching Critical Will, 2015.

Mian, Zia, and A. H. Nayyar. "Pakistan." In *Banning the Production of Fissile Materials for Nuclear Weapons: Country Perspectives on Challenges to a Fissile Material (Cut-Off) Treaty,* 37–41. Princeton, NJ: International Panel on Fissile Materials, 2008.

Mian, Zia, A. H. Nayyar, R. Rajaraman, and M. V. Ramana. *Fissile Materials in South Asia: Implications of the Indo-US Nuclear Deal.* Princeton, NJ: International Panel on Fissile Materials, 2006.

————. "Fissile Materials in South Asia and the Implications of the U.S.-India Nuclear Deal." *Science and Global Security* 14, no. 2/3 (January 2007): 117–43.

Mishra, Atul. "Necessary Oppositions: Domestic Debates on Iran." *Strategic Analysis* 36, no. 6 (November–December 2012): 892–98.

Mistry, Dinshaw. "The Unrealized Promise of International Institutions: The Test Ban Treaty and India's Nuclear Breakout." *Security Studies* 12, no. 4 (2003): 116–51.

Mohan, C. Raja. *Impossible Allies: Nuclear India, United States and the Global Nuclear Order.* New Delhi: India Research Press, 2006.

————. "India's Nuclear Exceptionalism." In *Nuclear Proliferation and International Security*, edited by Morten Bremer Mærli and Sverre Lodgaard, 96–117. London: Routledge, 2007.

Morgan, Forrest E., Karl P. Mueller, Evan S. Medeiros, Kevin L. Pollpeter, and Roger Cliff. *Dangerous Thresholds: Managing Escalation in the 21st Century.* Santa Monica, CA: RAND, 2008.

Mukherjee, Anit. "Correspondence: Secrecy, Civil-Military Relations and India's Nuclear Program." *International Security* 39, no. 3 (Winter 2014–15): 202–7.

Nagal, Balraj. "Strategic Stability—Conundrum, Challenge and Dilemma: The Case of India, China and Pakistan." *CLAWS Journal*, Summer 2015, 1–22.

Nagappa, Rajaram. "Technical Aspects of Hatf-9/Nasr Missile." In *Pakistan's Tactical Nuclear Weapons: Conflict Redux*, edited by Gurmeet Kanwal and Monika Chansoria, 157–70. New Delhi: KW Publishers, 2014.

Narang, Vipin. "Five Myths about India's Nuclear Posture." *Washington Quarterly* 36, no. 3 (Summer 2013): 143–57.

————. "Posturing for Peace: Pakistan's Nuclear Posture and South Asian Stability." *International Security* 34, no. 3 (Winter 2009–10): 38–78.

————. "Pride and Prejudice and Prithvis: Strategic Weapons Behavior in South Asia." In *Inside Nuclear South Asia*, edited by Scott D. Sagan, 137–83. Stanford, CA: Stanford University Press, 2009.

Nayan, Rajiv. "NPT and India: Accommodating the Exception." *Strategic Analysis* 34, no. 2 (2010): 309–21.

O'Donnell, Frank. *Launching an Expanded Missile Flight-Test Notification Regime.* Washington, DC: Stimson Center, 2017.

O'Donnell, Frank, and Yogesh Joshi. "Lost at Sea: The Arihant in India's Quest for a Grand Strategy." *Comparative Strategy* 33, no. 5 (2014): 466–81.

O'Donnell, Frank, and Harsh V. Pant. "Evolution of India's Agni-V Missile: Bureaucratic Politics and Nuclear Ambiguity." *Asian Survey* 54, no. 3 (May–June 2014): 584–610.

————. "The Evolution of India's National Security Apparatus: Persisting Structural Deficiencies." In *Handbook of Indian Defence Policy*, edited by Harsh V. Pant, 323–36. Oxford: Routledge, 2015.

Pan Zhenqiang. "China's No First Use of Nuclear Weapons." In *Understanding Chinese Nuclear Thinking*, edited by Li Bin and Zhao Tong, 51–78. Washington, DC: Carnegie Endowment for International Peace, 2016.

Pande, Savita. "Missile Technology Control Regime: Impact Assessment." *Strategic Analysis* 22, no. 6 (September 1999): 923–45.

Pant, Harsh V. *The China Syndrome: Grappling with an Uneasy Relationship.* New Delhi: HarperCollins India, 2010.

————. "India Comes to Terms with a Rising China." In *Strategic Asia 2011–12: Asia Responds to Its Rising Powers—China and India*, edited by Ashley J. Tellis, Travis Tanner, and Jessica Keough, 101–30. Seattle: National Bureau of Asian Research, 2011.

———. "India's Nuclear Doctrine and Command Structure: Implications for Civil-Military Relations in India." *Armed Forces and Society* 33, no. 2 (January 2007): 238–64.

———. "India's Relations with Iran: Much Ado about Nothing." *Washington Quarterly* 34, no. 1 (Winter 2011): 61–74.

———. *The US–India Nuclear Pact: Policy, Process and Great Power Politics.* New Delhi: Oxford University Press, 2011.

Patney, Vinod. "Air Power and Joint Operations: Doctrine and Organizational Challenges." *United Service Institution Journal* 133, no. 553 (July–September 2003): 366–87.

Pedrozo, Raul. "Close Encounters at Sea: The USNS *Impeccable* Incident." *Naval War College Review* 62, no. 3 (Summer 2009): 101–11.

Perkovich, George. "The Non-Unitary Model and Deterrence Stability in South Asia." In *Deterrence Stability and Escalation Control in South Asia*, edited by Michael Krepon and Julia Thompson, 21–40. Washington, DC: Stimson Center, 2013.

Posen, Barry R. *Inadvertent Escalation: Conventional War and Nuclear Risks.* Ithaca, NY: Cornell University Press, 1991.

Prakash, Arun. "National Security Reforms: Ten Years after the Kargil Committee Report." *United Service Institution Journal* 141, no. 590 (October–December 2012): 504–23.

Rajagopalan, Rajesh. "India: The Logic of Assured Retaliation." In *The Long Shadow: Nuclear Weapons and Security in the 21st Century*, edited by Muthiah Alagappa, 188–214. Stanford, CA: Stanford University Press, 2008.

———. "India's Doctrinal Options." In *Pakistan's Tactical Nuclear Weapons: Conflict Redux*, edited by Gurmeet Kanwal and Monika Chansoria, 193–214. New Delhi: KW Publishers, 2014.

———. "The Threat of Unintended Use of Nuclear Weapons in South Asia." *India Review* 4, no. 2 (2005): 214–32.

Rajagopalan, Rajesh, and Atul Mishra. *Nuclear South Asia: Keywords and Concepts.* New Delhi: Routledge India, 2014.

Rajaraman, R. "Estimates of India's Fissile Material Stocks." *Science and Global Security* 16, no. 3 (December 2008): 74–87.

———. "Implications of the Indo-US Nuclear Deal for India's Energy and Military Programmes." In *Indo-US Nuclear Deal: Seeking Synergy in Bilateralism*, edited by P. R. Chari, 123–42. New Delhi: Routledge, 2013.

———. "India." In *Banning the Production of Fissile Materials for Nuclear Weapons: Country Perspectives on Challenges to a Fissile Material (Cut-Off) Treaty*, 22–26. Princeton, NJ: International Panel on Fissile Materials, 2008.

———. "India's Nuclear Arms Control Quandary." *Bulletin of the Atomic Scientists* 66, no. 2 (March 2010): 27–36.

Rajiv, S. Samuel C. "India and Iran's Nuclear Issue: Three Policy Determinants." *Strategic Analysis* 35, no. 5 (2011): 819–35.

Raman, S. Kalyan. "Operation Parakram: An Indian Exercise in Coercive Diplomacy." *Strategic Analysis* 26, no. 4 (2002): 478–92.

Ramana, M. V. "An Estimate of India's Uranium Enrichment Capacity." *Science and Global Security* 12, no. 1/2 (2004): 115–24.

———. "India." In *Assuring Destruction Forever*, 2015 ed., edited by Ray Acheson, 38–46. Geneva: Reaching Critical Will, 2015.

———. *The Power of Promise: Examining Nuclear Energy in India.* New Delhi: Penguin Books India, 2013.

Rangachari, T. C. A. "China's Role in South Asia: An Indian Perspective." In *Neighbourhood First: Navigating Ties under Modi*, edited by Aryaman Bhatnagar and Ritika Passi, 86–95. New Delhi: Observer Research Foundation, 2016.

Rehman, Iskander. "Drowning Stability: The Perils of Naval Nuclearization and Brinkmanship in the Indian Ocean." *Naval War College Review* 65, no. 4 (Autumn 2012): 64–88.

———. *Murky Waters: Naval Nuclear Dynamics in the Indian Ocean*. Washington, DC: Carnegie Endowment for International Peace, 2015.

———. "Tomorrow or Yesterday's Fleet? The Indian Navy's Operational Challenges." In *India's Naval Strategy and Asian Security*, edited by Anit Mukherjee and C. Raja Mohan, 37–64. Oxford: Routledge, 2016.

Rice, Condoleezza. *No Higher Honor: A Memoir of My Years in Washington*. New York: Simon & Schuster, 2011.

Rizvi, M. Mahtab Alam. "Interpreting India's Vision in West Asia: A Study of India-Iran Relations." *South Asian Survey* 18, no. 1 (2011): 81–92.

Saalman, Lora. "Between 'China Threat Theory' and 'Chindia': Chinese Responses to India's Military Modernization." *Chinese Journal of International Politics* 4 (2011): 87–114.

Sagan, Scott D. "The Evolution of Pakistani and Indian Nuclear Doctrine." In *Inside Nuclear South Asia*, edited by Scott D. Sagan, 219–64. Stanford, CA: Stanford University Press, 2009.

Sahgal, Arun. "China's Military Modernization: Responses from India." In *Strategic Asia 2012–13: China's Military Challenge*, edited by Ashley J. Tellis and Travis Tanner, 277–308. Seattle: National Bureau of Asian Research, 2012.

———. "The Diversified Employment of China's Armed Forces: An Indian Perspective." *CLAWS Journal*, Summer 2013, 209–19.

———. "Logic and Options for Use." In *Pakistan's Tactical Nuclear Weapons: Conflict Redux*, edited by Gurmeet Kanwal and Monika Chansoria, 85–114. New Delhi: KW Publishers, 2014.

Sarkar, Jayita. "The Making of a Non-Aligned Nuclear Power: India's Proliferation Drift." *International History Review* 37, no. 5 (2015): 933–50.

Sasikumar, Karthika. "India's Emergence as a Responsible Nuclear Power." *International Journal* 62, no. 4 (Autumn 2007): 825–44.

Saxena, Jyotika. "Regime Design Matters: The CTBT and India's Nuclear Dilemma." *Comparative Strategy* 25, no. 3 (2006): 209–29.

Schelling, Thomas C. "Bargaining, Communication and Limited War." *Conflict Resolution* 1, no. 1 (March 1957): 19–36.

Shankar, Mahesh, and T.V. Paul. "Nuclear Doctrines and Stable Strategic Relationships: The Case of South Asia." *International Affairs* 92, no. 2 (January 2016): 1–20.

Shankar, Vijay. "Tactical Nuclear Weapons: A Step Closer to the 'Abyss.'" In *Pakistan's Tactical Nuclear Weapons: Conflict Redux*, edited by Gurmeet Kanwal and Monika Chansoria, 19–38. New Delhi: KW Publishers, 2014.

Sharma, Anand. *Ballistic Missile Defence: Frontier of the 21st Century*. New Delhi: Centre for Air Power Studies and Knowledge World, 2011.

Singh, Jasjit. "Planning Military Power for the Future." *Air Power Journal* 2, no. 4 (Winter 2005): 57–72.

———. "Why Nuclear Weapons?" In *Nuclear India*, edited by Jasjit Singh, 9–25. New Delhi: Knowledge World, 1998.

Singh, Jaswant. "Against Nuclear Apartheid." *Foreign Affairs* 77, no. 5 (September–October 1998): 41–52.

———. *A Call to Honour: In Service of Emergent India*. New Delhi: Rupa, 2006.

Small, Andrew. *The China-Pakistan Axis: Asia's New Geopolitics*. Gurgaon: Random House India, 2015.

Sood, V. K., and Praveen Sawhney. *Operation Parakram: The War Unfinished*. New Delhi: Vision Books, 2003.

Srivastava, Anupam, and Seema Gahlot. "The Influence of Bureaucratic Politics on India's Nuclear Strategy." In *Strategy in the Second Nuclear Age: Power, Ambition, and the Ultimate Weapon*, edited by Toshi Yoshihara and James R. Homes, 133–60. Washington, DC: Georgetown University Press, 2012.

Subrahmanyam, K. "India's Nuclear Policy: 1964–1998." In *Nuclear India*, edited by Jasjit Singh, 26–53. New Delhi: Knowledge World, 1998.

———. "Nuclear Force Design and Minimum Deterrence Strategy for India." In *Future Imperilled: India's Security in the 1990s and Beyond*, edited by Bharat Karnad, 176–95. New Delhi: Viking, 1994.

———. "Nuclear Tests: What Next?" *India International Centre Quarterly* 25, no. 2/3 (Summer/Monsoon 1998): 52–62.

Subramaniam, Arjun. "The Strategic Role of Air Power: An Indian Perspective on How We Need to Think, Train and Fight in the Coming Year." *Air and Space Power Journal* 22, no. 3 (Fall 2008): 56–66.

Sundarji, K. *Effects of Nuclear Asymmetry on Conventional Deterrence*, Combat Paper No. 1 (Mhow, India: College of Combat, 1981).

———. "Imperatives of Indian Minimum Nuclear Deterrence." *Agni* 2, no. 1 (1996): 17–22.

———. "Nuclear Deterrence: Doctrine for India—Part 1." *Trishul* 5, no. 2 (1992): 43–60.

———. "Nuclear Deterrence: Doctrine for India—Part 2." *Trishul* 6, no. 1 (1993): 42–60.

Talbott, Strobe. *Engaging India: Diplomacy, Democracy and the Bomb*. Washington, DC: Brookings Institution Press, 2004.

Tellis, Ashley J. "China's Military Space Strategy." *Survival* 49, no. 3 (Autumn 2007): 41–72.

———. "The Evolution of US-India Ties: Missile Defense in an Emerging Strategic Relationship." *International Security* 30, no. 4 (Spring 2006): 113–51.

———. "India's Emerging Nuclear Doctrine: Exemplifying the Lessons of the Nuclear Revolution." *NBR Analysis* 12, no. 2 (May 2001): 1–110.

———. *India's Emerging Nuclear Posture: Between Recessed Deterrence and Ready Arsenal*. Santa Monica, CA: RAND, 2001.

———. "No Escape: Managing the Enduring Reality of Nuclear Weapons." In *Strategic Asia 2013–14: Asia in the Second Nuclear Age*, edited by Ashley J. Tellis, Abraham M. Denmark, and Travis Tanner, 3–34. Washington, DC: National Bureau of Asian Research, 2014.

———. *Troubles, They Come in Battalions: The Manifold Travails of the Indian Air Force*. Washington, DC: Carnegie Endowment for International Peace, 2016.

———. "What Should We Expect from India as a Strategic Partner?" In *Gauging U.S.-Indian Strategic Cooperation*, edited by Henry D. Sokolski, 231–58. Carlisle, PA: US Army War College, 2007.

Tellis, Ashley J., C. Christine Fair, and Jamison J. Moby. *Limited Conflicts under the Nuclear Umbrella: Indian and Pakistani Lessons from the Kargil War*. Santa Monica, CA: RAND, 2001.

Venkataraman G. *Bhabha and His Magnificent Obsessions*. Hyderabad: Sangam, 1994.

Walker, William. "Nuclear Enlightenment and Counter-Enlightenment." *International Affairs* 83, no. 3 (2007): 431–53.

Waltz, Kenneth. *The Spread of Nuclear Weapons: More May Be Better*, Adelphi Paper No. 171. London: International Institute for Strategic Studies, 1981.

Wang Xiaoxuan. "SLOC Security and International Cooperation." In *Beyond the Wall: Chinese Far Seas Operations*, edited by Peter A. Dutton and Ryan D. Martinson, 91–94. Newport, RI: US Naval War College, 2015.

Winner, Andrew C. "The Future of India's Undersea Nuclear Deterrent." In *Strategy in the Second Nuclear Age: Power, Ambition, and the Ultimate Weapon*, edited by Toshi Yoshihara and James R. Homes, 161–80. Washington, DC: Georgetown University Press, 2012.

Wortzel, Larry M. "PLA Contingency Planning and the Case of India." In *The People's Liberation Army and Contingency Planning in China*, edited by Andrew Scobell, Arthur S. Ding, Philip C. Saunders, and Scott W. Harold, 225–50. Washington, DC: National Defense University Press, 2015.

Wu Riqiang. "Certainty of Uncertainty: Nuclear Strategy with Chinese Characteristics." *Journal of Strategic Studies* 36, no. 4 (2013): 579–614.

———. "How China Practices and Thinks about Nuclear Transparency." In *Understanding Chinese Nuclear Thinking*, edited by Li Bin and Zhao Tong, 219–50. Washington, DC: Carnegie Endowment for International Peace, 2016.

Xia Liping. "On China's Nuclear Doctrine." *Journal of China and International Relations* 3, no. 1 (2015): 167–96.

Xu Weidi. "China's Security Environment and the Role of Nuclear Weapons." In *Understanding Chinese Nuclear Thinking*, edited by Li Bin and Zhao Tong, 19–50. Washington, DC: Carnegie Endowment for International Peace, 2016.

Zhang Hui. "China." In *Assuring Destruction Forever*, 2015 ed., edited by Ray Acheson, 22–28. Geneva: Reaching Critical Will, 2015.

INDEX

Page numbers in italic indicate tables.

ABOUT THE AUTHORS

Yogesh Joshi is a nuclear security postdoctoral fellow at the Center for International Security and Cooperation (CISAC), Stanford University. Before joining CISAC, Joshi was an associate fellow in the Strategic Studies Program at the Observer Research Foundation, New Delhi. He received his PhD from Jawaharlal Nehru University specializing in Indian foreign and security policy. He is also an alumnus of Columbia University's Summer Workshop on Military Operations and Analysis (SWAMOS) and the Woodrow Wilson Center's International Nuclear History Boot Camp. At CISAC he is finishing a book manuscript on the history of India's nuclear submarine program. He previously held fellowships at George Washington University, King's College London, and the Carnegie Endowment for International Peace, Washington, DC. His research has appeared or is under review in *Asian Security, International History Review, International Affairs, Survival, US Naval War College Review, Comparative Strategy, Harvard Asia Quarterly, India Review, Asia Policy, Journal of Asian Security and International Affairs, War on the Rocks, World Politics Review,* and *The Diplomat.* He has coauthored two books: *The US "Pivot" and Indian Foreign Policy: Asia's Emerging Balance of Power* and *Indian Nuclear Policy: Oxford India Short Introductions.*

Frank O'Donnell is a Stanton Junior Faculty Fellow at the Belfer Center of Science and International Affairs at Harvard University and a nonresident fellow in the South Asia Program at the Stimson Center. His research investigates the intersections among strategic cultures, technical force developments, deterrence conceptions, and stability challenges within nuclear rivalries, with special reference to South Asia. His writings on these themes have appeared in journals such as *Asian Survey, Comparative Strategy, Contemporary Security Policy, Orbis,* and *Survival.* He has provided testimony to the UK House of Commons Foreign Affairs Committee and regularly comments on Asian security issues for various media. He received his PhD in defense studies from King's College London.